LINGUISTIC SURVEYS OF AFRICA

Volume 12

PRACTICAL ORTHOGRAPHY OF
AFRICAN LANGUAGES
bound with
ORTHOGRAPHE PRATIQUE DES
LANGUES AFRICAINES
bound with
THE DISTRIBUTION OF THE
SEMITIC AND CUSHITIC
LANGUAGES OF AFRICA
bound with
DISTRIBUTION OF THE NILOTIC
AND NILO-HAMITIC LANGUAGES
OF AFRICA
and
LINGUISTIC ANALYSES

PRACTICAL ORTHOGRAPHY OF AFRICAN LANGUAGES

INTERNATIONAL AFRICAN INSTITUTE

LONDON AND NEW YORK

First published in 1930 by Oxford University Press

This edition first published in 2018
by Routledge
2 Park Square, Milton Park, Abingdon, Oxon OX14 4RN

and by Routledge
711 Third Avenue, New York, NY 10017

Routledge is an imprint of the Taylor & Francis Group, an informa business

© 1930 International African Institute

All rights reserved. No part of this book may be reprinted or reproduced or utilised in any form or by any electronic, mechanical, or other means, now known or hereafter invented, including photocopying and recording, or in any information storage or retrieval system, without permission in writing from the publishers.

Trademark notice: Product or corporate names may be trademarks or registered trademarks, and are used only for identification and explanation without intent to infringe.

British Library Cataloguing-in-Publication Data
A catalogue record for this book is available from the British Library

ISBN: 978-1-138-08975-4 (Set)
ISBN: 978-1-315-10381-5 (Set) (ebk)
ISBN: 978-1-138-09586-1 (Volume 12) (hbk)
ISBN: 978-1-138-09621-9 (Volume 12) (pbk)
ISBN: 978-1-315-10552-9 (Volume 12) (ebk)

Publisher's Note
The publisher has gone to great lengths to ensure the quality of this reprint but points out that some imperfections in the original copies may be apparent.

Disclaimer
The publisher has made every effort to trace copyright holders and would welcome correspondence from those they have been unable to trace.

INTERNATIONAL INSTITUTE OF AFRICAN
LANGUAGES AND CULTURES

MEMORANDUM I

Revised Edition

PRACTICAL ORTHOGRAPHY OF AFRICAN LANGUAGES

Published by the OXFORD UNIVERSITY PRESS *for the*
INTERNATIONAL INSTITUTE OF AFRICAN
LANGUAGES AND CULTURES
22 CRAVEN STREET
LONDON, W.C. 2
1930

PRINTED IN GREAT BRITAIN

PRACTICAL ORTHOGRAPHY OF AFRICAN LANGUAGES

INTRODUCTION

THE first edition of the *Practical Orthography of African Languages*, consisting of 3,500 copies (3,000 in English and 500 in German) has been sold out within two years. This fact proves that the problem of finding a practical and uniform method of writing African languages has aroused widespread interest, and that the efforts of the Institute towards the solution of the problem have met with considerable response.

The second edition is being printed in English, French, and German.

Up to the present, the principles of orthography recommended by the Institute have been accepted for the following languages: Fante, Twi, Ga, Ewe on the Gold Coast; Efik, Ibo, Yoruba, and partially for Hausa in Nigeria; for Mende, Temne, Soso, Konno, Limba in Sierra Leone; Shilluk, Nuer, Dinka, Bari, Latuko, Madi, and Zande in the Sudan; in Mashonaland it is proposed for a written language to be called Shona, based on the closely related dialects of Karanga, Zezuru, Ndau, Korekore, and Manyika. In the Union of South Africa and in other parts of the continent the introduction of the new orthography is under discussion at present. A number of books for school and mission use have appeared in the new orthography in several of the above-named languages, and others are in preparation. Further information about these can be obtained on request from the Institute.

The aim of the recommendations of the Institute has been, and is, the unification and simplification of the orthography of African languages. Over large areas which have political, geographical, or linguistic unity an unsatisfactory state of affairs is found to exist at the present time owing to lack of agreement as to the general principles of writing down the languages, and as to the letters to be used and the meanings attached to them. In Africa to-day conditions of life are such that many thousands of natives leave their home districts and, either with or without their families, settle temporarily or permanently in districts where their mother tongue is not understood. Thus, for everyday intercourse, for church and school life, or in order to read a newspaper, they are obliged to learn another language. It would obviously be a great advantage if in the orthography of the new language, the value of the letters were the same, or as nearly as possible the same, as those they have already learnt for their mother tongue. Moreover, in many parts of Africa, children in the early stages of school life receive instruction through the medium of the mother tongue, and later in a language which is used over a wider area. The change from mother tongue to another language may not be very difficult for the Negro, because of his linguistic ability and because the two languages are generally closely related, and their construction, grammar, idiom, and vocabulary are often very similar. But if the two languages are written with two different systems of orthography, confusion is likely to arise, and unnecessary difficulty is placed in the path of the learner. In such cases the promotion of uniformity is clearly an important need of the moment.

Another urgent need is expressed in the second purpose of the Memorandum, viz. the simplification of orthography. The number of ways in which speech-sounds are represented to-day in Africa is overwhelming. In every case the basis is the Latin alphabet.[1] As many African languages contain sounds for which the Latin letters are inadequate and which nevertheless must be distinguished in writing, many methods of representing these sounds have been devised. The only systematic orthography which has been used to any considerable extent is that of R. Lepsius, described in his *Standard Alphabet* (2nd edition, London and Berlin, 1863). It is not necessary here to insist upon the scientific value of this alphabet, and especially of the enlarged and improved forms which Meinhof has devised for the particular needs of African languages, and the alphabets which have sprung from it (e.g. the *Anthropos* alphabet of P. W. Schmidt). It is possible by means of this system to represent speech-sounds with great accuracy.

For the practical use of the native, however, the Lepsius and *Anthropos* alphabets have notable disadvantages, in that they make extensive use of diacritic marks above and below the letters. For practical purposes in everyday life diacritic marks constitute a difficulty and a danger. In the first place it is found that in current writing these marks are liable to be altered so as to be unrecognizable and even omitted altogether, as every one who has had to read written texts in African languages will readily acknowledge. Such alterations and omissions of diacritic marks are also frequently found in print. For example, in Yoruba and in other Nigerian languages the horizontal line which Lepsius used in writing 'open' e and o has been replaced sometimes by a vertical line and sometimes by a dot. In the Lepsius alphabet, however, the dot has the opposite meaning to the horizontal line, and is used to indicate a 'close' vowel. A. T. Sumner has published handbooks in the Mende, Temne, and Sherbro languages (Freetown, 1917, 1921, and 1922). In the first of these, close vowels are represented by a dot under the letter and the open vowels are unmarked; in the Temne and Sherbro books the

---

[1] The few cases where Africans have invented their own alphabet or where a negro language has been written in Arabic characters need not be considered, as there is little likelihood of these scripts spreading further.

usage is reversed, the open vowels being represented by a dot under the letter and the close vowels remaining unmarked. In Sotho school-books open e and o have been printed in four different ways.[1]

In the Introduction to the *Standard Alphabet* (p. xii) the following statement is found: 'For the uncritical Native ... many of the diacritical marks may be dispensed with, or will gradually drop off of themselves.' This expected dropping off has certainly taken place, but proper distinction has not been made in what may and what may not be dispensed with.

The following are some further drawbacks to the use of diacritics. Letters with diacritic marks give a blurred outline to words and thus impair their legibility. Again, a letter consisting of two, three, or four separate elements is much more difficult to grasp and much more likely to strain the eyes than a simple letter. This objection is particularly true of diacritic marks under the letters, as these are most easily overlooked in reading and forgotten in writing.[2] Some existing alphabets are so overloaded with diacritic marks that a glance at them is sufficient to show that they are unsatisfactory from a practical point of view. When native pupils are no longer under the supervision of a teacher in school they simply drop most of the diacritics in writing.[3]

Economic considerations also support the case for uniformity and for the use of letters without diacritic marks. If the types in use differ from language to language and have to be stocked to meet every special case, European printers are less likely to undertake the production of African books than if similar type can be used over large speech-areas.[4] In printing-types diacritic

---

[1] A. N. Tucker, *Suggestions for the Spelling of Transvaal Sesuto* (p. 5).

[2] 'With the spread of religion over the world, the missionaries, usually educated men, have left, as has been said, examples of their erudition: but unfortunately they have shown little knowledge of typography, as is evidenced by the selection made by them of the miscellaneously accented characters with which they have unhappily endowed the scripts of many countries.'—*Typographical Printing Surfaces*, by Legros and Grant, 1916, p. 535.

'Our use to-day of a large number of diacritical marks attests the persistent deficiencies of our alphabet.'—*The Psychology and Pedagogy of Reading*, by E. B. Huey, 1913, p. 222.

'However, all the systems of phonetic writing and marking, often most carefully worked out from the philological and logical points of view, have been conspicuously lacking in revision from the psychological and pedagogical sides.'—Huey, p. 358.

'Too often, as in the working out of systems of phonetic spelling by philologists, a system excellent from the philological or logical standpoint has lacked fitness to the psychic or hygienic conditions involved in reading.'—Huey, p. 430.

[3] At the Language Conference at Rejaf (Sudan), 1928, it was authoritatively stated that experience in the schools of the Northern Sudan showed that about 50 per cent. of the diacritic marks were omitted in the writing of Arabic script.

[4] It may be mentioned here that there are now on the market typewriters of

marks are apt to break off, and they wear out more quickly than the letter itself, so that more frequent renewals are necessary.

All these facts, together with practical experience, have led us to recommend the introduction of a few new letters, which in view of their legibility and the suitability of their cursive forms are clearly to be preferred to ordinary Roman letters with diacritic marks attached. The adoption of these letters will put an end to the multiplicity of signs in use at present; each new letter is, moreover, a simple uniform symbol and not a conglomeration of two or more elements. Diacritic marks are manifestly a makeshift, and a practical alphabet for current use should not be constructed of makeshifts. The representation of each sound (or rather each phoneme, see p. 14) by one separately designed letter should be considered as an essential principle of orthography. Such difficulty as there may be in new letters lies in the fact that for Europeans (but not for the African child who is beginning to learn to read) these letters are unfamiliar and strike us as strange. It is difficult to find any other objections to them.

Although the above objection has not much intrinsic weight, it must nevertheless be taken into consideration to some extent in constructing a system that is to be of general practical use. For this reason, in the alphabet proposed the number of new letters is reduced to a minimum, and the principle of representing each essential sound by a separate symbol is not always rigidly adhered to. Thus in some cases—as for instance in the representation of palatal consonants—it has been thought advisable to resort to 'digraphs' or groups of two letters to indicate single sounds. Diacritic marks too have not been altogether banished: they are used to show 'central' vowels, nasalized vowels, and tones. Such departures from the general principles are made for two reasons: firstly because due regard must be given to forms of spelling which have long been established in many parts of Africa, and secondly because an alphabet which involves too radical a change from existing alphabets would have little prospect of general acceptance. In many parts of Africa traditions of spelling have existed for some time, and these one should endeavour to preserve in so far as they are not inconsistent with the production of a simple, practical, and unified alphabet. For example, the writing of palatal consonants with digraphs avoids the introduction of a diacritic mark or new letters; moreover, digraphs are already commonly used for this purpose, particularly for **ny,** which occurs in so many languages.

Diacritic marks are recommended for certain purposes, and notably to indicate nasalization and tones, because in these particular cases the advantages

---

various makes containing the new letters recommended by the Institute. The difference in price between these and the ordinary typewriter is negligible. The Institute will gladly furnish further information about these machines.

PRACTICAL ORTHOGRAPHY OF AFRICAN LANGUAGES 7

resulting from their use greatly outweigh their inherent drawbacks; it would be a manifest impossibility to introduce new letters for all nasalized vowels and all vowels with special tones. The marks which we recommend for nasalization and for tones are already widely used. For many languages, however, marks to show nasalization and tone are not required; and where they are essential, it is generally possible to reduce them to a manageable number.

It will thus be seen that the intention of this Memorandum is to show how existing orthographies may be modified and improved. It is hoped that the proposals here set forth, grounded as they are on scientific phonetic principles, may serve as a working basis and bring the ideals of unity and simplicity of writing nearer realization.

This Memorandum is not a document providing ready-made alphabets for every African language. For many languages the materials requisite for drawing up satisfactory alphabets are not yet available. Even when the sound-system of a language is known, an alphabet can only be constructed by an expert in the language, who must take into consideration its phonetic and grammatical structure, and sometimes also historical and geographical facts. How far this can be done and how far existing conditions have to be taken into account is discussed in the article by D. Westermann in vol. ii of *Africa* noted below.

In this second edition recommendations are made for the writing of various sounds and sound-groups which were not included in the first edition, but which have recently been under consideration by the Institute. It is hardly necessary to add that there still remain many African sounds for which we are not yet in a position to make recommendations.

The question of the orthography of African languages is discussed in the following articles, reports, and books:

(1) A. Lloyd James: 'The Practical Orthography of African Languages', in *Africa*, i, pp. 125–9. (1928)
(2) I. Carl Meinhof, II. Daniel Jones, 'Principles of Practical Orthography for African Languages', in *Africa*, i, pp. 228–39.
(3) A. Lloyd James, 'Phonetics and African Languages', in *Africa*, i, pp. 358–71.
(4) R. F. G. Adams and Ida C. Ward, 'The Arochuku Dialect of Ibo', in *Africa*, ii, pp. 57–70.
(5) D. Westermann, 'The Linguistic Situation and Vernacular Education in British West Africa', in *Africa*, ii, pp. 337–51.
(6) *A Common Script for Twi, Fante, Ga and Ewe*. Report by Prof. D. Westermann. Ordered by H. E. the Governor to be printed. Gold Coast Government Printer, Accra, 1927.
(7) *Report of the Rejaf Language Conference*. Published by the Sudanese Government. London, 1928.

(8) *Alphabets for the Efik, Ibo and Yoruba Languages.* Recommended by the Education Board, Lagos. London, 1929.
(9) *Alphabets for the Mende, Temne, Soso, Kono and Limba Languages.* International Institute of African Languages and Cultures. London, 1929.
(10) A. N. Tucker, *Suggestions for the Spelling of Transvaal Sesuto.* Memorandum VII of the International Institute of African Languages and Cultures.
(11) A. N. Tucker, *The Comparative Phonetics of the Suto-Chwana Group of Bantu Languages.* Longmans, Green & Co., 1929.
(12) R. A. C. Oliver, 'Psychological and Pedagogical Considerations in the making of Textbooks', in *Africa*, iii, pp. 293–304.
(13) *The New Script and its Relation to the Languages of the Gold Coast.* Published by the Crown Agents for the Colonies, London, 1930.

REPRESENTATION OF SOUNDS

1. The Institute recommends that African languages should be written on a Romanic basis according to the following scheme.

Consonants.

2. (i). **b, d, f, h, k, l, m, n, p, s, t, v, w, z** shall have their English values, subject to the General Principles mentioned in §§ 20–31, and to the following special conditions:

- (*a*) When it is necessary to distinguish between aspirated and unaspirated **p, t, k**, the simple letters shall be employed to represent the unaspirated sounds, and the aspirated sounds shall be represented by **ph, th, kh**. **ph** is thus to be pronounced as in *loop-hole* (and not as **f**), **th** as in *at home* (not as in *thin or then*), **kh** as in *back-hand*.
- (*b*) When it is necessary to distinguish between dental or alveolar **t** and **d** and retroflex (cerebral) **t, d**, the ordinary letters shall be used for the dental or alveolar sounds and the special letters **ṭ, ḍ** for the retroflex sounds. (Alveolar consonants are those formed by pressing the tongue-tip against the teeth-ridge, while the retroflex consonants are those which have the tongue-tip placed somewhat further back, so that it touches the roof of the mouth just behind the teeth-ridge or even further back still.) In Ewe the words **du** (town) and **ḍu** (powder), **da** (snake) and **ḍa** (hair) must be distinguished.

(ii) **ɡ** shall have its hard value as in *get, go*.

r shall stand for the rolled lingual (tongue-tip) **r** of Scottish pronunciation or for the fricative **r** of Southern English.

x shall be used to represent the Scotch sound of *ch* in *loch* (the German *ach*-sound). When in any language the German *ich*-sound occurs in addition to the *ach*-sound, and the use of the two is determined by the character of the neighbouring vowel, both can be written with **x**.

y shall have its consonantal value as in *you, yet*.

ty, dy, ny, ly, sy, zy may be used to represent palatal **t, d, n, l, s, z**.

ky, ɡy may be used to represent palatal or 'fronted' **k, ɡ**.

When a palatal consonant is preceded by a vowel, a kind of **i**-sound can often be heard between the two. This arises from the palatal character of the consonant and is an unavoidable 'glide'; thus the sound-group **anya** is often heard as **ainya** and has therefore been written **ainya** by some authors. But as this **i** is only the 'on-glide' to the palatal consonant and not an independent sound, it is not necessary or advisable to write it; the group should be written **anya** not **ainya**.

kp, gb shall be used for the labio-velar consonants of many Sudanic languages.

(iii) It is recommended that the following special consonant letters be used to supplement the ordinary Roman letters (subject to General Principles, § 31):

ŋ for the 'velar *n*', i.e. for the sound of *ng* in English *sing*, German *singen*.

ƒ for 'bilabial *f*', as in Ewe **ƒu** (bone), **ƒo** (to beat), which have to be distinguished from **fu** (feather), **fo** (to tear off). The symbol **f** has also been suggested instead of **ƒ**.

ʋ for 'bilabial *v*', i.e. the German sound of *w* in *schweben, schwimmen*. In Ewe the words **ʋu** (boat), **ʋə** (python) have to be distinguished from **vu** (to tear), **və** (to be finished).

ʃ for the English sound of *sh*, French *ch*, German *sch*.

ʒ for the English sound of *s* in *pleasure*, French *j*. The symbol **ɉ** has also been recommended for this sound.

ɣ for the 'voiced velar fricative' sound as in the colloquial pronunciation of *g* in German *Lage*.

' for the 'glottal stop', as in Hausa **a'a** (no).

(iv) It is recommended that the Affricate Consonants be represented by groups of two letters thus: **pf** as in German *hüpfen*, **bv** the corresponding voiced sound, **ts** as the German *z*, **dz** the corresponding voiced sound, **tʃ** the sound of English *ch*, **dʒ** the sound of English *j*. In some cases it is advisable to dispense with **tʃ** and **dʒ** and use the single letters **c** and **j** in their place.

(v) It is recommended that consonants pronounced with simultaneous 'glottal stop' be represented thus: **p', t', k', s', ts'**, &c.; e.g. Hausa **k'ofa** (door). It seems preferable to write the ' before the **y** in the combination of ' and **y** occurring in Hausa, as in **'ya'ya** (children).

(vi) *Implosive Sounds.* Implosive sounds are consonants of plosive nature formed by a sucking in of the air.[1] In many languages glottal closure accompanies an implosive consonant, but the exact nature of the sound is not yet definitely known in every case. To represent the peculiar character of these sounds, the ordinary letters preceded by an apostrophe are recommended: thus **'b, 'd, 'g**.

It frequently happens that a language contains only one implosive sound, namely implosive *b*; for such a case the special letter ɓ is recom-

---

[1] The sucking in is often very weak.

mended. The letter ɗ is recommended for use in those languages where implosive *d* also occurs.

In many dialects of Ibo an implosive *b* is found, while in other dialects the corresponding sound is **ɓb**. For Union Ibo the spelling **ɓb** has been adopted, because this notation is used in neighbouring languages and in some of the existing Ibo literature.

(vii) *Dental Sounds*. In the new orthographies for Bari, Nuer, Dinka, Shilluk, and other Sudanic languages where the distinction between dental **t, d, n** and alveolar **t, d, n** is found, the notation **th, dh, nh** has been adopted for the dental sounds. Such a device is only possible in languages which do not contain aspirated **t**.

(viii) *Lateral Sounds*. A decision is likely to be reached in South Africa itself in the near future as to the writing of the lateral sounds and clicks which occur in South African languages. We therefore give here only the present spelling and the letters suggested by Dr. C. M. Doke.

Present Spelling.	Doke.	
tl	tl	for laterally exploded **t**.
tlh	tlh	for aspirated **tl**.
hl	ɬ	for lateral **s** (voiceless fricative **l**).
dhl	ɮ	for lateral **z** (voiced fricative **l**).

The current use of **hl** and **dhl** to represent single sounds is far from satisfactory. In comparison with this Dr. Doke's suggestions, even though they introduce two new letters, are an improvement.

(ix) *Clicks*. The letters at present in use in South Africa to represent clicks are:
   c for the dental click
   q for the retroflex click
   x for the lateral click.
There exist also the following click-combinations:

c	ch	nc	nch	ǵc	ŋc	ŋǵc
q	qh	nq	nqh	ǵq	ŋq	ŋǵq
x	xh	nx	nxh	ǵx	ŋx	ŋǵx

(Here **nc, nq, nx** indicate **n** followed by a click, while **ŋc, ŋq, ŋx** denote clicks completely nasalized throughout.)

As the letters **c** and **x** are used in other languages to represent quite different sounds, and as the clicks are sounds of a very special nature, it has been suggested that special signs should be used for them. The following letters have been recommended:

ʇ for **c**
ʗ for **q**
ʖ for **x**

It should be noted, however, that the only important languages containing clicks are found in South Africa. Moreover, even if the new symbols for the clicks were adopted, it would still be necessary to use the letters ǥ and ŋ in special conventional senses differing from those which they have in other languages, namely ǥ for denoting voice, and ŋ for denoting nasalization (not a separate nasal consonant).

It is therefore doubtful whether in these circumstances the introduction of new symbols for the clicks themselves is feasible.[1]

In Nama, a dialect of Hottentot, other symbols for clicks have been used for some time. These are:

/ for the dental click;
≠ for the alveolar click;
! for the retroflex click;
// for the lateral click.

As Nama is a language of little importance and somewhat removed from the other languages in which clicks occur, it will no doubt be best not to alter the existing spelling.

(x) *Labialization.* In the new alphabet for the Shona dialects the letters s̬ and z̬ have been adopted to represent labialized s and z.

A symbol seems desirable for 'front labialization' which plays an important part in the grammar of the languages of the Suto-Chwana group. Tucker has suggested ɥ for this purpose (see *Suggestions for the Spelling of Transvaal Sesuto,* pp. 15–18).

Vowels.

3. The vowel letters **a, e, i, o, u** shall have the so-called 'Italian' values. In cases where it is necessary to distinguish between a 'close' e and an 'open' e,[2] the letter e shall represent the close vowel and the special letter ɛ shall be used for the open vowel. And when it is necessary to distinguish between a 'close' o and an 'open' o[3], the letter o shall represent the close vowel and the special letter ɔ shall be used for the open vowel.

4. When a language contains a 'middle' o in addition to a close o and an open o, as in Ibo, the letter ɵ is recommended to represent the 'middle' o.

5. *Central Vowels.* There exist vowels of a 'neutral' or intermediate character, which are neither 'front' (like **i, e**) nor 'back' (like **u, o**). Such a sound is the first vowel in the English words *about, along.* There are numerous varieties of central vowels: some have lip-rounding and others

---

[1] In writing Zulu and Xosa, if x is retained to represent the lateral click, it has been suggested that χ be used to denote the 'velar fricative' (the Scotch *loch*-sound).

[2] As between the French *é* and *è*.

[3] As between the French vowels in *Beaune* and *bonne*.

have not; some are nearer to the front series and are therefore more e-like, while others are nearer to the back series and are more o-like.

6. When a language contains only one central vowel and this is e-like, the letter ə is recommended for representing it. The letter o with the diacritic mark ¨, thus ö, is recommended for the representation of an o-like central vowel. When in any language there are several central vowels which must be distinguished, it is difficult to avoid the use of diacritic marks. For example, in Nuer besides o, ə, and a there are three central vowels which cannot well be represented otherwise than by ö, ə̈, and ä.

Diphthongs.

7. It is recommended that diphthongs be represented by groups of letters, e.g. ai, ɛi, ei, au, əi. Ya and wa might also be regarded as diphthongs and could be written ia, ua, &c. But as the spellings ya and wa are in common use, their retention is recommended.

Nasalization.

8. It is recommended that nasalized vowels be represented by the sign ~ placed over the vowel-letter.

9. It is not necessary in every case to indicate the nasalization of a vowel, particularly when a nasal consonant (m, n, ny, ŋ) precedes or follows it. Even in some cases where no nasal consonant is present the nasal sign can be omitted. For example, in Mende the word for 'in' is pronounced hũ, but as no other word occurs in the language in any way resembling it—i.e. there is no hu—there can be no doubt about the meaning. For this reason, and because the word is such a common one, it has been decided to leave out the nasalization mark in this word.

10. Good illustrations as to when and how far the use of nasalization marks can be omitted will be found in the *New Ga Primer, Teachers' Handbook*, by C. P. Moir, Chapter I, Notes on the new Ga Script (London, 1929).

11. The use hitherto made in certain languages of the letter n to indicate nasalization is not to be recommended, as it undoubtedly leads to misunderstanding.

Length.

12. It is recommended that long or doubled sounds be represented by doubling the letter. This applies to both consonants and vowels. Examples: Luganda siga (sow (verb)), sigga (scorpion); Akan əmã (he gives), əmmã (he does not give); Ewe godo (yonder), godoo (around), fa (to be cool), faa (freely).

13. In some cases, especially where the lengthening of a vowel can be used for expressing two different meanings, the mark · following the letter may be used to denote length.

14. Vowel-length, like nasalization, need not always be marked. It will suffice to mark it in those cases where vowel-length is the only method of distinguishing words otherwise alike in all respects, but which differ in meaning or in grammatical usage.

Tones.

15. In books for Africans, tones, generally speaking, need only be marked when they have a grammatical function, or when they serve to distinguish words alike in every other respect; and even then they may be sometimes omitted when the context makes it quite clear which word is intended. As a rule, it will suffice to mark the high or the low tone only.

16. For marking tones an accent above the vowel is recommended: thus high tone á, low tone à. Rising and falling tones may be represented, if necessary, by ǎ and â respectively, and mid tone by ȧ. Examples: Ewe **mí** (we), **mi** (you, pl.); **lé** (seize), **le** (be), Efik **mî** (me), **mí** (here), **mi** (my), **efé** (shed), **efe** (flying squirrel), **éfe** (which (interrog.)), **éfě** (it flies). (The syllables here unmarked have low tones.)

17. Professor D. Jones recommends the following more comprehensive system of tone marks: ā for a high-level tone, a̱ for a low-level tone, á for a high-rising tone, a̗ for a low-rising tone, à for a high-falling tone, a̖ for a low-falling tone, â for a rise-fall, and ǎ for a fall-rise.

18. This system may be recommended for those languages in which a more precise method of tone-marking is necessary, and for scientific purposes. In certain languages, e.g. the Kru-group, even these tone-marks are not sufficient to show the whole tonal system of the language. It should be stated once more, however, that this Memorandum is concerned with the representation of tones only in so far as their marking is necessary for the understanding of the African.

Table of Sounds.

19. The letters recommended by the Institute are classified and set out systematically in the Sound Chart on p. 15.

GENERAL PRINCIPLES
DEFINITIONS
1. *Phonemes.*

20. It often happens that two distinct sounds occur in a language, but the Native is not aware that they are different, or at most regards one of them as an unimportant variety of the other. This happens where one of the sounds occurs only in certain positions in connected speech, while the other never occurs in those positions.

21. Thus in English the k's in *keep* and *collar* are different sounds, but the use of these sounds is determined by the following vowel. Hence we regard

		Bi-labial	Labio-dental	Dental and Alveolar	Post-alveolar	Retroflex (Cerebral)	Palatal	Velar	Laryngal
CONSONANTS	Explosive	p b		t d		ʈ ɖ	ty dy ky gy	k g	ʼ
	Implosive	ɓ		ɗ					
	Affricate	pf bv		ts dz	tʃ dʒ (=c j)			kx	
	Nasal	m		n			ny	ŋ	
	Lateral { Explosive			tl dl					
	Fricative			ɬ ɮ					
	Frictionless			l			ly		
	Rolled and Flapped			r					
	Fricative	ɸ β	f v	s z	ʃ ʒ		sy zy	x ɣ	h
	Semi-vowel	w					y	(w)	
VOWELS	Close	(u)					i	u	
	Half-close	(o)					e	o	
	Half-open	(ǝ)					ɛ	ɔ	e
	Open								a

them as two varieties of **k**. The same applies to the **k**'s in the French *qui, quoi,* and the German *Kiel, Kuh.*

22. Again, there are languages in which the sound ŋ occurs only in the groups ŋk, ŋg, ŋw, ŋh but not in any other circumstances. In such a language the ŋ may be regarded as a variety of **n**, and these combinations can be written **nk, ng, nw, nh**. For instance, the *n* in the Italian *banca, lungo* has the sound ŋ; but since ŋ does not occur in Italian as an independent sound (e. g. before a vowel), it may be regarded as a variety of **n**. On the contrary, in English and German, ŋ is not a variety of **n**, because both occur in identical positions; compare English *sin, sing* (phonetically **sin, siŋ**), German *sinnen, singen* (phonetically **zinən, ziŋən**).

23. There exist languages and dialectal variants of languages showing a tendency to give the velar pronunciation to every final nasal consonant, i.e. to substitute ŋ for every final **m** or **n**. If the pronunciation with **m** and **n** exists and ŋ is not found as a separate phoneme, it is better to write **m** and **n** and ignore the velar pronunciation.

24. If, on the other hand, ŋ is found in a language as a separate phoneme, it is recommended that the sound should be written ŋ wherever it occurs, that is to say not only before vowels but also before **k, g,** &c.

25. In Zulu there exist a 'close' **e** and an 'open' **e**. These sounds are, however, used in accordance with a certain principle of vowel harmony. Therefore they may for practical purposes be regarded as one speech-unit in Zulu, and may be written with the single letter **e**. In the Akan language of West Africa the **w** in **wu, wo,** and **wɔ** is quite a distinct sound from the **w** in **wi, we,** and **wɛ**, but as the use of the two sounds is determined by the following vowel, they may be considered for practical purposes as one. In Kikuyu the sound **g** only occurs in the group ŋg, but the related sound ɣ occurs in other positions though never after ŋ; **g** and ɣ may, therefore, be treated as a single entity in Kikuyu. In Chwana a **d**-like variety of **l** is used before **i** and **u**, but an ordinary **l** is used before all other vowels. The distinction is negligible from the point of view of the Natives.

26. The term *Phoneme* is used to denote any small family of sounds which may be regarded as a single entity for reasons such as those applying to the above examples.

27. In very many cases phonemes consist of only one sound. Thus *phoneme* and *sound* are identical in the case of English **f, m, n, v**, since the pronunciation of these sounds is not appreciably affected by neighbouring sounds in the sentence.

28. It is phonemes that serve to distinguish one word from another in every language. Thus the phonemes **n** and ŋ distinguish words in English and German, as mentioned above. Close and open **e** and **o** (i.e. **e** and **ɛ**, **o** and **ɔ**) distinguish words in French, most West African languages, Chwana,

PRACTICAL ORTHOGRAPHY OF AFRICAN LANGUAGES

Suto, and many other languages in other parts of Africa; they are separate phonemes in those languages.

2. *Diaphones*.

29. Very often different speakers of the same language pronounce the same word in somewhat different ways. For instance, the value of the *a* in *bad* is different in different parts of England. In French and in German *r* is sounded by some with the tip of the tongue and by others with the uvula.

30. The term *Diaphone* is used to denote a normal sound together with the variants of it heard from different speakers of the same language.

PRINCIPLES OF ORTHOGRAPHY

31. The following general principles should be observed in fixing the orthography of any particular language:
    (1) The orthography of a given language should be based on the principle of one letter for each phoneme of that language. This means that whenever two words are distinguished in sound they must also be distinguished in orthography.
    (2) The existence of diaphones must be recognized and allowed for. Thus Fante speakers of Akan pronounce the syllable **di** as **dzi** and **ti** as **tsi**; but the orthography **di, ti** is adequate for covering both pronunciations. Again, the Hausa **f** is pronounced in some dialects as labiodental **f** and in others as bi-labial ***f*** and in others as **p**; but the letter **f** can be used in orthography with the necessary conventions as to dialectal pronunciations.
    (3) It may sometimes be convenient to depart from a strictly phonetic system, in order to avoid writing a word in more than one way. Thus it is better to write in Luganda **soka oleke** (wait a bit), although the pronunciation is **sok oleke**. Similarly, it is better to write in Akan **ɔ hwɛ no** (he saw him), although in many districts the final **o** is not pronounced. Again, it is preferable to write always the same form of the Akan word **hwɛ**, in spite of the fact that it is actually pronounced **hwe** when followed by a syllable containing **i** or **u** (as in **ɔ hwɛ mu**).

Similar considerations hold good for numerous other cases of vowel harmony in Akan and in other languages.

It must, however, be very definitely stated that the rules governing vowel harmony and assimilation in Akan and other languages are often numerous and complicated. It is not possible to formulate them once for all by means of a simple rule. The extent to which these phenomena should be reflected in current spelling must depend upon the special phonetic and grammatical usages of each particular language.

(4) As a concession to existing usage an ordinary Roman letter may sometimes be used in place of one of the special new letters, when the sound denoted by the Roman letter does not occur in the language. Thus **f** may be used instead of **ƒ** in writing Sechwana, because the labio-dental **f** does not occur in that language. Similarly, **s** may be used instead of **ʃ** in writing Oshikuanyama because an ordinary **s** does not occur in that language. Again, if every **t** in a language is retroflex, the letter **t** can be used to represent it; it is not necessary to employ the special symbol for the retroflex sound. In Hausa there exists a **ts** combined with glottal stop (**ts'**); this sound is replaced in some dialects by **s'** and in others by **t'**. As, however, the language has no **ts** *without* glottal stop, it is recommended that the sound be written simply **ts** without marking the glottal stop.

CAPITAL LETTERS AND WRITTEN FORMS

32. A table is subjoined showing the printed capital forms of the most important of the special letters, also the handwriting forms of both small and capital letters. Information as to the precise forms of other letters may be had on application to the Institute.

Roman.	Italic.	Written Forms.	Roman.	Italic.	Written Forms.
a A	*a A*	a 𝒶	l L	*l L*	l ℒ
b B	*b B*	b ℬ	m M	*m M*	m 𝓂
ɓ Ɓ	*ɓ Ɓ*	ɓ ℬ	n N	*n N*	n 𝓃
c C	*c C*	c C	ŋ Ŋ	*ŋ Ŋ*	ŋ 𝓃
d D	*d D*	d 𝒟	o O	*o O*	o 𝒪
ɖ Ɖ	*ɖ Ɖ*	ɖ or dʼ 𝒟	ɔ Ɔ	*ɔ Ɔ*	ɔ 𝒪
e E	*e E*	e ℰ	p P	*p P*	p 𝒫
ɛ Ɛ	*ɛ Ɛ*	ɛ ℰ	r R	*r R*	r or ɼ ℛ
ə Ə	*ə Ə*	ə Ə	s S	*s S*	s or ʃ 𝒮
f F	*f F*	f ℱ	ʃ Σ	*ʃ Σ*	ʃ ℱ
ƒ Ƒ	*ƒ Ƒ*	ƒ ℱ	t T	*t T*	t 𝒯
g G	*g G*	g 𝒢	u U	*u U*	u 𝒰
ɣ Ɣ	*ɣ Ɣ*	ɣ Ɣ	v V	*v V*	v V or ʋ 𝒱
h H	*h H*	h ℋ	ʋ Ʋ	*ʋ Ʋ*	ʋ Ʋ or ʋ 𝒱
x X	*x X*	x 𝒳	w W	*w W*	w 𝒲
i I	*i I*	i ℐ	y Y	*y Y*	y 𝒴
j J	*j J*	j 𝒥	z Z	*z Z*	z 𝒵
k K	*k K*	k 𝒦	ʒ Ʒ	*ʒ Ʒ*	ʒ Ʒ

ALPHABETICAL ORDER OF THE LETTERS

The following is recommended as the alphabetical order of the principal letters:

a b ɓ c d ɖ e ɛ ə f ƒ g ɣ h x i j k l m n ŋ o ɔ p r s ʃ t u ʋ w y z ʒ '

Nasal vowels should follow ordinary vowels, and central vowels should follow nasal vowels, thus: o õ ö. Other new letters should follow those from which they are derived: thus ɖ should follow d, and ṣ should follow s. If special letters are introduced to represent clicks, it is suggested that they be placed at the end of the alphabet.

It is recommended that in vocabularies and dictionaries words beginning with digraphs (**dy, dz, dʒ, kp, ts, tʃ**, &c.) be placed in separate groups following all the words beginning with simple **d, k, t,** &c.

Names of the Consonant Letters.

b	ɓ	c	d	ɖ	f	ƒ	g	ɣ	h	x	j	k	l	m	n
be	ɓa	ce	de	ɖa	ef	iƒ	ga	ɣe	ha	ex	je	ke	el	em	en
	(tʃe)										(dʒe)				

ŋ	p	r	s	ʃ	t	v	ʋ	w	y	z	ʒ	'
iŋ	pe	ra	es	iʃ	te	ve	ʋi	wa	ya	ze	ʒi	a'a

SPECIMENS OF THE RECOMMENDED ORTHOGRAPHY

(The specimens illustrating the languages marked * are taken from books in which the new orthography is employed.)

*Akan.**

Ɔdɔ dwo nc ani, nc yam ye, odo nyɛ ahõoyaw, odɔ nyɛ ahoahoa, ɛŋhoraŋ, ɛnyɛ nehõ sɛnea ɛmfata, ɛŋhwehwɛ nea ɛyɛ ne aŋkasa de, ne bo ŋhaw no, ɛmfa bone ŋhyɛ ne yam, ne ani nye nea ɛntẽɛ hõ, na ɛne nokware ani gye, etie a ade nnyina, egye ade nnyina di, enya ade nnyina mu anidaso. Ɔdɔ to ntwa da. Na afei gyidi, odo, anidaso na etrã ho, na odɔ na ɛne mu kɛse.

(From 'Ɛha amanne kwaŋ so aware Ɛso Ɖhyira', p. 7).

Bambara.

Kŋo sogo bee yi i nyogõ la dye k u be dlo dõ u ko sogo o sogo bee ka na ni nyo more more ye. Sogo bee nana n ata ye. Suruku ba e o me mi ŋke a y ala muru ba ta, a bina a da la dia la.

Chwana.

Tlhaloxanyɔ ya tlou xoŋwe yane ekete ke ya motho. Betʃwana ba boxolo-xolo bare tlou ekile ya foloxɛla mo nokeŋ ya Sampisi, ya fitlha ya nwa.

Erile e santse e nwa, ya utlwa kwena e e kapa ka selɔpɔ, ere e e xɔxɛla mo metsiŋ. Kefa tlou e inola kwena, e e tʃholetsa ka selɔpɔ, e e kakamara, e e isa ko naxeŋ, kxakalakxakala le noka. Erile e fitlha ko likakeŋ ya baya kwena fa fatshe, yare: 'kana orile oa m polaya? Sala jalo hɛ, ke bonɛ xore a o tla tshela kwa ntlɛ xa metse!'

Duala.

Ngokolɔ na dibobɛ ba ta dikɔm, ba yenga babo babanɛ ponda yɛsɛ. Nde ba ta ba ja o ekwali bunya bɔo, nde na ngokolɔ e kwalanɛ dibobɛ na: A dikɔm lam la ndolo, na malangwea nde oa na mbalɛ, bato ba si masenga, be ndɔki.

(From a text in *Africa*, vol. ii, p. 72, Jan. 1929.)

Efik.

Tiŋ enyin tim se uŋwana oro, neŋere tiene enye; ke ntre ke afo edikut inua-otop oro; tuak, ndien mɔ eyeteme fi se afo edinamde. Ndien ŋkokut ke ndap mi nte owo oro otibide itɔk efege. Ekem enye ika-ikaha kaŋa anyan usuŋ ikpɔŋ ufɔk esie; ndien kadaŋemi ŋwan esie ye nditɔ esie ekutde, mɔ etɔŋɔ ndifiori ŋkot enye, ete afiak edi; edi enye esin nuenubok ke utɔŋ, efege itɔk, ete, 'Uwem! uwem! nsi-nsi uwem!'

Ewe.*

Asime. Asi ɖina le tefe geɖewo le ŋkeke ene sia ŋkeke ene megbe. Ame geɖewo va foa fu ɖe afima. Wotsɔa bli, te, mɔli, agbeli, fofoŋ, fetri, agbitsa, atadi kple kutsetse bubu geɖewo, ɖetifu, de, nɛʃi, amidzẽ, nɛmi, yɔkumi kple nu bubu geɖewo va dzrana. Ga si woxɔna la, wotsɔnɛ ƒlea avɔ, ɖeti, atama, sukli, kple ŋudowɔnu siwo wohiã. Ɖeviwo lɔ̃a asimedede.

(From 'Eʋegbegbalẽxɛxlẽ na Gɔmedzelawo', p. 64.)

Ga.*

Dʒata ko hi ʃi yɛ dʒeŋ a·hu. Agbɛnɛ egbɔ hewɔ lɛ enyẽẽ emomo hewalɛ na· doŋŋ. Enɛ hewɔ lɛ eyakã ʃi yɛ ebu lɛ mli akɛ ehe mi· ye. Koloi lɛ ba· eŋo ekome-kome ni amɛbasra· lɛ yɛ ebu lɛ mli. Osɔ le enɛ fɛ̃ hewɔ lɛ ete koni eyasra dʒata helatʃɛ nɛ. Beni ete lɛ ebotee bu lɛ mli. Edamɔ sɛ ʃoŋŋ ni ebi dʒata lɛ akɛ, 'Helatʃɛl te oyɔ teŋŋ?'

(From the *New Ga Primer*, by C. P. Moir, Part 2, p. 24.)

Ila.

Uʃɛsu udi kwizɛulu, nadiile iʒina dyako, nabuzize buɔneki bwako, nalu-tʃitwe luzando lwako anʃi ano ubudi kwizɛulu. Σidyo nʃi tubula utupe bwasunu. Utulekelɛle milandu, bubɔna mbu tubalekelɛle kale obadi milandu kudi uswɛ. Utatuenʒa mu kutepaulwa, utuʋune ku bubiabe. Ukuti buɔneki mbu bwako, iinsana, obulɛmu, ʃikwense o ʃikwense.

Kikuyu.

Idɛ wito we igoro, reetwa reaku nereamorɔɔ. Odamaki waku ookɛ. Ɔ orea wɛndɛtɛ wɛ, newekagwɔ goko de, ɔ ta orea wekagwɔ kou igoro. Tohɛ omode iriɔ ciito cia gotoigana. Na otorɛkɛrɛ madire maito, ɔ ta orea idue torɛkagera area mare na madire maito. Na ndogatotwarɛ magɛriɔ-ine, nɔ kohɔnɔkia otohɔnɔkagiɛ ooru-ine.

Lokele.

Bowase atolimba onɔkɔ.
Mbuu esoofeta.
Bosokola ngwa nda liulu, inde koicakae anyo.
Itɔɔ kwa ʃa ombolo wa koba.
Loo loca okuki, angowa ae kosinga.

Mende.*

Mu gɔnɛi gbe, ngi mayomboi manyɛingɔ, tɛli lɔ hu kɛ kolei.
Ngi yamɛisia gbe kea ta vo dão.
A kulɔlɔ a foloi kɛ kpindii.
Ta hani manɛma tɛnga nyina mia.
Ta hei kpɛ, ngi wolii mia a sɛsia.
Ngi longɔ i ye hanii hou ngi lenga va.

(From 'Koyɛima kaa Gɔlɔisia', Yehalayɛi, p. 25.)

Nyanja.

Mphepo yakumpoto ndidzua zinali kumenyana, imodzi yaizo inati ine ndiri wamphamvu kupambana iwe, ndipo inzace inati iai ine ndiri wamphamvu kupambana iwe. Koma zinaona mlendo mmodzi alikupita anabvala ntsaru yorimba ndithu, zinapaŋgana ndani abvule ntsaru yamlendo uyu adzaitanidwa wamkulu kupambana mnzace. Mphepo yakumpoto inaomba kwambiri koma iŋgakhale inaomba ndithu, mlendo uja anagwiritsa ntsaru yace. Ndipo mphepo yakumpoto inalephera kumbvula ntsaru, ndipo dzua linaturuka ndikutentha ndithu. Mlendo anamasula ntsaru yace ndikucotsa yontse, ndipo mphepo yakumpoto inati wanditha ndiwe mfumu.

Pedi.

Moleta ŋwedi o leta lefsifsi.
Moruswana xe o tshela lefao o eletʃa o moŋ.
Pshiu tʃa tlou xa di pataxanywe.
Mpʃa e tala e bolaya ka xo tsoxɛla.
A e tswhe dibza.
Mokxola morithi xa se modudi wa ɔna.

Xa o tʃhaba pula o tʃhabe modumɔ; xa o tʃhaba marotholodi a pula, ea xonɛla. (Mma, tʃaka xe diapꭒa se ʃetʃe; ke pꭒhapꭒha diatla, ka lesa tʃampholoxa ka maxetla.)[1]

Shilluk.*

Ya yito ki gin dɔc. Agin? Ya yiti riŋo. Dɔc, kani yuk othal wa. Riŋo mi awany ki kɛli lum. Kani loth o yiejo nak. Yanythɛnho anaki yiec ma gir. Kɛtho wak dway yuk. Ya yito ki tɔŋ mia ma dɔc. Ya dwato bɛth ki loth anan. Gin cam athal? Ḍɛ! Ḍɛ wa bɛ cam. Wa ocamo anan.

(From 'Wanyo Kipa Tiiŋ Gwɛt' No. 1, p. 11.)

Shona (Zezuru Dialect).

Ruŋgano rwaTsuro naHamba.

Ʋakafurirana kundocera tsime. Ɖino Tsuro akaramba. Hamba wakaenda kundotṣaga ʋanaΣumba. Ɖino ʋanaΣumba ʋakacera tsime. Ɖino Tsuro wakauya kuzoɓa mvura. Akauya namaɗende ake. Akawana Hamba aripo. Akamuwona, akatiza.

Rimŋe zuʋa akawana Hamba akahwanda mumvura. Ɖino akaɗa kucera mvura. Hamba akaɓata ruwoko rwaTsuro. Ɖino Tsuro akati, 'Rega kundiɓata.' Tsuro akati, 'Rega, ndinokutṣagira huci.' Hamba waregera Tsuro. Ɖino Tsuro wakapa huci kunaΣumba. Tsuro wakati, 'Rega, nditaŋge ndakusuŋga sekuru'. Ɖino Tsuro wakayisa mabge muhuci. Akayisa mabge mukanwa maΣumba. Ɖino Tsuro wakasimuka oroʋa Σumba.

Shona (Karanga Dialect).

Σuro icinyeŋgere-ʃumba.

Rimŋe zuʋa ʃuro yakaʃoŋgana neʃumba, ikati, 'Sekuru munotṣakei?' Σumba ikati, 'Ndinovima.' Σuro ikati, 'Cihendei kugomo, muŋgondoʋata makaita majaɗa pamukwara wemhuka, ini ndigondodziŋge-mhuka mugomo, imi makagaridzira.' Nambera ʃuro inonyeŋgere-ʃumba, kuti ʃumba igotakwa nebge rinokuŋguruswa mugomo neʃuro. Ɖino ʃumba yakandoʋatapo, ndokuhwa hurumatanda dziciʋirima dzicibvo-mugomo. Σumba ndokuʋata paɗiʋi, mabge aya ndokupfuʋura. Σumba ndokudzokera paya payasiyiwa neʃuro, ndokuʋata ᶎe yakaita maneɗe. Ɖino ʃuro ndokuʋaŋga, ndokuti, 'Ndakaŋguʋa ndarubvira rwokuʋuraye-ʃumba!' Ɖino ikati icitore-ɓaŋga rokuʋuraye-ʃumba, ʃumba ndokuɓate-ʃuro, mambaʋa ndokuwadzuka, ʃuro ndokutiza icidziŋgana neʃumba. Σuro ndokupinda mugwiriŋgwindi, ʃumba ndokuɓato-mŋise weʃuro. Σuro ikati, 'Mandikoniwa maɓato-mudzi!' Σumba ndokuregedza. Σuro ikati, 'Ohii, hamuzandikoniwa!' Ndokugara mumŋena kuṣika ʃumba yainda.

---

[1] In this sentence the symbol ꭒ suggested by Tucker for 'front-labialization' is used provisionally (see Section 2 (x), p. 12).

PRACTICAL ORTHOGRAPHY OF AFRICAN LANGUAGES

Soso.

Woŋ fafe, naxaŋ na ariana, i xili xa sɛniyeŋ. I yamanɛ xa fa. I sago xa niɲa dunia ma, alɔ a niɲaxi ariana kɛnaxai. Woŋ ki to woŋma lɔxɔ o lɔxɔ doŋse ra. Anuŋ ixa woŋma fekobi kafari, alɔ woŋtaŋ nee kafarima kɛnaxai naxaŋ fekobi niɲa woŋ ra. Anuŋ i nama woŋ raso fekobi maniɲa. Kɔnɔ i xa woŋ rakisi fekobi ma. Katugu itaŋ naŋ gbe yamanɛ ra, anuŋ sɛmbɛ anuŋ yigi ra abada anuŋ abada.

Swahili.

Akanena yule mtume: 'Ee Muungu wangu, aliyecukua feza mtu mgine, na aliyeuawa mgine, amezulumiwa yule.' Mwenyiezi Muungu akamʃuʃia walii akamwambia: 'Wewe tazama ibada yako, na ukitaka mambo haya, si kazi yako.' Akamwambia: 'Baba yake yule wa kwanza alimnyaɲanya dinar alf katika mali za babae yule kijana, hamleta yule kijana kuja twaa mali ya babae. Na yule mcanja kuni alimua babae yule wa kwanza hamleta kijana kuja kutoa kisasi tya babae.'[1]

Temne.*

Hawa ɔ yi ro rɔ su.
A lɔkɔ o lɔkɔ ɔ ti kɔ ro karaŋde.
Hawa ɔ ti karaŋ akafa kɔtɔtɔkɔ kaake.
Ɔ karaŋ mump mɔfino o yema ŋa.
Anfɔm ŋa Hawa ɔ bonɛ ŋa tɔk karaŋ ka ɔwan kaŋaŋ.
Hawa ɔ karaŋ akafa ka ɔkas koŋ yi ɔya kɔŋ.
Aŋ yema yi ɔbana.

(From 'Atafa Takaraŋ ta Koyɛima', Kɔtɔtɔkɔ, p. 13).

Xosa.

Kwathi xa umoya wase zantsi wauphikisana ne laŋga ukuɓa ŋguwuphina onamanḳa kuɓo ɓoɓaɓini, kwa fika umhambi ambethe iŋguɓo efudumeleyo. Ɓavumelana ukuɓa oŋgaqala a mendze umhambi ukuɓa alaɬe iŋguɓo yakhe woɓa woyisile. Utheke umoya wase zantsi wavuthuza ŋgawo oŋke amanḳa awo, kwathi okukhona uvuthuzayo kwaɓa kokukhona umhambi ayisondezayo iŋguɓo yakhe. Ekupheleni umoya wase zantsi wancama. Laza ke lona ilaŋga la khanya ŋgokuʃuʃu, waza umhambi wayilaɬa iŋguɓo. Wavumake umoya wase zantsi ukuɓa lilaŋga elinamanḳa.

---

[1] In view of the fact that there are not many Swahili words containing ŋ immediately followed by a vowel, it is suggested that the sound-group ŋg be represented by the spelling **ng**. It would be more consistent, from the point of view of the native, to write it **ŋg**, but the use of **ng** has the advantage of involving less change from the orthography hitherto used.

Yoruba.

Ida li akɔ. Aroko tu ilɛ. Ɔmɔbiri̇̄ wɛ ɔwɔ rɛ. Onịle ra iʃu. Ki ɛ duro de wa nihīyi titi awa o fi lɔ si ɔhū. Ɩ̣wɔ su adi. Apɔ̃ da ɛkɔ̃. Aŋwɔ aroko ro oko. Ɛ nyī fa kɛkɛ. Awa bɛ nyi. Alase se onjɛ. Ʃile mɛta ni yi. Mo ri ɛgbɔ̃. Ewurɛ jɛ koriko. Ɔrɔ otitɔ li o ŋsɔ. Ɩ̣wɔ ŋlu agogo ile-ɛkɔ wa.

Zulu.

Aɓelungu ɓahamba ngemikhumbi, ɓayizingele. Ɓaphatha imikhonto eminingi emikhulu, enezintlenǩa, nezintambo nemiphongolo emingi. Ɓathi qedi ɓafike elwanǩe umkhomo uɓonakale, ɓasondela kaɫe ɓathekelezele intambo emkhontweni ɓawugwaze.

(Adapted from the version in Doke's *Phonetics of Zulu*, p. 279.)

ORTHOGRAPHE PRATIQUE DES LANGUES AFRICAINES

INSTITUT INTERNATIONAL DES LANGUES
ET CIVILISATIONS AFRICAINES

LONDON AND NEW YORK

First published in 1930 by Oxford University Press

This edition first published in 2018
by Routledge
2 Park Square, Milton Park, Abingdon, Oxon OX14 4RN

and by Routledge
711 Third Avenue, New York, NY 10017

Routledge is an imprint of the Taylor & Francis Group, an informa business

© 1930 International African Institute 1930

All rights reserved. No part of this book may be reprinted or reproduced or utilised in any form or by any electronic, mechanical, or other means, now known or hereafter invented, including photocopying and recording, or in any information storage or retrieval system, without permission in writing from the publishers.

Trademark notice: Product or corporate names may be trademarks or registered trademarks, and are used only for identification and explanation without intent to infringe.

British Library Cataloguing-in-Publication Data
A catalogue record for this book is available from the British Library

ISBN: 978-1-138-08975-4 (Set)
ISBN: 978-1-315-10381-5 (Set) (ebk)
ISBN: 978-1-138-09586-1 (Volume 12) (hbk)
ISBN: 978-1-138-09621-9 (Volume 12) (pbk)
ISBN: 978-1-315-10552-9 (Volume 12) (ebk)

Publisher's Note
The publisher has gone to great lengths to ensure the quality of this reprint but points out that some imperfections in the original copies may be apparent.

Disclaimer
The publisher has made every effort to trace copyright holders and would welcome correspondence from those they have been unable to trace.

INSTITUT INTERNATIONAL DES LANGUES ET
CIVILISATIONS AFRICAINES

ORTHOGRAPHE PRATIQUE DES LANGUES AFRICAINES

INSTITUT INTERNATIONAL DES LANGUES
ET CIVILISATIONS AFRICAINES

26 RUE DE LA PÉPINIÈRE, PARIS
1930

PRINTED IN GREAT BRITAIN

ORTHOGRAPHE PRATIQUE DES LANGUES AFRICAINES

INTRODUCTION

LA première édition de *l'Orthographe pratique des langues africaines*, tirée à 3,500 exemplaires (3,000 en Anglais et 500 en Allemand) a été épuisée en moins de deux ans. Ceci prouve que le problème qui consiste à trouver une méthode pratique et uniforme d'écrire les langues africaines, a excité beaucoup d'intérêt, et que les efforts de l'Institut pour résoudre ce problème ont été généralement appréciés.

La deuxième édition paraît en Anglais, en Français, et en Allemand.

Actuellement, les principes d'orthographe recommandés par l'Institut ont été acceptés pour les langues suivantes: Fanté, Twi, Gan, Ewe (Côte d'Or); Efik, Ibo, Yoruba, et en partie pour Hausa (Nigérie); pour Mendé, Temne, Soso, Konno, Limba (Sierra Leone); Shilluk, Nuer, Dinka, Bari, Latuko, Madi, Zande (Soudan); enfin ils sont proposés pour une langue littéraire qui s'appellera Shona et qui est basée sur les dialectes très voisins les uns des autres parlés dans le Mashonaland, c'est-à-dire Karanga, Zezuru, Ndau, Korekore, Manyika. Dans l'union de l'Afrique du Sud et dans d'autres parties du continent noir la question d'adopter l'orthographe nouvelle est à l'étude en ce moment même. Bon nombre d'ouvrages scolaires et religieux, employant notre orthographe, ont été publiés dans plusieurs des langues susnommées, d'autres sont en préparation. Des détails seront fournis sur demande par l'Institut.

Ce qu'a recherché et ce que recherche l'Institut, c'est d'unifier et de simplifier l'orthographe des langues africaines.

A l'heure actuelle, dans de vastes territoires qui pourtant ont une unité politique, géographique ou linguistique, il existe un état de choses malheureux provenant de désaccords quant aux principes à suivre pour écrire les langues indigènes, quant aux lettres à employer et quant à la valeur à leur attribuer. Dans l'Afrique contemporaine, les conditions économiques sont telles que bien des milliers d'indigènes, accompagnés ou non de leurs familles, quittent leur pays natal et se fixent momentanément ou d'une manière permanente dans des districts où leur langage maternel n'est pas compris. En conséquence, tant pour les relations quotidiennes que pour l'école ou l'église, ou simplement pour lire un journal, ils sont obligés d'apprendre une langue nouvelle. Il saute aux yeux qu'il y aurait tout avantage pour eux, si dans l'orthographe de cette langue, la valeur des lettres était la même, ou à peu près la même, que dans leur langue maternelle. En outre, dans beaucoup de parties de l'Afrique, les enfants des petites classes scolaires reçoivent leur première instruction dans leur langue maternelle; plus tard ils étudient une langue répandue sur un territoire plus vaste. Le passage de l'une à l'autre peut ne pas être très difficile pour les nègres, à cause de leurs aptitudes linguistiques naturelles, et parce que les deux langues sont généralement très voisines, très semblables en structure, en grammaire, en phraséologie et en vocabulaire. Mais si les deux langues sont écrites en deux systèmes orthographiques différents, il y aura confusion, et l'élève aura à surmonter des difficultés inutiles. Dans des cas de ce genre, il est évidemment très important d'unifier les systèmes.

Il n'est pas moins important de poursuivre notre deuxième but, qui est de simplifier. Le nombre de méthodes employé aujourd'hui pour représenter les sons des langues africaines est effrayant. C'est toujours l'alphabet latin qui sert de base.[1] Mais comme beaucoup de langues africaines possèdent des sons que l'alphabet latin ne peut pas rendre, et qui pourtant doivent être distingués par l'écriture, on a imaginé de nombreux moyens pour les représenter. La seule orthographe systématique qui ait été largement employée est celle de R. Lepsius, décrite dans son *Standard Alphabet* (2ᵉ Édition, Londres et Berlin, 1863). Il est superflu d'insister ici sur la valeur scientifique de cet alphabet, surtout sous la forme élargie et améliorée que Meinhof a construite spécialement pour les langues africaines, et sous celle de divers alphabets dérivés, par exemple l'alphabet *Anthropos* de P. W. Schmidt. Ce système permet de représenter les sons du langage avec une très grande exactitude.

Mais, pour l'usage courant des indigènes, les alphabets Lepsius et *Anthropos* ont de grands inconvénients, dûs surtout à l'emploi considérable qu'ils font de signes diacritiques au-dessus et au-dessous des lettres. Pour l'usage courant, les signes diacritiques constituent une difficulté et un danger. Tout d'abord en écriture cursive, ces signes risquent d'être modifiés au point d'être méconnaissables, ou même d'être entièrement omis: quiconque a lu des textes manuscrits en une langue africaine confirmera cette assertion. Même dans les textes imprimés, ces altérations se retrouvent souvent. Par exemple, en Yoruba et dans d'autres langues de Nigérie, la ligne horizontale dont Lepsius se sert pour marquer les e et o ouverts, est remplacée tantôt par une ligne verticale et tantôt par un point; tandis que dans l'alphabet Lepsius le point a une valeur opposée et sert à marquer une voyelle fermée. A. T. Sumner a publié des manuels en Mende, en Temne, et en Sherbro. En Mende, les voyelles fermées sont affectées d'un point sous la lettre et les

[1] Nous pouvons négliger les rares cas d'alphabets inventés par les indigènes eux-mêmes pour représenter leurs langues, ou d'applications de l'alphabet arabe aux langues africaines, parce qu'il n'est guère probable que l'usage puisse s'en répandre.

voyelles ouvertes ne sont pas marquées; en Temne et en Sherbro c'est le contraire, les voyelles ouvertes sont affectées d'un point sous la lettre et les voyelles fermées ne sont pas marquées. Dans les livres scolaires Sotho les e et les o ouverts sont indiqués de quatre manières différentes.[1]

Dans l'Introduction au *Standard Alphabet* (p. xii) on trouve la phrase suivante: 'Pour l'usage d'indigènes non disposés à la critique, beaucoup de diacritiques peuvent être supprimés, ou bien ils tomberont d'eux-mêmes.' Effectivement, ils sont tombés en grand nombre dans l'usage, mais sans qu'on ait distingué ceux qui peuvent s'omettre sans inconvénient de ceux qui sont nécessaires.

Voici, d'ailleurs, d'autres inconvénients des diacritiques. Les mots qui en sont accompagnés prennent un air confus qui les rend moins lisibles. Une lettre formée de deux, trois ou quatre éléments séparés est plus difficile à saisir par le regard, et fatigue la vue beaucoup plus qu'une lettre simple. Cet inconvénient est surtout grave pour les diacritiques placés sous les lettres: ce sont ceux qu'on néglige le plus souvent dans la lecture et qu'on est disposé à omettre en écrivant.[2]

Certains alphabets sont tellement surchargés de diacritiques, qu'un coup d'œil superficiel suffit pour en faire sentir la défectuosité pratique. Les élèves indigènes, quand ils ne sont plus sous la surveillance d'un maître d'école, négligent simplement presque tous les diacritiques.[3]

On peut aussi faire valoir des considérations économiques en faveur de l'uniformisation des alphabets, et contre l'usage des diacritiques. Si les

---

[1] A. N. Tucker, *Suggestions for the Spelling of Transvaal Sesuto* (International Institute of African Languages and Cultures, 1929).

[2] Voici quelques citations significatives:

'Tout en propageant la religion dans le monde, les missionnaires, qui sont ordinairement des gens d'éducation supérieure, ont laissé des monuments de leur science, comme on l'a remarqué avec raison; malheureusement ils se sont montrés peu experts dans l'art de la typographie, preuve en soit le choix de lettres accentuées au petit bonheur dont ils ont tristement encombré les alphabets de nombreux idiomes.' *Typographical Printing Surfaces*, par Legros et Grand, 1916, p. 535.

'Notre usage actuel d'un grand nombre de signes diacritiques suffit à démontrer l'imperfection persistante de notre alphabet.' — *The Psychology and Pedagogy of Reading*, par E. B. Huey, 1913, p. 222.

'Tous les systèmes d'écriture et de figuration phonétique, souvent admirablement construits au point de vue de la philologie et de la logique, sont gravement défectueux du point de vue psychologique et pédagogique.' — Huey, p. 358.

'Trop souvent, comme dans l'élaboration de systèmes phonétiques par des linguistes, un système excellent du point de vue philologique et logique s'est trouvé défectueux en ce qui regarde les conditions psychiques et hygiéniques de la lecture.' Huey, p. 430.

[3] À la conférence linguistique de Rejaf (Soudan), il a été affirmé officiellement, d'après les expériences faites dans les écoles du Soudan septentrional, qu'environ 50% des diacritiques étaient négligés dans l'écriture arabe.

caractères employés diffèrent d'une langue à l'autre, et s'il faut se les procurer spécialement pour chaque cas particulier, les imprimeurs européens seront moins disposés à entreprendre la publication de livres indigènes que si pour de vastes régions on emploie la même série de caractères.[1]

Puis, dans les caractères d'imprimerie, les diacritiques se brisent facilement, et s'usent plus rapidement que le corps de la lettre, d'où nécessité de renouveler le caractère plus souvent.

Toutes ces considérations et les expériences faites nous ont amenés à recommander l'introduction de quelques lettres nouvelles, qui, au point de vue de la facilité de lecture et d'écriture, valent mieux que les lettres romaines accompagnées de diacritiques. L'adoption de ces lettres mettra fin à la multiplicité de signes en usage jusqu'ici; et chaque lettre nouvelle est une lettre simple, au lieu d'être une agglomération de deux éléments au moins. Les diacritiques ne sont évidemment qu'un pis-aller; or un alphabet pratique destiné à l'usage courant ne doit pas être construit sur des pis-allers. La représentation de chaque son (disons plutôt de chaque phonème, v. p. 14) par une lettre spéciale doit être considérée comme un principe essentiel d'une bonne orthographe.

La seule difficulté que présentent les nouvelles lettres, c'est qu'elles sont nouvelles pour les Européens, et en conséquence elles nous font un effet bizarre. Il serait difficile de leur opposer une autre objection.

Si peu importante que soit cette objection à un point de vue intrinsèque, il faut pourtant en tenir compte en quelque mesure en construisant un alphabet destiné à l'usage pratique universel. Pour cette raison, l'alphabet que nous recommandons ne contient qu'un minimum de nouvelles lettres; et le principe de représenter chaque son essentiel par un signe spécial n'est pas appliqué dans toute sa rigueur. Ainsi dans quelques cas — par exemple pour les consonnes palatales — on a cru devoir employer des 'digraphes' ou groupes de deux lettres pour représenter des sons uniques. Les diacritiques aussi n'ont pas été complètement éliminés: on les emploie pour les voyelles 'centrales', la nasalisation, les tons musicaux. Ces accrocs faits aux principes généraux se justifient par deux raisons. D'abord parce qu'il faut tenir compte des systèmes orthographiques employés depuis longtemps dans beaucoup de parties de l'Afrique; ensuite parce qu'un alphabet différant trop sensiblement de ceux en usage aurait peu de chances d'être accepté partout. Il y a bien des régions de l'Afrique où existe depuis assez longtemps une tradition orthographique: il y a lieu de la respecter pour autant qu'elle ne va pas à

---

[1] A ce propos il est bon de mentionner qu'on trouve maintenant dans le commerce des machines à écrire de différents types contenant les nouvelles lettres recommandées par l'Institut. La différence de prix entre ces machines et celles à caractères usuels est négligeable. L'Institut fournira volontiers tous les renseignements relatifs à ces machines.

l'encontre des principes d'un alphabet simple, pratique et uniforme. Par exemple la coutume d'écrire les consonnes palatales au moyen de digraphes évite l'élaboration de lettres nouvelles ou l'emploi de diacritiques; puis, les digraphes sont ici d'un usage général et uniforme, en particulier pour **ny**, qui se trouve dans beaucoup de langues. Quant aux diacritiques, nous les recommandons dans certains cas, en particulier pour marquer la nasalisation et les tons musicaux, parce qu'ici les avantages dépassent de beaucoup les inconvénients; de fait, il serait impossible d'avoir des lettres spéciales pour toutes les voyelles nasalisées, ou pour toutes les voyelles affectées d'un ton spécial. Les diacritiques que nous recommandons à cet usage sont déjà très employés. Mais il y a beaucoup de langues pour lesquelles il est superflu de marquer la nasalisation ou le ton musical; et dans celles où il est nécessaire d'employer les diacritiques spéciaux, il est généralement possible d'en réduire le nombre suffisamment pour ne pas être gêné.

On voit donc que le but de ce Mémoire est de montrer comment les orthographes déjà en usage peuvent être modifiées et améliorées. Nous espérons que nos propositions, qui sont basées sur des principes de phonétique scientifique, serviront de base pratique de discussion et nous rapprocheront de notre idéal, qui est l'unité et la simplicité.

Ce Mémoire n'est pas un document pouvant fournir un alphabet tout prêt pour toutes les langues africaines. Dans bien des langues, nous manquons encore d'éléments indispensables pour construire un alphabet pratique. Même quand le système de sons d'une langue est suffisamment connu, un tel alphabet ne peut être mis debout que par quelqu'un qui connaît la langue à fond, et qui peut tenir compte de sa structure phonétique et grammaticale, parfois même de certaines considérations historiques et géographiques. L'article de D. Westermann dans le second volume de la revue *Africa* (v. plus bas) montre bien comment la chose peut être faite, et dans quelle mesure on peut tenir compte des situations existantes.

Dans cette deuxième édition nous avons inséré des recommandations relatives à divers sons et groupes de sons non mentionnés dans la première, mais que l'Institut a pris en considération récemment. Il est à peine besoin de dire qu'il reste bien des sons africains pour lesquels nous ne sommes pas à même de donner des avis.

La question de l'orthographe des langues africaines est discutée dans les articles et ouvrages suivants:

(1) A. Lloyd James: 'The Practical Orthography of African Languages', *Africa*, i, pp. 125–9.
(2) I. Carl Meinhof, II. Daniel Jones, 'Principles of Practical Orthography for African Languages', *Africa*, i, pp. 228–39.
(3) A. Lloyd James, 'Phonetics and African Languages', *Africa*, i, pp. 358–71.
(4) R. F. G. Adams and Ida C. Ward, 'The Arochuku Dialect of Ibo', *Africa*, ii, pp. 57–70.

(5) D. Westermann, 'The Linguistic Situation and Vernacular Education in British West Africa', *Africa*, ii, pp. 337–51.
(6) *A Common Script for Twi, Fante, Ga and Ewe*. Report by Prof. D. Westermann. Ordered by H. E. the Governor to be printed. Gold Coast Government Printer, Accra, 1927.
(7) *Report of the Rejaf Language Conference*. Published by the Sudanese Government, Londres, 1928.
(8) *Alphabets for the Efik, Ibo and Yoruba Languages*. Recommended by the Education Board, Lagos, Londres, 1929.
(9) *Alphabets for the Mende, Temne, Soso, Kono and Limba Languages*. International Institute of African Languages and Cultures.
(10) A. N. Tucker, *Suggestions for the Spelling of Transvaal Sesuto*. Memorandum VII of the International Institute of African Languages and Cultures.
(11) A. N. Tucker, *The Comparative Phonetics of the Suto-Chwana Group of Bantu Languages*. Longmans, Green & Co., 1929.
(12) R. A. C. Oliver, ' Psychological and Pedagogical Considerations in the making of Text-books', *Africa*, iii, pp. 293–304.
(13) *The New Script and its Relation to the Languages of the Gold Coast*. Published by the Crown Agents for the Colonies, Londres, 1930.

REPRÉSENTATION DES SONS

Consonnes.

1. L'Institut recommande d'écrire les langues africaines en se basant sur l'alphabet romain, en observant les indications suivantes :

2. (i) **b, d, f, h, k, l, m, n, p, s, t, v, w, z** sont à employer avec leurs valeurs ordinaires, en se conformant aux principes généraux exposés aux paragraphes 20–31, et en observant les conditions suivantes :

(*a*) Quand il est nécessaire de distinguer entre **p, t, k**, aspirés et non aspirés, on emploiera les lettres simples pour représenter les consonnes non aspirées, et **ph, th, kh** pour les consonnes aspirées. **ph** doit donc se prononcer comme dans l'Anglais *loop-hole* (Danois *penge*), non pas comme **f**; **th** comme dans l'Anglais *at home* (Danois *tale*), non pas comme dans l'Anglais *thin* ou *then*; **kh** comme dans l'Anglais *back-hand* (Danois *komme*). (*b*) Quand il est nécessaire de distinguer entre **t, d** dentales ou alvéolaires et **t, d** rétroflexes (cérébrales), on emploiera les lettres ordinaires pour les sons dentals ou alvéolaires et les lettres spéciales **ṭ ḍ** pour les sons rétroflexes. (Nous appelons alvéolaires les consonnes pour lesquelles la pointe de la langue s'appuie contre la racine des dents supérieures; rétroflexes celles pour lesquelles elle s'appuie contre le palais plus en arrière, soit juste avant les gencives soit plus en arrière encore. En Ewe il faut distinguer **du** 'ville' et **ḍu** 'poudre', **da** 'serpent' et **ḍa** 'cheveu'.

(ii) **ɡ** doit toujours avoir sa valeur d'explosive comme dans *gant, gui* (Anglais *get, go*).

r s'emploie soit pour la roulée linguale telle qu'elle se prononce dans la campagne française et en Écosse, soit pour le r fricatif de l'Anglais méridional.

x représente le son de l'Allemand *ach*, de l'Écossais *loch*, de l'Espagnol *bajo*. Si dans une langue on trouve aussi le son de l'Allemand *ich*, mais que l'emploi en est déterminé entièrement par l'influence des sons voisins, on peut aussi l'écrire **x**.

y aura la valeur qu'il a dans *yole* (Anglais *you, yet*). **ty, dy, ny, ly, sy, zy**, peuvent s'employer pour des **t, d, n, l, s, z** palatals; **ky, ɡy** pour des **k, ɡ** palatals ou palatalisés.

Quand une consonne palatale est précédée d'une voyelle, on entend souvent une espèce de **i** entre les deux: ceci est un 'son transitoire' inévitable, dû au caractère palatal de la consonne. Ainsi **anya** s'entend souvent comme **ainya**, et a été écrit **ainya** par quelques auteurs. Mais comme cet **i** n'est qu'un son transitoire et non un son indépendant, il n'est pas nécessaire ni utile de le représenter : il vaut mieux écrire **anya**.

kp, gb sont à employer pour les consonnes labio-vélaires fréquentes dans les langues du Soudan.

(iii) Nous recommandons l'emploi des lettres-consonnes suivantes, en plus des lettres romaines ordinaires (en se conformant aux Principes Généraux, § 31).

ŋ pour la nasale vélaire, c'est-à-dire le son de *ng* dans l'Anglais *sing*, l'Allemand *singen*.

ƒ pour *f* bilabial, comme dans les mots Ewe **ƒu** 'os', **ƒo** 'battre', à distinguer de **fu** 'plume', **fo** 'arracher' — On a aussi proposé **f** au lieu de ƒ.

ʋ pour *v* bilabial, c'est-à-dire le *w* de l'Allemand *schweben, schwimmen*. En Ewe il faut distinguer **ʋu** 'bateau', **ʋə** 'python', de **vu** 'déchirer', **və** 'être achevé'.

ʃ pour le *ch* français, *sh* anglais, *sch* allemand.

ʒ pour le *j* français, *s* de l'Anglais *pleasure*. — On a aussi proposé **ɉ** pour ce son.

ɣ pour la fricative vélaire voisée, le *g* de l'Allemand *Lage* (prononciation familière nord-allemande) et de l'Espagnol *luego*.

' pour la plosive laryngale, comme dans le Hausa **a'a** 'non'.

(iv) Pour les affriquées, nous recommandons l'emploi de groupes de lettres, comme suit : **pf** comme dans l'Allemand *hüpfen*, **bv** pour le son voisé correspondant, **ts** comme le *z* allemand, **dz** comme dans l'Italien *zitto*, **tʃ** comme le *ch* anglais, **dʒ** comme le *j* anglais. Dans quelques cas on conseille de remplacer **tʃ, dʒ** par les lettres simples **c, j**.

(v) On recommande de représenter comme suit les consonnes formées avec fermeture simultanée de la glotte : **p', t', k', s', ts'**, etc. ; par exemple : Hausa **k'ofa** 'porte'.—Pour **y** accompagné de cette fermeture, il paraît préférable d'écrire le ' en premier : Hausa **'ya'ya** 'enfants'.

(vi) *Sons implosifs*. Nous appelons ainsi des consonnes de nature plosive formées par succion de l'air (succion souvent très faible). Dans beaucoup de langues il y a fermeture de la glotte en même temps que consonne implosive ; mais la nature exacte des sons résultants n'a pas encore pu être déterminée dans tous les cas. Pour représenter le caractère particulier de ces sons, nous recommandons l'usage d'une apostrophe précédant la lettre usuelle : **'b, 'd, 'g**.

Il arrive souvent qu'une langue possède une seule implosive, qui est *b* : alors on conseille d'employer une lettre spéciale, **ɓ**. On peut aussi employer **ɗ** dans les langues qui ont un *d* implosif.

En Ibo, certains dialectes ont un **b** implosif là où d'autres emploient

gb. Pour l'Ibo littéraire on a adopté l'orthographe **gb**, parce que cette notation est déjà employée dans une partie de la littérature Ibo et dans des langues voisines.

(vii) *Consonnes dentales*. Dans les nouvelles orthographes des langues Bari, Nuer, Dinka, Shilluk, et autres langues soudanaises qui distinguent entre **t,d,n** dentals et alvéolaires, on a adopté la notation **th,dh,nh**, pour la variété dentale. Cet expédient n'est possible que pour les langues ne possédant pas de **t** aspiré.

(viii) *Sons latéraux*. Une décision sera probablement prise prochainement en Afrique du Sud, au sujet des sons latéraux et des clicks existant dans les langues de cette région. En conséquence nous donnons simplement ici la notation en usage actuellement et celle suggérée par le Dr. C. M. Doke.

Notation actuelle.	*Doke.*	
tl	tl	t avec explosion latérale
tlh	tlh	tl aspiré
hl	ɬ	s latéral (1 soufflé fricatif)
dhl	ɮ	z latéral (1 voisé fricatif)

La notation courante **hl, dhl** est loin d'être satisfaisante. Les suggestions du Dr. Doke, quoiqu'impliquant deux nouvelles lettres, constituent un progrès appréciable.

(ix) *Clicks*. On emploie actuellement, dans l'Afrique du Sud, les lettres suivantes pour représenter les clicks :
    c pour le click dental
    q pour le click rétroflexe
    x pour le click latéral.
Il y a aussi les combinaisons suivantes :

c	ch	nc	nch	gc	ŋc	ŋgc
q	qh	nq	nqh	gq	ŋq	ŋgq
x	xh	nx	nxh	gx	ŋx	ŋgx

Ici **nc, nq, nx**, représentent **n** suivi d'un click, tandis que **ŋc, ŋq, ŋx**, représentent des clicks complètement nasalisés. Mais comme les lettres **c** et **x** sont employées dans d'autres langues pour des sons totalement différents, et que les clicks sont des sons d'une nature tout à fait spéciale, on propose de leur affecter des signes spéciaux. On a recommandé les signes suivants :
    ʇ pour c
    ʗ pour q
    ʖ pour x

Mais il est à noter que les seules langues importantes contenant des clicks sont celles de l'Afrique du Sud. En outre, pour les clicks en combinaison, il paraît nécessaire d'employer ɡ̊ et ŋ̊ avec une valeur particulière, ɡ̊ pour marquer la voix et ŋ̊ pour la nasalisation (et non pas pour une consonne nasale). Alors, on peut se demander si l'introduction de signes spéciaux pour les clicks eux-mêmes est avantageuse.[1]

En Nama, dialecte Hottentot, on emploie depuis assez longtemps d'autres signes pour les clicks, savoir:

/ pour le click dental
≠ pour le click alvéolaire
! pour le click rétroflexe
// pour le click latéral

Comme le Nama est une langue peu importante et assez éloignée des autres langues à clicks, il sera sans doute préférable de ne pas changer l'orthographe en usage.

(x) *Labialisation.* Dans le nouvel alphabet employé pour les dialectes Shona, on a adopté les signes ṣ, ẓ pour les s, z labialisés.

Il semble nécessaire d'avoir un modifieur pour exprimer la 'labialisation palatale' qui joue un rôle important dans les langues du groupe Suto-Tchwana. Tucker a suggéré le signe ɥ (Voir, *Suggestions for the Spelling of Transvaal Sesuto*, pp. 15–18).

Voyelles.

3. Les lettres **a, e, i, o, u**, sont employées avec les valeurs dites italiennes. Quand il est nécessaire de distinguer un e fermé et un e ouvert[2], on écrira e pour la voyelle fermée, et ɛ (lettre nouvelle) pour la voyelle ouverte. De même, quand il est nécessaire de distinguer un o fermé et un o ouvert[3], on écrira o pour la voyelle fermée et ɔ pour la voyelle ouverte.

4. Quand une langue contient un 'o moyen' intermédiaire entre o et ɔ, comme l'Ibo, on peut le représenter par ɵ.

5. *Voyelles centrales.* Il y a des voyelles d'un caractère neutre ou intermédiaire, qui ne sont ni 'd'avant' comme **i, e**, ni 'd'arrière' comme **u, o**. Telle est la première voyelle des mots Anglais *about, along*, et, en quelque mesure, celle du Français *cheval*. Il y a bien des variétés de voyelles centrales: les unes sont accompagnées d'action labiale, les autres ne le sont pas; les unes, plus avancées, se rapprochent de la série d'avant (**i, e**), les autres, plus retirées, de la série d'arrière (**u, o**).

6. Quand une langue ne possède qu'une seule voyelle centrale, plutôt voisine de e, nous recommandons de la représenter par ə. Pour une voyelle centrale tirant sur o, nous proposons un o frappé d'un tréma, donc ö. Quand

---

[1] Pour le Zulu et le Xosa, si on continue à employer x pour le click latéral, on a suggéré l'emploi de χ pour la fricative vélaire (Allemand *ach*, Écossais *loch*).

[2] Comme en Français *é, è*.

[3] Comme dans le Français *Beaune, bonne*.

il y a plusieurs voyelles centrales devant être distinguées, il est difficile d'éviter les diacritiques. En Nuer, par exemple, en plus de o, ǝ, a, il y a trois voyelles centrales, qui ne peuvent guère se représenter autrement que par ö, ɔ̈, ä.

Diphthongues.

7. Nous recommandons d'écrire les diphthongues par des groupes de lettres, p.e. **ai, ɛi, ei, au, ǝi**. Ya et wa, etc., pourraient aussi être regardés comme diphthongues et écrits **ia, ua**, etc.; mais les orthographes **ya** et **wa** étant déjà courantes il semble préférable de les conserver.

Nasalisation.

8. Nous conseillons de marquer la nasalisation des voyelles en frappant la lettre-voyelle du tilde ~ placé au-dessus.

9. Il n'est pas toujours nécessaire de marquer la nasalisation, surtout quand une consonne nasale (**m, n, ny, ŋ**) précède ou suit la voyelle. Dans certains cas, même où il n'y a pas de consonne nasale, on peut omettre le tilde. En Mende par exemple, le mot qui veut dire 'dans' se prononce **hũ**; mais comme la langue ne possède pas de mot **hu** ni rien qui y ressemble, il n'y a pas de danger de confusion. Comme, en outre, c'est un mot très commun, on a décidé d'omettre le tilde.

10. Quand et dans quelle mesure peut-on omettre le tilde? De bonnes indications là-dessus se trouvent dans le *New Ga Primer, Teacher's Handbook*, par C. P. Moir; Ch. I, 'Notes on the new Ga Scripts' (Londres, 1929).

11. L'emploi de la lettre **n** pour marquer la nasalisation, en usage jusqu'ici dans certaines langues, n'est pas à encourager, il produit fatalement des confusions.

Durée.

12. On conseille de marquer les sons longs ou redoublés en redoublant la lettre. Ceci s'applique aux consonnes et aux voyelles. Exemples: Luganda **siga** 'sème!' **sigga** 'scorpion'; Akan **ǝmã** 'il donne', **ǝmmã** 'il ne donne pas'; Ewe **godo** 'là-bas', **godoo** 'autour', **fa** 'rafraîchir', **faa** 'librement'.

13. Dans certains cas pourtant, surtout quand la durée d'une voyelle peut servir à distinguer le sens, le signe · après la lettre peut être employé pour indiquer la longueur.

14. La longueur, comme la nasalité, n'est pas toujours nécessaire à marquer. Il suffit de la marquer quand la durée de la voyelle constitue la seule différence entre des mots qui autrement seraient identiques, mais qui diffèrent par leur sens ou leur emploi grammatical.

Tons musicaux.

15. Dans les livres destinés aux Africains, il n'est en général nécessaire d'indiquer les tons que s'ils ont une fonction grammaticale, ou s'ils servent

à distinguer des mots identiques pour tout le reste. Même alors ils peuvent parfois s'omettre, quand le contexte rend le sens parfaitement clair. En général il suffit de marquer deux tons, aigu (haut) et grave (bas).

16. Pour représenter les tons, nous conseillons l'emploi d'un accent sur la voyelle: ainsi á aigu, à grave. Un ton montant peut au besoin s'indiquer ainsi ă, un ton descendant ainsi â, un ton moyen ainsi ā. Exemples: Ewe mí'nous', mi 'vous'; lé 'saisir', le 'être'; Efik mî 'moi', mí 'ici', mi 'le mien' efé 'hangar', efe 'écureuil volant', éfe 'lequel?', éfĕ 'il vole'. (Les syllabes non marquées ont le ton grave).

17. Le professeur D. Jones recommande un système de signes plus complet, savoir ā ton aigu-uniforme, a̱ ton grave-uniforme, á ton aigu-montant, a̱ ton grave-montant, à ton aigu-descendant, a̱ ton grave-descendant, â ton montant-descendant, ă ton descendant-montant.

18. Ce système se recommande pour les langues ayant une intonation compliquée, ainsi que pour les travaux scientifiques. Dans quelques langues, par exemple le groupe Kru, il serait encore insuffisant pour rendre justice à la variété des tons employés. Répétons encore, que dans ce Mémoire nous nous occupons de la représentation des tons seulement en tant que c'est nécessaire pour rendre les textes intelligibles aux Africains.

Tableau des Sons.

19. Les lettres recommandées par notre Institut sont classées et rangées en un ordre systématique dans le tableau de la page 15.

PRINCIPES GÉNÉRAUX
DÉFINITIONS

1. *Phonèmes.*

20. Il arrive souvent que deux sons bien distincts existent dans une langue, mais que ceux qui parlent cette langue comme leur langue maternelle ne perçoivent pas la différence, ou en tout cas les considèrent comme des variétés insignifiantes. Ceci a lieu régulièrement, quand l'un des deux sons ne se rencontre que dans certaines positions données, tandis que l'autre ne se trouve jamais dans ces mêmes positions.

21. Ainsi en Français le k de *qui* et celui de *quoi* sont bien différents; mais l'emploi de ces deux sons est entièrement déterminé par la qualité de la voyelle suivante. Nous les considérons donc comme deux variétés de k. Il en est de même des deux k dans l'Anglais *keep, collar*, ou dans l'Allemand *Kiel, Kuh*.

22. Il y a aussi des langues où le son ŋ se trouve seulement dans les combinaisons ŋk, ŋg, ŋw, ŋh, où n'apparaît jamais le son n. On peut alors considérer ŋ comme une simple variété de n, et écrire nk, ng, nw, nh. En

	Bi-labiales	Labio-dentales	Dentales et Alvéolaires	Post-alvéolaires	Rétroflexes (Cérébrales)	Palatales	Vélaires	Laryngales
CONSONNES								
Explosives	p b		t d		ṭ ḍ	ty dy ky gy	k ġ	ʼ
Implosives	ɓ		ɗ					
Affriquées	pf bv		ts dz	tʃ dʒ (=c j)			kx	
Nasales	m		n			ny	ŋ	
Latérales — Explosives			tl dl					
Latérales — Fricatives			ɬ ɮ					
Latérales — Sans friction			l			ly		
Roulées			r					
Fricatives	f v	f v	s z	ʃ ʒ		sy zy	x ɣ	h
Semi-voyelles	w					y	(w)	
VOYELLES								
Fermées	(u)					i	u	
Mi-fermées	(o)					e	o	
Mi-ouvertes	(e)					ɛ	ɛ	
Ouvertes						a		

Italien, par exemple, le *n*, de *banco, lungo*, se prononce ŋ; mais comme ŋ n'existe pas en Italien en tant que son indépendant (p.ex. devant voyelle), on peut considérer ce ŋ comme une variété de n. Au contraire, en Anglais et en Allemand, ŋ n'est pas une variété de **n**, parce que les deux sons se rencontrent dans les mêmes positions: comparez l'Anglais *sin, sing* (en phonétique **sin, siŋ**) l'Allemand *sinnen, singen* (en phonétique **zinən, ziŋən**).

23. Il y a des langues ou des variantes dialectales où existe une tendance à prononcer vélaires toutes les nasales finales, à substituer donc ŋ à m ou à **n** finals. Si la prononciation avec **m** ou **n** existe, et que ŋ ne se trouve pas comme phonème indépendant, il vaut mieux écrire toujours **m** ou **n** et ignorer la tendance à la prononciation vélaire.

24. Mais si ŋ existe dans la langue en tant que phonème indépendant, nous recommandons d'écrire ŋ partout où ce son se rencontre, devant **k** et **ġ** aussi bien que devant les voyelles.

25. En Zulu il existe un **e** fermé et un **e** ouvert. Mais ces voyelles sont employées suivant un certain principe d'harmonie vocalique; en pratique, donc, on peut les considérer comme une unité linguistique du Zulu, et toujours écrire **e**. En Akan, langue de l'Afrique occidentale, le **w** de **wu, wo, wɔ**, est très différent de celui de **wi, we, wɛ**; mais l'usage de ces deux sons étant déterminé par la voyelle suivante, on doit les considérer comme ne faisant qu'un. En Kikuyu le son **ġ** ne se trouve que dans le groupe **ŋġ**, tandis qu'ailleurs figure le son voisin ɣ, lequel par contre ne se trouve jamais après ŋ: alors **ġ** et ɣ peuvent se considérer comme ne faisant qu'un en Kikuyu. En Tchwana on emploie devant **i** et **u** une variété de **l** ressemblant à **d**, devant les autres voyelles un **l** ordinaire: la différence est négligeable du point de vue des indigènes.

26. On emploie le mot *phonème* pour désigner une petite famille de sons voisins les uns des autres, qui peut être considéré comme une unité linguistique pour des raisons de ce genre.

27. Dans beaucoup de cas un phonème ne comprend qu'un seul son. Les noms *phonème* et *son* peuvent s'employer indifféremment pour les consonnes **f, m, n, v** en Français et en Anglais, car la prononciation de ces consonnes n'est pas influencée d'une manière appréciable par les sons qui les entourent.

28. Ce sont les phonèmes qui, dans toutes les langues, peuvent servir à distinguer un mot d'un autre. Ainsi comme nous l'avons vu, les phonèmes **n** et ŋ distinguent des mots en Anglais et en Allemand. Les variétés fermées et ouvertes de **e** et de **o** (c.-à-d. e–ɛ, o–ɔ) distinguent des mots en Français, dans la plupart des langues Ouest-africaines, en Tchwana, en Soto, et dans beaucoup d'autres langues; dans ces langues, ce sont des phonèmes distincts.

2. *Diaphones.*

29. Souvent les mêmes mots sont prononcés d'une manière un peu dif-

férente par des personnes parlant la même langue. Ainsi en Français et en Allemand, les uns prononcent *r* du bout de la langue, les autres de la luette. En Anglais, la voyelle de *bad* se prononce diversement dans diverses parties du pays.

30. On emploie le terme *diaphone* pour désigner un son normal avec les variantes de ce son telles que les prononcent diverses personnes parlant la même langue.

PRINCIPES D'ORTHOGRAPHE

31. Voici les principes généraux à observer pour fixer l'orthographe d'une langue donnée :
(1) L'orthographe d'une langue doit se baser sur le principe : Une lettre pour chaque phonème de la langue. Autrement dit, chaque fois que deux mots se distinguent par le son, ils doivent aussi se distinguer par l'écriture.
(2) Il faut reconnaître l'existence des diaphones et en tenir compte. Ainsi les Fanté parlant la langue Akan prononcent **di** comme **dzi** et **ti** comme **tsi**; mais l'orthographe **di ti** suffit pour les deux variétés de prononciation. En Hausa, certains dialectes prononcent le **f** labio-dental, d'autres un ƒ bilabial, d'autres encore **p**; mais on peut employer toujours **f**, en tenant compte des prononciations dialectales par des conventions appropriées.
(3) Il est parfois préférable de sacrifier la rigeur phonétique, pour éviter d'écrire le même mot de plusieurs manières différentes. Ainsi en Luganda, il vaut mieux écrire **soka oleke** 'attends un peu', quoiqu'en fait on dise **sok oleke**. De même en Akan il vaut mieux écrire ɔ **hwɛ no** 'il l'a vu', quoique dans beaucoup de régions le **o** final disparaisse. En Akan encore, il est préférable de toujours écrire **hwɛ**, bien que ce mot devienne **hwe** quand la syllabe suivante contient un **i** ou un **u**, comme dans ɔ **hwɛ mu**.
Il y a lieu d'agir de même pour de nombreux cas d'harmonie vocalique en Akan et dans d'autres langues.
Toutefois, notons expressément que les règles qui gouvernent l'harmonie vocalique et l'assimilation en Akan et dans d'autres langues, sont souvent nombreuses et compliquées, et ne peuvent pas se définir une fois pour toutes par une règle simple. Seule la structure phonétique et grammaticale de chaque langue peut déterminer jusqu'à quel point l'orthographe courante doit tenir compte de ces phénomènes.
(4) Par manière de concession à l'usage établi, on peut parfois employer une lettre romaine à la place d'une lettre nouvelle appropriée, quand le son proprement représenté par la lettre romaine n'existe pas dans la langue. Ainsi on peut employer **f** au lieu de ƒ en Tchwana, parce

que le **f** labio-dental n'existe pas dans cette langue. De même en Oshikuanyama on peut écrire **s** pour **ʃ** parce que cette langue ne possède pas le **s** ordinaire. De même encore, si une langue ne possède que le **t** rétroflexe, on peut écrire **t**, sans recourir au signe spécial de la consonne rétroflexe. En Hausa il y a un **ts** uni à une occlusion glottale, donc **ts'** (remplacé par **s'** ou par **t'** dans certains dialectes). Mais comme la langue n'a pas de groupe **ts** sans occlusion glottale, nous conseillons d'ignorer celle-ci et d'écrire simplement **ts**.

MAJUSCULES ET FORMES ÉCRITES

32. Nous donnons ci-dessous les majuscules imprimées des lettres nouvelles les plus importantes et les formes manuscrites des lettres tant petites que grandes. L'Institut fournira sur demande des détails sur la forme exacte d'autres lettres.

Romaines.	Italiques.	Manuscrites.	Romaines.	Italiques.	Manuscrites.
a A	a A	a A	l L	l L	l L
b B	b B	b B	m M	m M	m M
ɓ Ɓ	ɓ Ɓ	ɓ Ƃ	n N	n N	n N
c C	c C	c C	ŋ Ŋ	ŋ Ŋ	ŋ Ŋ
d D	d D	d D	o O	o O	o O
ɖ Ɖ	ɖ Ɖ	ɖ ou dʼ Ɖ	ɔ Ɔ	ɔ Ɔ	ɔ Ɔ
e E	e E	e E	p P	p P	p P
ɛ Ɛ	ɛ Ɛ	ɛ Ɛ	r R	r R	r ou ɼ R
ə Ə	ə Ə	ə Ə	s S	s S	s ou ʃ S
f F	f F	f F	ʃ Σ	ʃ Σ	ʃ ʃ
ƒ Ƒ	ƒ Ƒ	ƒ Ƒ	t T	t T	t T
g G	g G	g G	u U	u U	u U
ɣ Ɣ	ɣ Ɣ	ɣ Ɣ	v V	v V	v V ou v V
h H	h H	h H	ʋ Ʋ	ʋ Ʋ	ʋ ou ʋ Ʋ
x X	x X	x X	w W	w W	w W
i I	i I	i I	y Y	y Y	y Y
j J	j J	j J	z Z	z Z	z Z
k K	k K	k K	ʒ Ʒ	ʒ Ʒ	ʒ Ʒ

ORDRE ALPHABÉTIQUE DES LETTRES

Nous recommandons d'écrire les principales lettres selon l'ordre alphabétique suivant:

a b ɓ c d ɖ e ɛ ə f ƒ g ɣ h x i j k l m n ŋ o ɔ p r s ʃ t u v ʋ w y z ʒ '

Les voyelles nasalisées doivent suivre les voyelles ordinaires, les voyelles centrales suivre les nasalisées: ainsi o õ ö. D'autres nouvelles lettres doivent suivre celles dont elles sont dérivées : ɖ doit suivre d, ʂ suivre s. Si on introduit des lettres spéciales pour les clicks, on propose de les mettre à la fin de l'alphabet. Dans les vocabulaires et dictionnaires, on conseille de placer les mots commençant par des digraphes (**dy, dz, dʒ, kp, ts, tʃ**, etc.) en groupes séparés, à la suite de tous les mots commençant simplement par **d, k, t** etc.

Noms des consonnes.

b	ɓ	c	d	ɖ	f	ƒ	g	ɣ	h	x	j	k	l	m	n
be	ɓa	ce	de	ɖa	ef	if	ga	ɣe	ha	ex	je	ke	el	em	en
		(tʃe)									(dʒe)				

ŋ	p	r	s	ʃ	t	v	ʋ	w	y	z	ʒ	'
iŋ	pe	ra	es	iʃ	te	ve	ʋi	wa	ya	ze	ʒi	a'a

SPÉCIMENS DE L'ORTHOGRAPHE RECOMMANDÉE

(Les spécimens marqués d'un astérisque * sont tirés de livres où la nouvelle orthographe est employée.)

Akan.*

Ɔdɔ dwo ne ani, ne yam ye, ɔdɔ nyɛ ahõɔyaw, ɔdɔ nyɛ ahoahoa, ɛŋhoraŋ, ɛnyɛ nehõ sɛnea ɛmfata, ɛŋhwehwɛ nea ɛyɛ ne aŋkasa de, ne bo ŋhaw no, ɛmfa bone ŋhyɛ ne yam, ne ani nye nea ɛntɛ̃ɛ hõ, na ɛne nokware ani gye, etie a ade nnyina, egye ade nnyina di, enya ade nnyina mu anidaso. Ɔdɔ to ntwa da. Na afei gyidi, ɔdɔ, anidaso na etrã hɔ, na ɔdɔ na ɛne mu kɛse.

(Tiré de 'Ɛha amanne kwaŋ so aware Ɛso Ɖhyira', p. 7.)

Bambara.

Kŋo sogo bee yi i nyogõ la dye k u be dlo dõ u ko sogo o sogo bee ka na ni nyo more more ye. Sogo bee nana n ata ye. Suruku ba e o me mi ŋke a y ala muru ba ta, a bina a da la dia la.

Tchwana.

Tlhaloxanyɔ ya tlou xoŋwe yane ekete ke ya motho. Betʃwana ba boxolo-xolo bare tlou ekile ya foloxɛla mo nokeŋ ya Sampisi, ya fitlha ya nwa. Erile e santse e nwa, ya utlwa kwena e e kapa ka selɔpɔ, ere e e xɔxɛla mo metsiŋ. Kefa tlou e inola kwena, e e tʃholetsa ka selɔpɔ, e e kakamara, e e isa ko naxeŋ, kxakalakxakala le noka. Erile e fitlha ko likakeŋ ya baya kwena fa fatshe, yare : 'kana orile oa m polaya ? Sala jalo hɛ, ke bɔnɛ xore a o tla tshela kwa ntlɛ xa metse !'

Duala.

Ngɔkɔlɔ na dibobɛ ba ta dikɔm, ba yenga babɔ babanɛ ponda yɛsɛ. Nde ba ta ba ja o ekwali bunya bɔɔ, nde na ngɔkɔlɔ e kwalanɛ dibobɛ na : A dikɔm lam la ndolo, na malangwea nde oa na mbalɛ, bato ba si masenga, be ndɔki.

(Tiré d'un texte dans 'Africa', vol. ii, p. 72, janv. 1929.)

Efik.

Tiŋ enyin tim se uŋwana oro, neŋere tiene enye; ke ntre ke afo edikut inua-otop oro ; tuak, ndien mɔ eyeteme fi se afo edinamde. Ndien ŋkokut ke ndap mi nte owo oro otibide itɔk efege. Ekem enye ika-ikaha kaŋa anyan usuŋ ikpɔŋ ufɔk esie; ndien kadaŋemi ŋwan esie ye nditɔ esie ekutde, mɔ etɔŋo ndifiori ŋkot enye, ete afiak edi; edi enye esin nuenubɔk ke utɔŋ, efege itɔk, ete, 'Uwem ! uwem! nsi-nsi uwem !'

Ewe.*

Asime. Asi ɖina le tefe geɖewo le ŋkeke ene sia ŋkeke megbe. Ame geɖewo va ʃoa ʃu ɖe afima. Wotsoa bli, te, mɔli, agbeli, fofoŋ, fetri, agbitsa, atadi kple kutsetse bubu geɖewo, ɖetifu, de, nɛʃi, amidzẽ, nɛmi, yɔkumi kple nu bubu geɖewo va dzrana. Ga si woxɔna la, wotsonɛ ʃlea avɔ, ɖeti, atama, sukli, kple ŋudɔwɔnu siwo wohiã. Ðeviwo lɔa asimedede.

(Tiré de 'Eʋegbegbalẽxexlẽ na Gɔmedzelawo', p. 64.)

Ga.*

Dʒata ko hi ʃi yɛ dʒeŋ a·hu. Agbɛnɛ egbo hewo lɛ enyẽẽ emomo hewalɛ na· doŋŋ. Enɛ hewo lɛ eyakã ʃi yɛ ebu lɛ mli akɛ ehe mi· ye. Koloi lɛ ba· eŋo ekome-kome ni amɛbasra· lɛ yɛ ebu lɛ mli. Osɔ le enɛ fẽ hewo lɛ ete koni eyasra dʒata helatʃɛ nɛ. Beni ete lɛ ebotee bu lɛ mli. Edamɔ sɛ ʃoŋŋ ni ebi dʒata lɛ akɛ, 'Helatʃɛ! te oyo teŋŋ?'

(Tiré de 'New Ga Primer', par C. P. Moir, Part 2, p. 24.)

Ila.

Uʃɛsu udi kwizɛulu, nadiile iʒina dyako, nabuzize buɔneki bwako, nalu-tʃitwe luzando lwako anʃi ano ubudi kwizɛulu. Σidyo nʃi tubula utupe bwasunu. Utulekelɛle milandu, bubɔna mbu tubalekelɛle kale obadi milandu kudi uswɛ. Utatuenʒa mu kutepaulwa, utuʋune ku bubiabe. Ukuti buɔneki mbu bwako, iinsana, obulɛmu, ʃikwense o ʃikwense.

Kikuyu.

Idɛ wito we igoro, reetwa reaku nereamoroɔ. Odamaki waku ookɛ. Ɔ orea wɛndɛtɛ wɛ, newekagwɔ goko de, ɔ ta orea wekagwɔ kou igoro. Tohɛ omode iriɔ ciito cia gotoigana. Na otorɛkɛrɛ madire maito, ɔ ta orea idue torɛkagera area mare na madire maito. Na ndogatotwarɛ magɛriɔ-ine, nɔ kohonɔkia otohonɔkagiɛ ooru-ine.

ORTHOGRAPHE PRATIQUE DES LANGUES AFRICAINES

Lokele.

Bowase atolimba ɔnɔkɔ.
Mbuu esoofeta.
Bosokola ngwa nda liulu, koicakae anyo.
Itɔɔ kwa ʃa ombolo wa koba.
Loo loca okuki, angowa ae kosinga.

Mende.*

Mu gɔnɛi gbe, ngi mayomboi manyɛingɔ, tɛli lɔ hu kɛ kolei.
Ngi yamɛisia gbe kea ta vo dão.
A kulɔlɔ a foloi kɛ kpindii.
Ta hani manɛma tɛnga nyina mia.
Ta hei kpɛ, ngi wolii mia a sɛsia.
Ngi longɔ i ye hanii hou ngi lenga va.
(Tiré de 'Koyɛima kaa Gɔlɔisia', Yehalayɛi, p. 25.)

Nyanja.

Mphepo yakumpoto ndidzua zinali kumenyana, imodzi yaizo inati ine ndiri wamphamvu kupambana iwe, ndipo inzace inati iai ine ndiri wamphamvu kupambana iwe. Koma zinaona mlendo mmodzi alikupita anabvala ntsaru yorimba ndithu, zinapaŋgana ndani abvule ntsaru yamlendo uyu adzaitanidwa wamkulu kupambana mnzace. Mphepo yakumpoto inaomba kwambiri koma iŋgakhale inaomba ndithu, mlendo uja anagwiritsa ntsaru yace. Ndipo mphepo yakumpoto inalephera kumbvula ntsaru, ndipo dzua linaturuka ndikutentha ndithu. Mlendo anamasula ntsaru yace ndikucotsa yontse, ndipo mphepo yakumpoto inati wanditha ndiwe mfumu.

Pedi.

Moleta ŋwedi o leta lefsifsi.
Moruswana xe o tshela lefao o eletʃa o moŋ.
Pshiu tʃa tlou xa di pataxanywe.
Mpʃa e tala e bolaya ka xo tsoxɛla.
A e tswhe dibza.
Mokxola morithi xa se modudi wa ɔna.
Xa o tʃhaba pula o tʃhabe modumo; xa o tʃhaba marotholodi a pula, ea xonɛla.
(Mma, tʃaka xe diapᶙa a se ʃetʃe; ke pᶙhapᶙha diatla, ka lesa tʃampholoxa ka maxetla.)[1]

Shilluk.*

Ya yito ki gin dɔc. Agin? Ya yiti riŋo. Dɔc, kani yuk othal wa. Riŋo mi awany ki kɛli lum. Kani loth o yiejo nak. Yanythɛnho anaki yiec ma

[1] Dans cette phrase le signe ᶙ suggéré par Tucker pour la labialisation palatale, est employé provisoirement. V. Section 2 (x), p. 12.

gir. Kɛtho wak dway yuk. Ya yito ki tɔŋ mia ma dɔc. Ya dwato bɛth ki loth anan. Gin cam athal ? Ɖe ! Dɛ wa bɛ cam. Wa ocamo anan.
(Tiré de 'Wanyo Kipa Tiiŋ Gwɛt', No. 1, p. 11.)

Shona (dialecte Zezuru).

Ruŋgano rwaTsuro naHamba.
ʋakafurirana kundocera tsime. ⱬino Tsuro akaramba. Hamba wakaenda kundotṣaga ʋanaƩumba. ⱬino ʋanaƩumba ʋakacera tsime. ⱬino Tsuro wakauya kuzoƁa mvura. Akauya namaɗende ake. Akawana Hamba aripo. Akamuwona, akatiza.
Rimɲe zuʋa akawana Hamba akahwanda mumvura. ⱬino akaɗa kucera mvura. Hamba akaƁata ruwoko rwaTsuro. ⱬino Tsuro akati, 'Rega kundiƁata.' Tsuro akati, 'Rega, ndinokutṣagira huci.' Hamba waregera Tsuro. ⱬino Tsuro wakapa huci kunaƩumba. Tsuro wakati, 'Rega, nditaŋge ndakusuŋga sekuru'. ⱬino Tsuro wakayisa mabge muhuci. Akayisa mabge mukanwa maƩumba. ⱬino Tsuro wakasimuka orova Ʃumba.

Shona (dialecte Karanga).

Ʃuro icinyeŋgere-ʃumba.
Rimɲe zu a ʃuro yakaʃoŋgana neʃumba, ikati, 'Sekuru munotsakei ?' Ʃumba ikati, 'Ndinovima.' Ʃuro ikati, 'Cihendei kugomo, muŋgondoʋata makaita majaɗa pamukwara wemhuka, ini ndigondodziŋge-mhuka mugomo, imi makagaridzira.' Nambera ʃuro inonyeŋgere-ʃumba, kuti ʃumba igotakwa nebge rinokuŋguruswa mugomo neʃuro. ⱬino ʃumba yakandoʋatapo, ndokuhwa hurumatanda dziciʋirima dzicibvo-mugomo. Ʃumba ndokuvata paɖiʋi, mabge aya ndokupfuʋura. Ʃumba ndokudzokera paya payasiyiwa neʃuro, ndokuvata ẓe yakaita maneɗe. ⱬino ʃuro ndokuvaŋga, ndokuti, 'Ndakaŋguʋa ndarubvira rwokuvuraye-ʃumba !' ⱬino ikati icitore-Ɓaŋga rokuvuraye-ʃumba, ʃumba ndokuƁate-ʃuro, mambaʋa ndokuwadzuka, ʃuro ndokutiza icidziŋgana neʃumba. Ʃuro ndokupinda mugwiriŋgwindi, ʃumba ndokuƁato-mɲise weʃuro. Ʃuro ikati, 'Mandikoniwa maƁato-mudzi !' Ʃumba ndokuregedza. Ʃuro ikati, 'Ohii, hamuzandikoniwa !' Ndokugara mumɲena kuṣika ʃumba yainda.

Soso.

Woŋ fafe, naxaŋ na ariana, i xili xa sɛniyeŋ. I yamanɛ xa fa. I sago xa niɲa dunia ma, alɔ a niɲaxi ariana kɛnaxai. Woŋ ki to woŋma lɔxɔ o lɔxɔ doŋse ra. Anuŋ ixa woŋma fekobi kafari, alɔ woŋtaŋ nee kafarima kɛnaxai naxaŋ fekobi niɲa woŋ ra. Anuŋ i nama woŋ raso fekobi maniɲa. Kɔnɔ i xa woŋ rakisi fekobi ma. Katugu itaŋ naŋ gbe yamanɛ ra, anuŋ sɛmbɛ anuŋ yigi ra abada anuŋ abada.

ORTHOGRAPHE PRATIQUE DES LANGUES AFRICAINES

Swahili.

Akanena yule mtume: 'Ee Muungu wangu, aliyecukua feza mtu mgine, na aliyeuawa mgine, amezulumiwa yule.' Mwenyiezi Muungu akamʃuʃia walii akamwambia; 'Wewe tazama ibada yako, na ukitaka mambo haya, si kazi yako.' Akamwambia; 'Baba yake yule wa kwanza alimnyaŋanya dinar alf katika mali za babae yule kijana, hamleta yule kijana kuja twaa mali ya babae. Na yule mcanja kuni alimua babae yule wa kwanza hamleta kijana kuja kutoa kisasi tya babae.'[1]

Temne.*

Hawa ɔ yi rɔ rɔ su.
A lɔkɔ o lɔkɔ ɔ ti kɔ ro karaŋde.
Hawa ɔ ti karaŋ akafa kətɔtɔkɔ kaake.
Ɔ karaŋ mump məfinɔ ɔ yema ŋa.
Anfəm ŋa Hawa ɔ bonɛ ŋa tək karaŋ ka ɔwan kaŋaŋ.
Hawa ɔ karaŋ akafa ka ɔkas kɔŋ yi ɔya kɔŋ.
Aŋ yema yi ɔbana.

(Tiré de 'Atafa Takaraŋ ta koyɛima', Kətɔtɔkɔ, p. 13.)

Xosa.

Kwathi xa umoya wase zantsi wauphikisana ne laŋga ukuɓa ŋguwuphina onamanƙa kuɓo ɓoɓaɓini, kwa fika umhambi ambethe iŋguɓo efudumeleyo. Ɓavumelana ukuɓa oŋgaqala a mendze umhambi ukuɓa alaɬe iŋguɓo yakhe woɓa woyisile. Utheke umoya wase zantsi wavuthuza ŋgawo oŋke amanaƙa awo, kwathi okukhona uvuthuzayo kwaɓa kokukhona umhambi ayisondezayo iŋguɓo yakhe. Ekupheleni umoya wase zantsi wancama. Laza ke lona ilaŋga la khanya ŋgokuʃuʃu, waza umhambi wayilaɬa iŋguɓo. Wavumake umoya wase zantsi ukuɓa lilaŋga elinamanƙa.

Yoruba.

Ida li akɔ. Aroko tu ilɛ. Ɔmɔbirĩ wɛ ɔwɔ rɛ. Onile ra iʃu. Ki ɛ duro de wa nihĩyi titi awa o fi lɔ si ohũ. Ḍwɔ su adi. Apɔ̃ da ɛkɔ̃. Aŋwɔ aroko ro oko. Ɛ nyĩ fa kɛkɛ. Awa bɛ nyi. Alase se onjɛ. Σile mɛta ni yi. Mo ri ɛgbɔ̃. Ewurɛ jɛ koriko. Ɔrɔ otitɔ li o ŋsɔ. Ḍwɔ ŋlu agogo ile-ɛkɔ wa.

Zulu.

Aɓelungu ɓahamba ngemikhumbi, ɓayizingele. Ɓaphatha imikhonto eminingi emikhulu, enezintlenƙa, nezintambo nemiphongolo emiŋgi. Ɓathi qedi ɓafike elwanƙe umkhomo uɓonakale, ɓasondela kaɬe ɓathekelezele intambo emkhontweni ɓawugwaze.

(Adapté de la version donnée par Doke, 'Phonetics of Zulu', p. 279.)

[1] Vu qu'il y a peu de mots Swahili contenant un ŋ immédiatement suivi d'une voyelle, ou propose d'écrire le groupe ŋg ainsi: **ng**. Il serait plus logique, au point de vue des indigènes, d'écrire ŋg; mais **ng** a l'avantage de ne pas changer les habitudes reçues.

PRINTED IN GREAT BRITAIN AT THE UNIVERSITY PRESS, OXFORD
BY JOHN JOHNSON, PRINTER TO THE UNIVERSITY

THE DISTRIBUTION OF THE SEMITIC AND CUSHITIC LANGUAGES OF AFRICA
An Outline of Available Information

M. A. BRYAN

LONDON AND NEW YORK

First published in 1947 by Oxford University Press

This edition first published in 2018
by Routledge
2 Park Square, Milton Park, Abingdon, Oxon OX14 4RN

and by Routledge
711 Third Avenue, New York, NY 10017

Routledge is an imprint of the Taylor & Francis Group, an informa business

© 1947 International African Institute 1947

All rights reserved. No part of this book may be reprinted or reproduced or utilised in any form or by any electronic, mechanical, or other means, now known or hereafter invented, including photocopying and recording, or in any information storage or retrieval system, without permission in writing from the publishers.

Trademark notice: Product or corporate names may be trademarks or registered trademarks, and are used only for identification and explanation without intent to infringe.

British Library Cataloguing-in-Publication Data
A catalogue record for this book is available from the British Library

ISBN: 978-1-138-08975-4 (Set)
ISBN: 978-1-315-10381-5 (Set) (ebk)
ISBN: 978-1-138-09586-1 (Volume 12) (hbk)
ISBN: 978-1-138-09621-9 (Volume 12) (pbk)
ISBN: 978-1-315-10552-9 (Volume 12) (ebk)

Publisher's Note
The publisher has gone to great lengths to ensure the quality of this reprint but points out that some imperfections in the original copies may be apparent.

Disclaimer
The publisher has made every effort to trace copyright holders and would welcome correspondence from those they have been unable to trace.

Due to modern production methods, it has not been possible to reproduce the fold-out maps within the book. Please visit www.routledge.com to view them.

THE DISTRIBUTION OF THE SEMITIC AND CUSHITIC LANGUAGES OF AFRICA

An Outline of Available Information

COMPILED BY

M. A. BRYAN

Published for the
INTERNATIONAL AFRICAN INSTITUTE
by the
OXFORD UNIVERSITY PRESS
LONDON NEW YORK TORONTO
1947

Oxford University Press, Amen House, London E.C.4
EDINBURGH GLASGOW NEW YORK TORONTO MELBOURNE
WELLINGTON BOMBAY CALCUTTA MADRAS CAPE TOWN
Geoffrey Cumberlege, Publisher to the University

PRINTED IN GREAT BRITAIN
AT THE UNIVERSITY PRESS, OXFORD
BY CHARLES BATEY
PRINTER TO THE UNIVERSITY

PREFACE

THE International African Institute has undertaken the preparation of a *Handbook of African Languages*, and for the past three years its research staff has been engaged on preparatory studies, including the scrutiny of available published and unpublished documents, consultations by correspondence and interview with linguistic experts, and surveys in the field. The present paper represents an analysis of the available information on the Semitic and Cushitic languages of Eritrea, Ethiopia, and the Anglo-Egyptian Sudan. It was decided to issue it at this stage in the hope that it might be of use to language students, and, more important, might provoke criticism and lead to further study.

The method of arrangement and classification used in this paper is based on a technique devised for the purpose by the Linguistic Advisory Committee of the Institute, which has been charged with the direction of the work on the Handbook.

The starting-point for the classification is not the large area but the individual language; related languages are grouped together into larger sections which have some linguistic significance, since the principal criteria of grouping are linguistic. Since the individual language is taken as the basic unit of classification, it is necessary to determine exactly what this unit is. In some cases this proves difficult, particularly where several dialects have been recognized within one language. Thus it is necessary to distinguish different types of basic unit: (1) a language without recognized dialectal variations; (2) a language with which is associated a number of relatively less important dialects; (3) a number of dialects no one of which appears to dominate. The term 'language' will be used for (1) and (2), but (3) will be termed a 'dialect cluster'. For purposes of classification, however, they are all treated as basic units.

In the case of the simple 'language', i.e. type (1), no subdivision is necessary; the other units, however, may be subdivided into dialects, that is, into something smaller than a unit. Useful or even necessary though this subdivision may be for purposes of reference, it must be emphasized that this is a kind of fragmentation, since the dialect is always smaller than the basic unit.

A number of adjacent units may be found to display a certain relationship. This gives rise to a 'group', and this term is reserved exclusively to denote a number of related languages or dialect clusters. Any loose use of this word, therefore, becomes undesirable in view of the precise linguistic significance given to it. The group is in fact the only other level of classification which appears in this system. The criteria governing the establishment of groups are linguistic; in certain cases, where these criteria are indecisive, it becomes necessary to take other factors into consideration.

Certain things must be observed about this use of only two essential levels of classification. Since the group is fundamental to the system wherever classification proves to be possible, it will sometimes be composed of one basic unit only. This will happen where a language or dialect cluster appears to have little relationship with neighbouring ones. On the other hand, a group may sometimes consist of several units between which there is an uneven closeness of relationship. While it is useful to know that certain members of the group are more closely related to each other than to the others, this does not justify the use of a term such as 'sub-group', which would have no clear meaning. Where we have an area in which the relationship between the languages is or appears to be insufficient to justify classification into groups, we are left with only the basic unit, i.e. language or dialect cluster. This will also be the case where a language is found with no apparent relationship to any other.

In view of the vast number of languages to be covered by the Handbook, it is necessary to arrange it in sections. Since common usage has loosely distinguished certain blocks of languages such as Semitic, Cushitic, &c., it is often convenient to make use of these terms. The word 'language-family' is, however, avoided as being of doubtful value for our purpose. When the languages of any section have been put into groups, no attempt is made to establish any larger linguistic unit, since the practical value of such larger units is questionable. In some cases, however, as in Bantu, there may be so many groups that it becomes desirable to arrange the groups in sets for ease of reference. This is done on a geographical basis, and the term 'zone' is used for this purpose. Even though linguistic considerations may govern the limits of the zones, the significance of the zones remains geographical, as they serve simply to make reference more easy.

Here, then, is a summary of the system adopted. The basic unit is the LANGUAGE or DIALECT CLUSTER. These basic units are put together into GROUPS. There are certain cases where it becomes necessary to list the subdivisions of the basic unit, i.e. the dialects. There are certain other cases where it may be convenient to use the term *zone*. The dialects and zones are, however, not essential parts of the system, which is concerned with Languages and Dialect Clusters in their Groups.

A bibliography of the sources consulted in the preparation of this paper is appended, and this includes also all the relevant published works of which information could be obtained. The bibliography, though annotated, does not claim to be critical.

The present work, as indicated in its sub-title, is not to be taken as anything but an outline. An authoritative study of these languages will be included in the Handbook. It has become clear, however, that such a definitive work could not be undertaken until the reliability of much of the existing material had been tested and the many important gaps in the data filled. It has been possible to collect a certain amount of information, but there must be much additional material in the hands of workers in the field of which we have no record. If the publication of this paper serves to reveal such gaps and leads to their being filled, and at the same time secures the collaboration of workers in the areas concerned, its purpose will have been achieved.

The compiler and the Linguistic Advisory Committee desire to express their indebtedness to all who have made available unpublished studies, have answered inquiries, and, in ways too numerous to mention, have put their knowledge and experience at the disposal of the Institute. In particular, acknowledgement is made to:

Dr. E. Cerulli	Capt. G. W. B. Huntingford
Dr. S. F. Nadel	Counsellor Retta
Major Duncanson	Mr. A. C. A. Wright

IDA WARD
Chairman, Linguistic Advisory Committee

NOTES

1. Names of languages and tribes are given as follows: The first name given is the officially recognized name of the language or tribe in the spelling used by the Government concerned. If this is not known, the first name given is the one most generally used.

    Alternative versions as used by various writers are given in brackets.

    Phonetic renderings of names are given, where known, in the 'Africa' orthography.

2. Where an authority is quoted without a footnote reference to a published work, the information was given personally.

SEMITIC LANGUAGES

TIGRE. LANGUAGE

Number of speakers: In Eritrea: Estimated by Cerulli at about 250,000, i.e. the majority of the Moslem section of the total population of Eritrea; estimated by Ullendorf:[1] 170,000; Nadel:[2] 168,000; Italian Census 1931: 113,000. In the Anglo-Egyptian Sudan: numbers not known.

Area where spoken: In Agordat, Keren, and Massawa Divisions, Eritrea, north of the TIGRINYA-speaking area; in the Anglo-Egyptian Sudan, north of the Eritrean border as far as the environs of Tokar.

Spoken by:

1. Some of the *BENI AMER* tribes in Eritrea (mainly in Agordat Division) and the Anglo-Egyptian Sudan.

    Note: The *BENI AMER* consist of a number of units sometimes referred to as sections, sometimes as tribes; some speak TIGRE, some BEJA, and some are bilingual.

2. Tribes of non-*BENI AMER* origin, assimilated or affiliated to the *BENI AMER*.
3. Autonomous tribes in Eritrea, mainly in Keren and Massawa Divisions.

BENI AMER tribes (see also BEJA):

In Eritrea:[3]

    DAGGA 4,000 (*a*), 12,000 (*b*), 12,000 (*c*). Bilingual: BEJA and TIGRE.
    AD OKUD (*AD 'UQUD*) 6,500 (*a*), 10,000 (*b*), 10,000 (*c*). Part of the tribe speak BEJA, part TIGRE.
    AD AL BAKHIT 3,400 (*a*), 4,000 (*b*), 3,400 (*c*). According to A. C. A. Wright, part of the tribe speak BEJA, part TIGRE.
    AD IBRAHIM 900 (*a*), 3,000 (*b*), 2,000 (*c*). The majority speak TIGRE, a few speak BEJA.
    AD GULTANA 400 (*a*), 1,500 (*b*), 4,000 (*c*).
    AD HASSARI (*ADHASERI, AD HASRI*) 300 (*a*), 500 (*b*), under 300 (*c*); also in the Anglo-Egyptian Sudan.[4]
    ELMAN (*AD ELMAN*) 550 (*a*), 200 (*b*), 300 (*c*). Bilingual; BEJA and TIGRE.
    AD TAULE (*TAULIAB*) 340 (*a*), 500 (*b*), 400 (*c*).
    AD SALA (*ASSALA, ABSADAB*) 530 (*a*), 700 (*b*), 400 (*c*).

---

[1] E. Ullendorf, *Exploration and Study of Abyssinia*, Asmara, 1945, p. 69.
[2] S. F. Nadel, *Races and Tribes of Eritrea*. Government Publication, B.M.A. Eritrea, 1943.
[3] Figures marked (*a*) taken from S. F. Nadel, 'Notes on Beni Amer Society', *Sudan Notes*, 1945 (based on a recent inquiry in Eritrea); (*b*) from the Italian Census of 1931; (*c*) from S. F. Nadel, *Races and Tribes of Eritrea*.
[4] C. G. and B. Z. Seligman, 'Note on the History and Present Condition of the Beni Amer (Southern Beja)', *Sudan Notes*, 1930.

In the Anglo-Egyptian Sudan:[1]

  EL HASA, round Tokar. Bilingual: BEJA and TIGRE.
  AWADAB
  GANIFRU
  ADHASAN
  EL GURESHAB. Bilingual: BEJA and TIGRE.
  ADKUKAL (KOKUDUAB). Bilingual: BEJA and TIGRE.

Tribes assimilated or affiliated to the BENI AMER in Eritrea:[2]

  ALGEDEN 800 (a), 1,500 (b), 500 (c), of negro origin.
  FEIDAB (FAIDAB) 800 (a), 3,000 (b), 1,500 (c); also in the Anglo-Egyptian Sudan ('EL SHEIKH WAD FAID').[1] They are a branch of the (autonomous) AD SHEIKH of Keren Division.
  AD SHEIKH GARABIT 1,500 (a), 1,000 (b), 2,000 (c), north-east of Agordat (a branch of the AD SHEIKH).
  AD SHERAF 1,300 (a), 2,000 (b), 1,000 (c). They claim ARAB origin, and are bilingual, speaking BEJA and TIGRE.
  BEIT AWAT 1,000 (a), 1,100 (b), 1,300 (c), of serf origin. The majority speak TIGRE, a few BEJA.
  BEIT JUK 150 (a), 150 (b), under 400 (c), said to be descended from TIGRINYA-speaking peoples on the plateau.

Autonomous tribes in Eritrea (mainly nomadic):[3]

Agordat Division

  SABDERAT about 3,000, on the Anglo-Egyptian Sudan border. Bilingual: TIGRE and ARABIC.
  BITAMA 150, of negro origin, possibly related to the KUNAMA, among whom they live.

Keren Division—South

  MARIA 25,000. Some members of the tribe have emigrated to the neighbourhood of Agordat and to Kassala in the Anglo-Egyptian Sudan.
  MENSA 5,000. A few speak TIGRINYA.

Keren Division—North

  BEIT ASGEDE, consisting of:
    HABAB 25,000.
    AD TEKLES 10,000.
    AD TEMARIAM 7,000.
  AD SHEIKH about 9,000, between the HABAB and AD TEKLES. They claim ARAB origin, but include serfs of BENI AMER origin, who speak BEJA as well as TIGRE.
  AD TSAURA ⎫
  AD MUALLIM ⎬ 4,000–5,000. They claim ARAB origin. The BEIT MALA,
  BEIT MALA ⎭ who speak BEJA as well as TIGRE, are also to be found in the Anglo-Egyptian Sudan.[1]

---

[1] Seligman, op. cit.
[2] Figures marked (a) taken from S. F. Nadel, 'Notes on Beni Amer Society', (b) from the Italian Census 1931, (c) from S. F. Nadel, *Races and Tribes of Eritrea*.
[3] Figures from S. F. Nadel, op. cit.

Massawa Division—Northern (Samhar) Plain

BELLU, descendants of the original inhabitants of BENI AMER country (sedentary).

AFLENDA (AFILANDA) 2,500 in Eritrea; also in the Anglo-Egyptian Sudan.[1] They are of BEJA and HADENDOWA origin, and were once part of the BENI AMER.

MES'HALIT 1,600, of mixed origin. According to Nadel[2] they are a mixture of ASSAORTA, AD TSAURA, ARAB, and DANAKIL; according to A. C. A. Wright they are Sudanese negroes in pilgrimage transit.

Massawa Division—Northern Foothills

A number of small tribes, of various origins, but now all speaking TIGRE:[3]

AD AHA 400.
AD SHUMA 2,500.
AD ASHKER 750.
GEDEM SIKTA 600.
NABARA 800.
WARIA, call themselves WAIRA, 1,700.

The following SAHO tribes speak TIGRE in addition to their own language:
TEROWA BEIT MUSHE 1,100.
IDIFER (IDDIFER) 900.

TIGRE is also spoken by the mixed population of the Dahlak Archipelago, and by the BILIN (BOGOS) as a second language.

Dialects: Differences of dialect have been noted between the speech of the interior and that of Massawa and the Dahlak Archipelago. Leslau's *Short Grammar of Tigre* is in the 'Mensa dialect', i.e. the dialect of TIGRE spoken by the MENSA tribe. D'Abbadie's dictionary is in the 'Massawa dialect'.

TIGRINYA (TIGRIÑA, TIGRIGNA, &c.). LANGUAGE

Note. The language takes its name from the Ethiopian province of Tigre (Tigrai), and is sometimes known as TIGRAI or TIGRAY; this name, however, leads to confusion with the TIGRE language, and the name TIGRINYA (with the AMHARIC ending -*nya*) is therefore now generally used.

Number of speakers: 382,000 in Eritrea.[4] Ullendorf[5] estimates the total at 1,300,000, of whom 500,000 are in Eritrea; Cerulli considers this to be an over-estimate.

Area where spoken: In Eritrea:[6] Hamasien (170,000) and Serae (114,000) Divisions; part of Akkele Guzai (81,000); also spoken by emigrants from the central plateau who have settled in the southern part of Keren Division (10,000) and in Agordat (4,000) and Massawa (3,000) Divisions.

---

[1] Seligman, op. cit.
[2] *Races and Tribes of Eritrea*, p. 27.
[3] For further details, see S. F. Nadel, *Races and Tribes of Eritrea*, pp. 28–9.
[4] Ibid.
[5] Op. cit., p. 68.
[6] Figures from S. F. Nadel, op. cit.

In Ethiopia: North of a line drawn from Lake Ashangi to River Takkaze and beyond it to River Angareb and to the Anglo-Egyptian Sudan border—i.e. the Tigrai Province. On either side of this line there are bilingual areas (AMHARIC and TIGRINYA): (*a*) Walqayt (Wolkeit) region, north of River Angareb (with a tendency for AMHARIC to gain ground); (*b*) Sallamti, south of River Takkaze (AMHARIC gaining ground); (*c*) Wofla, immediately south of Lake Ashangi, where the linguistic boundary is not clear cut and there appear to be some bilingual areas.

On the south-western border of the TIGRINYA-speaking area in the Avergelle district there is a bilingual zone (TIGRINYA and AGAU).

In the GALLA-speaking Azabo and Raia regions, TIGRINYA is also spoken.

Dialects: There are several dialects of TIGRINYA differing in vocabulary and morphological characteristics, e.g. the dialects spoken in Hamasien, Adua, Tanben, and Akkele Guzai.

AMHARIC (own name AMARINYA). LANGUAGE

Number of speakers: 3,000,000–5,000,000 (Ullendorf).[1]

Area where spoken: (*a*) as a spoken language, over a wide area of central and southern Ethiopia, south of a line drawn from Lake Ashangi along the rivers Takkaze and Angareb to the Anglo-Egyptian Sudan frontier. There are bilingual areas on both sides of this line (see TIGRINYA). The southern boundary of the AMHARIC-speaking area runs along the edge of the Ethiopian table-land to the Dankali depression, following the Blue Nile–Awash watershed (except for Addis Ababa which is south of the watershed), and along the Blue Nile to the Anglo-Egyptian Sudan frontier. (Within this area there are enclaves where other languages are spoken: GALLA, AGAU, SHINASHA, GUNZA, ARGOBBA.)

(*b*) As the official and literary language, throughout the Ethiopian State.

Dialects: The language is more or less uniform throughout, though there are minor phonetic and lexical differences between the dialects spoken in different parts of the country, notably Shoa.

HARARI. LANGUAGE

Number of speakers: Estimated by Cerulli at about 35,000.

Area where spoken: In Harar city.

Spoken by the population of the town of Harar, with the exception of the Shoan immigrants.

ARGOBBA. LANGUAGE

Number of speakers: See below (figures from Cerulli).

Area where spoken: (*a*) Ifat region, east of the Shoan plateau (about 2,000–2,500).
(*b*) In a few villages immediately south of Harar (not more than 300–400).

Note. According to Cerulli there are slight dialectal differences from one area to another. The language is fast disappearing in favour of AMHARIC in the Ifat area, and of GALLA near Harar.

[1] Op. cit., p. 67.

GURAGE (GURAGIE, GURAGUE, GOURAGHE, &c.). Dialect Cluster.

Number of speakers: Estimated by Cerulli at about 350,000.

Area where spoken: In Ethiopia, in an area immediately south of Shoa from the head of the valley of Lake Margherita to the middle course of the River Gibie.

Dialects: CHAHA (c'aha). The dialect used for poetry.
EZHA (eʒa). Closely akin to CHAHA.
MUHER (muhər).
GIETA (GYETA). Spoken in Yecerit region.
INNEMOR (ENNAMOR) (ənnamor).
INDAGEN (əndagəny).
and others.

Note: All these dialects are mutually intelligible and constitute the 'Western Dialect group' considered by Cohen[1] to be akin to AMHARIC.

Dialects: AYMALLAL (**aimallal**). Spoken south of Addis Ababa. This dialect is influenced by AMHARIC as spoken in Shoa.
WALANI

Note: These two dialects are mutually intelligible and constitute the 'Eastern Dialect group' considered by Cohen[2] to be akin to HARARI.

A dialect of GURAGE is also spoken, according to Cerulli, by a small group of fishermen on the islands of Lake Zwai.

GE'EZ. Language

This language is no longer spoken in everyday life, but is the recognized language for religious observances throughout the Coptic Church in Ethiopia and Eritrea. A large body of religious and historical literature in GE'EZ exists.

GAFAT is the name of a Semitic language now extinct, which was spoken south of Gojam on the Blue Nile until the middle of the nineteenth century.

CUSHITIC LANGUAGES

Zone I.   Northern. Language Group: BEJA.
Zone II. Central. Language Group: AGAU.
                    Language Group: SIDAMA.
Zone III. Eastern. Language Group: SAHO-AFAR.
                    Language Group: SOMALI.
                    Language Group: GALLA.
                    Language Group: BURJI-GELEBA.

ZONE I. NORTHERN

Language Group: BEJA
BEJA (own name TO-BEDAWIE, BEDAWIET). Dialect Cluster
Number of speakers (see under tribes, below).

[1] M. Cohen, *Études d'Éthiopien Méridional*, Paris, 1931.   [2] Op. cit.

Area where spoken: In Eritrea, throughout the greater part of Agordat Division (many areas, however, being bilingual—see TIGRE), extending east into Keren Division; in the Anglo-Egyptian Sudan, mainly in Kassala Province.

Spoken by:

BENI AMER and affiliated tribes (see also TIGRE).
In Eritrea:[1]

    DAGGA (see TIGRE).
    AD OMAR 5,500 (*a*), 5,700 (*b*), 7,600 (*c*).
    In five sections which claim the status of separate tribes:
        AD AL ALLAM
        AL HAMID AWAD (AD HAMAD AWAT)
        AD HUMBIRRA
        HASSAL
        SHENEIAB
    AD OKUD (see TIGRE).
    AD TOWAS 1,700 (*a*), 1,000 (*b*), 1,700 (*c*).
    SINKAT KEINAB (SINKATKENAB) 920 (*a*), 700 (*b*), 700 (*c*); also in the Anglo-Egyptian Sudan.[2]
    AD AL BAKHIT (see TIGRE).
    LABAT (LEBET) 700 (*a*), 2,500 (*b*), 2,000–3,000 (*c*); also in the Anglo-Egyptian Sudan.[3] They are of HADENDOWA origin and were originally a serf-clan, but have now been assimilated to the BENI AMER.
    AD NASEH (AD NAZI) 450 (*a*), 550 (*b*), 300 (*c*).
    AD ALI 370 (*a*), 1,000 (*b*), 300 (*c*).
    AD ELMAN (see TIGRE).
    HASHISH 300 (*a*), 300 (*b*), 400 (*c*). They are largely of HADENDOWA origin, affiliated to the BENI AMER.

In the Anglo-Egyptian Sudan:[3]

    EL HASA (see TIGRE).
    EL GURESHAB (see TIGRE).
    AD KUKAL (KOKUDUAB) (see TIGRE).
    BEDAWIB (IBDAWI), in the hill country near the Eritrean border.
    MUSER.
    LUBIS.
    SAQAIT.
    HADUGWEIAB.

Also spoken by:
BEIT MALA, in Keren Division, Eritrea, and the Anglo-Egyptian Sudan (see TIGRE).

---

[1] Figures marked (*a*) taken from S. F. Nadel, 'Notes on Beni Amer Society'; (*b*) from the Italian Census 1931; (*c*) from S. F. Nadel, *Races and Tribes of Eritrea*.
[2] C. G. and B. Z. Seligman, 'Note on the History and Present Condition of the Beni Amer (Southern Beja)', *Sudan Notes*, 1930.
[3] Seligman, op. cit.

BEJA-speakers in the Anglo-Egyptian Sudan:

Note: All these tribes are known as and acknowledge the name of *BEJA (BEGA)*.

HADENDOWA (HADENDOA, HADENDIWA), estimated by Nadel at 30,000–40,000, by Owen[1] at about 70,000. Their territory extends from north of Sinkat and Suakin to Khashm el Girba, south of Kassala.

AMARAR, 40,000–50,000, on the increase.[2] They live north of the *HADENDOWA*, in an area bounded roughly in the north by Latitude 21, in the south by a line drawn westwards from Port Sudan, in the east by the Red Sea, in the west by Wadi Oko; there are also some settled in the River Atbara area, and a floating population of a few thousands in Port Sudan.

Note: The *AMARAR* are said to speak the purest form of the BEJA language.

BISHARIN, estimated at about 15,000.[3] Their territory is divided into four regions: (*a*) the Gwineb, consisting of the eastern face of the hills and the coastal plain, including the hills up to the watershed between the khors flowing direct into the Red Sea and those which reach it via Wadi Diib in the west, or flow into the Nile; (*b*) the Atbai, comprising all the country from the coastal plain watershed to Wadi Gabgaba and from the Egyptian frontier to Wadi Amur, including the western slope of the hills; (*c*) the Tamarab, an area bounded on the north by Wadi Amur, on the west by the Kassala–Northern Province boundary and the east bank of the River Atbara as far upstream as Musha Mitareb (30 miles north of Goz Regeb), on the east by a line drawn from Musha Mitareb through Musmar to Sarara well in Wadi Amur; (*d*) the River, i.e. the River Atbara and the area to the south-west, bounded by a line drawn from Gersi to Um Shadida wells and eastwards to Goz Regeb.

Other BEJA-speakers in the Anglo-Egyptian Sudan:[4]

MORGHUMAB} round Tokar and Khor Arbat. (There are also some sections
KUMEILAB } of these tribes on the River Atbara and near Berber on the
KAMALAB   } Nile, but they do not speak BEJA.)

Some of the *ABABDA*, north of the *BISHARIN* in the deserts adjoining upper Egypt on the east, also speak BEJA as well as ARABIC.

ZONE II. CENTRAL

Language Group: AGAU

AGAU. DIALECT CLUSTER

Area where spoken: In Keren Division, Eritrea, and in scattered enclaves in the Ethiopian highlands north of the Blue Nile and Awash rivers.

---

[1] T. R. H. Owen, 'The Hadendowa', *Sudan Notes*, **20**, 2, 1937, p. 183.
[2] G. E. R. Sandars, 'The Amarar', *Sudan Notes*, **17**, 2, 1935, p. 215.
[3] G. E. R. Sandars, 'The Bisharin', *Sudan Notes*, **16**, 2, 1933, p. 144.
[4] Ibid., p. 122.

Note: Most of the speakers of AGAU dialects speak as second language TIGRE, TIGRINYA, or AMHARIC, according to the locality. Most of the AGAU dialects, with the exception of BILEN, are dying out.

Dialect: BILEN (BILIN, BELEIN).

Spoken by: BOGOS, also known as BILEN. 24,300 (*Races and Tribes*); Italian Census 1931: 24,466. In the southern part of Keren Division, Eritrea.

Note: Cerulli points out that this dialect, owing to the geographical isolation of the *BOGOS* from the other AGAU-speakers, differs somewhat from the other dialects in this cluster in that 'it has remained from some points of view in an archaic condition and is therefore of special linguistic interest'. Some differences have been noted between the forms of the dialect spoken by the two main sections of the *BOGOS*, the *BEIT TARKE* (*BET TARQE*) and the *BEIT TAWKE* (*BET TAQWE*) tribes.

Dialect: KHAMTA.

Area where spoken: In the Avergele (Avergalle) district of South Tigrai, Ethiopia.

Note: According to Cerulli, TIGRINYA is rapidly gaining ground in this area.

Dialect: KHAMIR.

Area where spoken: In the Lasta and Wag (Waag) regions in central Ethiopia.

Dialect: AWIYA.

Area where spoken: To the south of Gojam in Agaumeder, Ethiopia.

Note: This dialect has kept some lexical affinities with SIDAMA, according to Cerulli.

Conti Rossini[1] considers the dialects spoken in Agaumeder and in Damot to be 'two dialects of one language'.

Dialect: QUARA (KWARA) (**q'wara**). Also known as QUARINYA.

Area where spoken: In the region of the same name on the western shores of Lake Tana.

Dialect: QEMANT (KEMANT) (**q'əmant**).

Area where spoken: In the region of the same name on the northern shores of Lake Tana.

Dialect: KAYLA, also known as KAILINYA.

Spoken by the *FALASHA*, i.e. the *AGAU* Jews in the same region as the above—not more than 30,000 according to Cerulli.

Note: The three dialects QUARA, QEMANT, and KAYLA are closely akin.

---

[1] C. Conti Rossini, 'Note sugli Agau, 2. Appunti sulla lingua Awiyā del Danghelà.' (*Giorn. Soc. Asiatica It.* 1905), p. 125.

Language Group: SIDAMA.
Consists of: JANJERO   Language.
SIDAMO   Dialect Cluster.
OMETO   Dialect Cluster.
GIMIRA   Dialect Cluster.
KAFA   Dialect Cluster.
ANFILLO (MAO)   Language.
SHINASHA   Language.

Area where spoken: South-western Ethiopia.

Note: SIDAMO is the name of a tribe, and of their language, which belongs to this group (but see Moreno's classification on p. 19). From this is derived the name SIDAMA, originally a term used by the *GALLA* with the general meaning of 'Foreigners', but now adopted by Europeans as a linguistic term to denote this group of languages.

JANJERO. LANGUAGE

(An AMHARIC and GALLA name, adopted by Europeans. Also rendered YANGARO, &c.)

Spoken by: *JANJERO*—call themselves *YEMMA*, also rendered *YÄMMA*; called *YANGERO* by the *KAFA*, *JANJOR* by the *HADIA*, *ZINGERO* by the Abyssinians (the name 'Zingero' means 'monkey' in AMHARIC and is used as a nickname).

Area where spoken: In the upper valley of the River Gibie.

Note: Within the JANJERO language there are two 'special' languages, which have been noted by Cerulli:[1]
  (*a*) the 'royal language', used to the king only;
  (*b*) the 'language of respect', used to lesser chiefs.
The vocabulary of these 'special' languages contains many words not existing in the ordinary language.

SIDAMO. DIALECT CLUSTER

Dialect: HADIA—own name GUDIELA (GUDELLA).
Spoken by: *HADIA*—call themselves *GUDIELA*—between the Omo and Billate rivers, south and west of the GURAGE-speaking areas.
Dialect: KAMBATTA.
Spoken by: *KAMBATTA*, south of the *HADIA*.
Dialect: TAMBARO (**t'ambaro**).
Spoken by: *TAMBARO*, south of the *KAMBATTA*, north of the *WOLAMO*.
Dialect: ALABA.
Spoken by: *ALABA*, 40,000, (Moreno, quoting the Resident of Zwai, about 1940),[2] east of the *TAMBARO* on the left bank of the River Billate, between it and Lake Awasa, with centre Colito (Kolito).

[1] E. Cerulli, *Studi Etiopici*, 3, *Il linguaggio dei Giangerò*, Rome, 1938, pp. 61-4.
[2] M. M. Moreno. 'Nuove notizie sull' Alaba e sugli Alaba', *Rass. Studi Etiopici*, 1, 1941, p. 52.

Dialect: SIDAMO.

Spoken by: *SIDAMO*, on the hills forming the watershed between the Juba and Webi rivers, and Lake Margherita; to the east as far as the upper valley of the river Juba with its affluents, to the west as far as Lake Margherita, and to the north to Lake Awasa.

Dialect: DARASA.

Spoken by: *DARASA*, south of the *SIDAMO*.

OMETO. DIALECT CLUSTER

> *Note*: This name means 'men of the Omo' and is used by Europeans to designate the language of the people living in the middle basin of the Omo River, as far as Lake Margherita. OMETO is also known as 'Omo SIDAMA' or 'SIDAMA of the Omo'. Moreno[1] maintains that OMETO is a language 'fundamentally one as to grammar and vocabulary despite regional and dialectal differences'. It comprises a number of closely related dialects, which Cerulli subdivides into the Northern, Southern, and Western dialects. No one dialect appears to have precedence.

Dialect: WOLAMO (WALAMO).

Spoken by: *WOLAMO*, on the left bank of the River Omo, between it and River Billate, south of the *TAMBARO*.

> *Note*: The name Wolaitsa (Walaitsa, Walaitta) has been erroneously used by Europeans (Beke, &c.)[2] as a linguistic term; this is, however, only the singular of *WOLAMO*, the tribal name.

Dialect: ZALA.

Spoken by: *ZALA*.

Dialect: GOFA.

Spoken by: *GOFA*.

Dialect: BASKETO.

Spoken by: *BASKETO*.

> *Note*: The above dialects constitute the 'Northern' subdivision of the OMETO cluster, according to Cerulli.

> *Note*: The approximate position of these dialects is indicated on the map; their exact location is difficult to determine owing to the multiplicity of names used by different writers, and marked on their maps (see also *note* p. 17).

Dialect: BADDITU (name used by the *GALLA* and adopted by Europeans)—own name KOYRA.

Spoken by: *BADDITU*—call themselves *KOYRA*—south of Lake Margherita, east of Lake Ciamo (Ruspoli).

---

[1] *Introduzione alla lingua Ometo*, Milan, 1938, p. 15.

[2] C. T. Beke. 'On the Languages and Dialects of Abyssinia and the Countries to the South', *Proc. Philol. Soc.* **2**, 33, 1845, pp. 89–107.

Dialect: HARURO (the name used by d'Abbadie and therefore by Conti Rossini)[1]
—own name KACHAMA (k'ac'ama).

Spoken by: *HARURO*—call themselves *KACHAMA*; also known as *GAT-ZAMBA*. They are very few in number, perhaps 150, according to Cerulli, and are fishermen on the islands in Lake Margherita.

Dialect: ZAYSSE.

Spoken by: *ZAYSSE*, south of Lake Ciamo in a region of the same name.

Note: These three dialects constitute Cerulli's 'Southern' subdivision of the OMETO cluster.

Dialect: CHARA (c'ara).

Spoken by: *CHARA*, in the region of the same name on the right bank of the River Omo, south of the *KAFFA*.

Note: Numerous other names are given by various writers as names of dialects; many of these, however, are names of tribes or of geographical areas, and may or may not prove to be names of dialects. Some of those used by Moreno and others are:

Uba—the name of a district;
Dauro—the name of a district;
Kullo—the AMHARIC name for the above;
Waratta (Woratta)—a tribe living in this district;
Konta, Malo, Doko—tribal names;
Kucha, Borodda, Gamo, Kosha—names of districts.

There appear to be considerable dialectal variations, not only from tribe to tribe, but also from place to place within a tribe. Moreno[2] points out, for example, that a man may say he speaks 'Konta' because he is of the *KONTA* tribe, or 'Kullo' because he is from Kullo; this, however, does not necessarily mean that 'Konta' and 'Kullo' are two different dialects; two modes of speech both qualified as 'Kullo' may show greater differences than those found between one qualified as 'Kullo' and another qualified as 'Konta'.

GIMIRA. DIALECT CLUSTER

Note: The name GIMIRA (GIMIRRA, GHIMIRRA, &c.) has been adopted by Europeans as a linguistic term for a cluster of dialects. Originally it was the name given by the *GALLA* to a group of tribes comprising most of the speakers of these dialects (but not the *SHAKKO* and *MAJI*).

Area where spoken: In a roughly horseshoe-shaped territory stretching from the Gurrafarda range in the west to the territory of the *CHARA* in the east, south of the *MOCHA* and *KAFFA* (see also MAJI).

Dialects: From west to east the dialects are:
SHAKKO (SHAKO) in the Gurrafarda area—West.

---

[1] 'Contributi per la conoscenza della lingua haruro', *Rendiconti della R. Accad. dei Lincei*, 1937.
[2] *Introduzione alla lingua Ometo*, pp. 11-12 footnote.

BIENESHO
SHE (also known as DIZU) }—Centre.
KABA
NAO—East.

Note: According to Cerulli, NAO differs considerably from BIENESHO and SHAKKO.

Dialect: MAJI.

Spoken by: *MAJI*—call themselves *MAZI*—estimated by Cerulli at about 6,000–7,000; according to Chiomìo 5,000.[1] They live in an enclave to the south of the other GIMIRA-speaking peoples, separated from them and surrounded by speakers of SURI or SURO languages (MEKAN, TIRMA, &c.). Their main centre is Maji.

KAFFA (KAFA). DIALECT CLUSTER

Dialect: KAFFA (own name KAFFICHO (**kaffico**)).

Spoken by: *KAFFA*, who call themselves *KAFAA*; in AMHARIC, *KAFFA*: the spelling *KAFFA* is the usually accepted one. They are called *GOMARO* by the *GIMIRA* tribes. They live in an area between the Rivers Baro and Gojeb to the north and the *GIMIRA* tribes to the south.

Dialect: GARO (own name BOSHA).

Spoken by: *GARO*—call themselves *BOSHA*—north of the River Gojeb, west of the River Omo, north of the Konta and Dauro regions.

Dialect: MOCHA.

Spoken by: *MOCHA* (a *GALLA* name, which has been adopted by Europeans) —call themselves *SHEKA* (**ʃekka**)—west of the *KAFFA*, extending north across the River Baro.

ANFILLO (own name MAO). LANGUAGE[2]

Spoken by: *MAO* of Anfillo forest.

Note: The name Anfillo is purely geographical, but has been used by Ethiopians and Europeans to denote the inhabitants of Anfillo and their language.

The *MAO* are divided into two sections, both calling themselves and their languages MAO. The southern section in Anfillo forest have adopted the SIDAMA language of their overlords the *BUSASI* (*BUSHASHI*), now very few in number. This language contains some words of the original MAO language, which is still spoken by the northern section of the tribe on the River Dabus.

SHINASHA (own name BWORO (**bwɔrɔ**)). LANGUAGE

Note: The name GONGA is used by Beke and Conti Rossini[3] for this language; according to Cerulli, however, it is not a linguistic term but the name applied to

---

[1] G. Chiomìo. 'I Magi (Masi) nell' Etiopia del Sud-ovest', *Rass. Stud. Etiop.* **1**. 3, 1941, p. 282.
[2] V. L. Grottanelli. *I Mao*. Rome 1940.
[3] 'Studi su popolazioni dell' Etiopia. 5. Appunti di lingua gonga', *Rivista di Studi Orientali*, **6**. 1914.

the *SHINASHA* aristocracy. Moreno[1] uses the name GONGA as a group name for several languages and dialects (see his classification below).

Spoken by: SHINASHA—call themselves BWORO.

Area where spoken: On the Blue Nile (Abbai), far removed from all other speakers of SIDAMA languages.

According to Grottanelli[2] they live in four areas:

(*a*) in the Gubba region among the *GUMUZ*;
(*b*) in the south-eastern part of Wambera among the *GALLA*, about latitude 10° 30′;
(*c*) to the east, about the same latitude, on the southern border of Agaumeder district, among the *NAGA* (a section of the *GUMUZ*);
(*d*) farther south, on the left bank of the Blue Nile.

Dialects: Grottanelli[3] suggests that there are probably dialectal differences between these areas.

Note on the classification of the SIDAMA *languages*

The classification given above is based on that of Cerulli. Moreno's classification[4] differs in several respects. He avoids the use of the term SIDAMA altogether, and classifies SIDAMO and kindred dialects, with which he includes BURJI, under the general heading of 'Eastern Cushitic'. The other SIDAMA languages, which he calls 'Western Cushitic', he groups as follows (spelling adapted to correspond with that used in this work):

YAMNA		JANJERO.
OMETO:	Northern	GOFA, ZALA, UBA, MALO, WOLAMO, GAMO, BORODDA, KULLO, KONTA, KUCHA, HARURO.
	Western	CHARA, DOKO, BASKETO.
	Eastern	ZAYSSE, BADDITU.
GIMIRA		BIENESHO, SHE, SHAKKO, KABA, NAO, MAJI.
GONGA		SHINASHA (BWORO), KAFFA ('Caffino'), GARO (BOSHA), MOCHA (SHEKKA), ANFILLO.

ZONE III. EASTERN

Language Group: SAHO-AFAR
    Consists of: SAHO   Language.
                     AFAR   Language.

SAHO (SAO) (own name SAHO; called SHIHO by TIGRINYA-speakers).
LANGUAGE

Spoken by: SAHO.

---

[1] *Manuale di Sidamo*, Milan, 1940, p. 320.
[2] 'Gli Scinascia del Nilo azzurro ed alcuni lessici poco noti della loro lingua', *Rass. Stud. Etiopici*, **1.** 3, 1941, p. 244.   [3] Op. cit., p. 244.
[4] *Manuale di Sidamo*, Appendix 1, p. 320; see also *Grammatica della lingua Galla*, Milan, 1939, p. 19; *Introduzione alla lingua Ometo*, p. 17; 'Le mie indagini linguistiche nel Galla-Sidama' (*Oriente Moderno*, 1938).

Number of speakers: 48,000 (*Races and Tribes*); Italian Census 1931: 41,170.

Area where spoken: In the eastern part of Akkele Guzai Division and the southern part of Massawa Division, Eritrea; also in enclaves in Ethiopia, in the districts of Irob, Serukso, and other scattered parts of Agame.

Dialects: Dialectal differences exist, but they are not great, and the language may be regarded as uniform. The dialects spoken by the *ASSAORTA* and *HAZU* tribes, and that spoken in Irob district (Agame) have been noted.

Some sections of the *ASSAORTA* are bilingual (see under TIGRE).

AFAR (own name 'AFAR; also known as DANKALI). LANGUAGE

Spoken by: *DANAKIL* (a general name used by Europeans and others to denote a number of tribes).

Number of speakers: Estimated by Cerulli at not more than 250,000; of these, according to *Races and Tribes*, 27,800 are in Eritrea (Italian Census 1931: 21,679).

Area where spoken: In the southern part of Eritrea, south of the *SAHO*; in the northern part of French Somaliland; in Ethiopia from the boundaries of Eritrea and French Somaliland westwards as far as the River Awash at Mataha (south of Addis Ababa on the French railway).

Dialects: Dialectal differences are only slight, so far as is known, but although the chief characteristics of the language have been outlined, no deep studies have been made of its division into dialects.

AFAR and SAHO are very closely related.

Language Group: SOMALI

SOMALI. DIALECT CLUSTER

Number of speakers: Total number not known; according to A. C. A. Wright, probably over 1,000,000 (Italian Census 1931 gives 922,814 in Italian Somaliland, 623 in Eritrea).

Area where spoken: Along the coast of the Indian Ocean from the southern border of Dankalia on the Gulf of Tajura to the River Tana in Kenya. In the interior, as far as the confluence of the Dakhata and Webi Shebeli rivers and the region of Diredawa. This area includes the southern part of French Somaliland, British Somaliland, former Italian Somaliland, the northern and north-eastern parts of Kenya (part of the Northern Frontier District and the Tana River District), the Ogaden, and a considerable part of Harar region.

Outside this area there are colonies of *SOMALI* in areas where other languages are spoken; some of these are considerable, such as the colony of *SOMALI* from the Ogaden on the Chercher plateau, the Jidla and Galja'el groups in the regions of Afdam and Ma'eso, &c.

Dialects: SOMALI, which is one of the most widely spoken languages of Africa, consists of several main dialects, generally known by the names of the tribes speaking them, or of the regions where they are spoken. Though the speakers of these dialects make use of dialectal names, they each claim that their dialect is the true SOMALI.

The main dialects are:

Dialect spoken by the *ISSA (ISA)* and *GADABURSI* confederacies in French Somaliland; some in former Italian Somaliland (Italian Census 1931: 22,179). This includes the *IS'HAK (ISAQ)* tribes in the western part of British Somaliland (Berbera and Hargheisa regions).

> *Note*: For purposes of this classification the dialects spoken by these tribes have been treated as one entity. Nevertheless a number of variants have been noted, particularly between the forms of the dialect spoken by the western *(HABAR AWAL)* and eastern *(HABAR JALO)* tribes. (According to A. C. A. Wright, the dialect of the *HABAR JALO* is that spoken by the colonies of *SOMALI* seamen living in seaports in the British Isles—Cardiff, Sunderland, and Tilbury.)

Dialect spoken by the *DAROD* tribes in the eastern part of British Somaliland, the Ogaden, the northern part of former Italian Somaliland (Mijurtein and Obbia regions), and the *SOMALI* zone of Kenya. Italian Census 1931 gives 233,268 for Somalia.

> *Note*: This dialect, the most widespread of all the SOMALI dialects, is regarded as one for the purposes of this classification; there are, however, local variants, particularly in the form of the dialect spoken in the Ogaden, which is sometimes referred to as 'Ogaden SOMALI'.

Dialect spoken by the *HAWIYA (HAWIYYA)* tribes in former Italian Somaliland, in the lower valley of the Webi Shebeli, and along the coast from Mareg (south of Obbia) as far as the territory between Merka and Brava (Italian Census 1931: 299,717).

This dialect is also spoken by the following non-*SOMALI* peoples: *KAWOLE (KABOLE), SHABELE (SHEBELLE), MAKANE (MAKANNE),* and *SHIDLE,* negro peoples living along the rivers, also by the *WAGOSHA (GOSHA),* of mixed (slave) origin, who are bilingual, speaking SOMALI as well as their own (Bantu) language.

> *Note*: For purposes of this classification the dialect of the *HAWIYA* is regarded as one entity; variants have, however, been noted, particularly in the form of the dialect spoken by the *ABGAL* tribes.

Dialect spoken by the *SAB* tribes, to the west of *HAWIYA* territory, as far as the River Juba; these include the following tribes (figures from the Italian Census 1931): *DIGIL* (23,569), *RAHANWEIN (RAHANWEN)* (254,020), *TUNI (TUNNI)* (16,741).

This is said to be the dialect spoken by the *RENDILE (RENDILLE)* estimated at about 6,000, in the North-West Frontier District of Kenya, mostly in the country south and south-west of Marsabit.

Also spoken by the non-*SOMALI* outcaste peoples *GABAWEIN (GOBAWEIN),* probably of negro origin, and *WAREBEI (WARABEI).*

Language Group: GALLA

GALLA (own name OROMO). DIALECT CLUSTER

(The name GALLA is an Ethiopic name, now used by Europeans.)

Area where spoken: An area including the western portion of the Ethiopian highlands, roughly between the River Gojeb in the south and the Blue Nile in the north; a large part of the southern Shoa provinces and part of Wollo; in the south the areas occupied by the *ARUSSI*, the region of Bali, and most of the Harar plateau. In the low-lying lands towards the Indian Ocean GALLA is spoken in a vast territory stretching from the River Galana Sagan to the east of Lake Stephanie, the valley of the Ganale Doria, and the frontiers of Kenya; in Kenya it is spoken in the Northern Frontier District and in part of the Tana River District.

Dialects: There are several dialects, but all are recognized as being OROMO:

Dialects spoken by the *MACHA* (**macc'a**) tribes in western Ethiopia, west of the River Gibie as far as the Anglo-Egyptian Sudan border.

Dialects spoken by the *TULAMA* tribes, east of the River Gibie, in the *GALLA* zone of Shoa Province.

Dialects spoken by the *ITTU* and *ARUSSI* tribes, on the highlands of Chercher and in the area between the River Awash, the valley of the Webi Shebeli and the upper course of the Ganale Doria.

The dialect spoken by the *GALLA* of Harar may perhaps be included with these.

Dialects spoken by the *BORANA* tribes in the lowlands to the south of the great lakes and in Northern Frontier District, Kenya. With these may perhaps be included the dialect of GALLA spoken in Wollo.

Dialect spoken by the *BARARETTA* and *KOFIRA* tribes in Tanaland Province, Kenya.

> *Note*: This dialect used to be distinguished from the others by the name of 'Southern GALLA language', but its affinity with the dialect of the *BORANA* should now be recognized, according to Cerulli.

GALLA is also spoken by the *WATA* (*WATTA*) in various parts of Ethiopia[1] and by the *SANYA* and *BONI* on the Kenya coast, with whom Huntingford includes the *ARIANGULU* (**ariaŋgulu**) and whom he describes as 'GALLA-speaking with traces of a former unclassifiable language of their own'.

Language Group: BURJI-GELEBA

    Consists of: BURJI   Language.
                  KONSO   Language.
                  GELEBA   Language.
                  and other languages or dialects.

> *Note*: Very little is known as yet about the languages and dialects in this group, and a great deal of the information about them is misleading. In spite of the work of Cerulli (who first postulated the existence of the group[2]) and Moreno, these remain among the least known of the Cushitic languages.

---

[1] The *WAITO* (*WAYTO*) on Lake Tana, however, are not GALLA-speaking.
[2] 'Il linguaggio degli Amar Cocchè e quello degli Arbore', *Rass. Stud. Etiopici*, **2**. 3, 1942.

BURJI, also known as BAMBALA. LANGUAGE

Note: The name by which the language is known to Europeans is that of the principal locality in the BURJI-speaking area.

Spoken by: BAMBALA, called AMARO by the GALLA, round Burji in an area south of Lake Ciamo (Ruspoli) between the River Sagan on the west and its affluent the Bishan Guracha on the south.

Note: According to Moreno,[1] BURJI is akin to SIDAMO, DARASA, &c. Cerulli, however,[2] classifies it with KONSO and other languages in this group.

KONSO. LANGUAGE

Spoken by: KONSO, south of Lake Ciamo in the bend of the River Sagan.

GELEBA. LANGUAGE

Note: This is the officially recognized name of the language and of its speakers, in Ethiopia at least, although English writers often use the name MARILLE; it is not known by what name the speakers themselves call it.

Spoken by: GELEBA (also rendered GELLABA, GELLEB, GELUBBA, &c.); also known as MARILLE[3] (MERILLE, MARLE, &c.), also as RESHIAT (RECHIAT, RACHIAT, RUSIA, &c.), and as DATHANAIC (DATHANIK, DASANEK, &c.). According to Chiomìo,[4] DASANEK is the original name of a tribe of which the GELEBA are a part. They live north of Lake Rudolf, mostly on the right bank of the Omo River, but some are found on the left bank on the lower part of its course, and they extend into Kenya on the eastern shores of Lake Rudolf. They are estimated to number about 2,140 adult males.[5]

To this group belong also the languages or dialects spoken by the following tribes:

ARBORE, north of Lake Stephanie, on the low ground (the AMARR occupying the high ground). They probably number less than 3,000.[6]

Note: The language of which Donaldson Smith[7] gives a vocabulary headed 'Arbore-Amarr' is ARBORE, not AMARR. The two have also been confused by Wellby,[8] but are quite distinct, AMARR being related to BAKO and other non-Cushitic languages.

TSAMAI or TSAMAKO in Kule region, on the River Galana Dule, affluent of the Sagan. The name KULE, by which they are also known, is, as da Casotto[9] points out, a geographical name only. They number about 1,000.

[1] See his classification given on p. 19.
[2] 'Il linguaggio degli Amar Cocchè e quello degli Arbore nella zona del Lago Stefania', *Rass. Stud. Etiopici*, **2**. 3, 1942.
[3] Not to be confused with the MURLE in the Anglo-Egyptian Sudan, a branch of whom is also said to live on the Omo river.
[4] 'I Magi (Masi) nell' Etiopia del sud-ovest', *Rass. Studi Etiopici*, **1**. 3, 1941, p. 300.
[5] MS. notes on the MARILLE by Shackleton, in the possession of A. C. A. Wright.
[6] V. L. Grottanelli, quoting Zavattari, in 'I Niloti dell' Etiopia allo stato attuale delle nostre conoscenze', p. 580. [7] *Through Unknown African Countries*, London, 1897, pp. 445–6.
[8] *Twixt Sirdar and Menelik*, London, 1901, pp. 407–8.
[9] G. da Casotto. 'Note sulle popolazioni dell' alto e medio Galana, 3. Gli Ṣamai (o Ṣamacò) del Cule', *Studi Etiopici*, 1945, pp. 167–78.

GARDULLA
GIDOLE   } on the hills between Lake Ciamo and the *KONSO*.
GOWAZE

Many other names are given by various writers as those of tribes living in the Omo-Rudolf-Stephanie area, and some statements have been made about their languages. It is, however, uncertain which of these names are tribal and which geographical, and further research is needed before any definitive linguistic classification can be attempted.[1]

[1] For a further discussion of this problem, see M. A. Bryan, 'A Linguistic No-man's Land', *Africa*, **15**. 4, 1945, pp. 188–205, and V. L. Grottanelli, 'I Niloti dell' Etiopia allo stato attuale delle nostre conoscenze'.

BIBLIOGRAPHY
SEMITIC LANGUAGES

Abbreviations of Titles of Periodicals used in this Bibliography

In general, abbreviations used are in accordance with the International Code, with the exception of the following:
M.S.O.S. Mitteilungen des Seminars für orientalische Sprachen (Berlin).
G.L.E.C.S. Groupe Linguistique d'Études Chamito-Sémitiques.

Note: Readers are referred to *Bibliography of the Semitic Languages of Ethiopia*, by Wolf Leslau, New York: The New York Public Library, 1946 (referred to throughout as 'Leslau, Bibl.'), an exhaustive and annotated bibliography of the Semitic languages. Only those works which are not included in that book are given here.

TIGRE

FLEISCH, HENRI. 1944. Les verbes à allongement vocalique interne dans le sémitique (Études de grammaire comparée). Paris: Travaux et mémoires de l'Institut d'Ethnologie, **43**. Pp. xxx+532.
    Part 2, Chaps. 3–7, deal with Tigrinya, Tigre, Amharic, Harari, Argobba and Gurage.
LITTMANN, ENNO. Die Diminutivbildung im Tigrē. Ann. Ist. Univ. Orient. Napoli, Nuova serie, **2**, 1943. Scritti dedicati alla memoria di Francesco Gallina, pp. 89–103.

TIGRINYA

ANON. 1920. Embaiz'... Libro di lettura italiana–tigrai. Pp. 215. Asmara: Tipografia Francescana.
—— 1912. Manuale d'istruzione italiano–tigrai. Pp. about 300. Asmara: Tipografia Francescana.
—— 1917. Manuale d'istruzione italiano–tigrai. Pp. 215. Asmara: Tipografia Francescana.
—— 1912. Manuale tigray–italiano–francese. Roma.
—— 1907, 1915. Sillabario ghëz–amarico–tigrigna. *See also under* AMHARIC.
BURCO, G. 1936. Vocabolario tascabile italiano–tigrino. Pp. 190. Milan: Ed. Boll. Bibliogr. musicale.
CARAGLIO, EGIDIO DA. 1916. Manuale di letture scelte italiane–tigrine. Pp. 455. Asmara: Tipografia Francescana.
CONTI ROSSINI, CARLO. 1942. Proverbi tradizioni e canzoni tigrine. Pp. 332. A cura dell' Uficio Studi del Ministero dell' Africa Italiana.
    Contains also grammatical notes, &c. Reviewed by Cerulli (Ann. Afr. Italiana, 1942).
FLEISCH, HENRI. Les verbes à allongement vocalique interne.... *See under* TIGRE.
LITTMANN, ENNO. Tigriña-Sprichwörter. Z. dtsch. morgenländ. Ges. 1943.
—— Nachtrag zu 'Tigriña-Sprichwörter'. Z. dtsch. morgenländ. Ges. **98.** 1, 1944.
SAVOIA, EUGENIO DI, and SIMONINI, G. Proverbi tigrini. Rass. Studi Etiop. **3.** 1. 1943, pp. 3–35.

AMHARIC

ANON. Sillabario ghëz–amarico–tigrigna. *See under* TIGRINYA.
—— 1917. Sillabario amarico–italiano. Pp. 72.
—— 1936. Prontuario per l'esame del corso di amharico del Prof. B. Ducati. Pp. 39. Rome: Ist. Coloniale Fascista (lithogr.).
ALONE, J. P. H. M., revised by STOKES, D. 4th edition 1946. Short manual of the Amharic language (with vocabularies). Pp. 206. London: Macmillan. *See* Leslau, Bibl. for 1st edition 1909.
ERIKSSON, OLLE. 1921. Méthode de lecture et de langage en Amharique. Pp. 120. Mission Suédoise.
FLEISCH, H. Les verbes à allongement vocalique interne.... *See under* TIGRE.

FUSELLA, LUIGI. Proverbi amarici. Rass. Studi Etiop. **2.** 3, 1942, pp. 282–311.
—— Esempi di omografi amarici. Ann. Ist. Univ. Orient. Napoli, Nuova serie, **2,** 1943. Scritti dedicati alla memoria di Francesco Gallina, pp. 243–57.
MITTWOCH, EUGEN. Popular Amharic texts. J. R. Afr. Soc. ('Africa' supplement), **41.** 165, 1942, pp. 261–9.
TOSELLI, GIOVANNI. 1937. Dizionario italiano–amarico e amarico–italiano. 1. Italiano–amarico. Pp. 956. Torino: Ist. Missioni Consolata (lithogr.).
VALDIERI, FEDELE DA. 1945. Il verbo amarico in tavole sinottiche. Classificazione—coniugazione —sintassi, con trascrizione italiana di ogni parola amarica. Pp. xi+64. Roma.
Favourably reviewed by Cerulli (Osservatore Romano, 8. 4. 1945).

Unpublished material
WALKER, CRAVEN HOWELL. An Amharic grammar in the Shoan dialect, with exercises and notes. MS. (152 pp. foolscap+additional notes) in possession of the International African Institute.

HARARI
FLEISCH, H. Les verbes à allongement vocalique interne. . . . *See under* TIGRE.
SANTIS, R. DE. Piccoli testi Harari. Riv. Studi Orient. **18,** 1940, pp. 286–398.

ARGOBBA
FLEISCH, H. Les verbes à allongement vocalique interne. . . . *See under* TIGRE.

GURAGE
FLEISCH, H. Les verbes à allongement vocalique interne. . . . *See under* TIGRE.

CUSHITIC LANGUAGES

GENERAL
ASSIRELLI, ODDONE. Il sistema pronominale nelle lingue etiopo–cuscitiche. Studi Etiopici raccolti da Conti Rossini. 1945. Roma: Ist. per l'Oriente. Pp. 59–77.
CERULLI, ENRICO. Le trilittéralisme en couchitique. G.L.E.C.S. **1,** pp. 85–7.
—— La Racine monosyllabique (consonne+voyelle ou voyelle seule) en couchitique. G.L.E.C.S. **3,** pp. 33–6.
COLIZZA, GIOVANNI. Le lingue kuschitiche. G. Soc. Asiatica ital. **3,** 1889, pp. 128–39.
FERRARIO, BENIGNO. Il pronome personale cuscitico. Actes du XXe Congr. Int. des Orientalistes (Bruxelles, 5–10 Sept. 1938). Louvain, 1940, pp. 73–5.

1. BEJA
ALMKVIST, HERMANN, also known as ALMQUIST. Die Bischari-Sprache in Nord-Ost Afrika. Vol. I [Grammar], 1880 or 1881 [Vol. 2, Dictionary, in the press in 1883]. Upsala.
HALÉVY [J.]. [A grammatical note on Hadendoa.] Rev. linguistique, **3,** 1869.
Contains grammatical notes.
HARTMANN, —. Die Bejah. Z. Ethn. 1882.
Contains grammatical notes.
LUCAS, L. On natives of Suakin, and Bishareen vocabulary. J. R. anthrop. Inst. **7,** 1876.
MEINHOF, CARL. 1912. Die Sprachen der Hamiten. Pp. xvi+256. Abh. Hamb. Kol. Inst. **9.** Chap. 5. Bedauye; comparative vocabulary, pp. 230–40. Reviewed by Conti Rossini (Riv. Studi Orient. **6**). *See also under* SOMALI.
—— Sprachstudien im egyptischen Sudan. No. 44. Bedauye. Z. Kol. Sprachen, **9,** 1919–20.
MÜLLER, —. [A grammatical note.] Orient und Occident, 1864.
MUNZINGER, WERNER. 1864. Ostafrikanische Studien. Schaffhausen.
Pp. 341–69, short grammar and vocabulary of 'Tobedauie'.
PERINI, R. Gl'idiomi parlati nella nostra colonia. Boll. Soc. Geogr. ital., serie 3, **5,** 1892, pp. 60–3.
Contains vocabularies in Italian, Arabic, Tigre, Tigrinya, Saho, Dankali, Hadendoa, Baria, Baza. *See* Leslau, Bibl.; *see also under* SAHO, AFAR.

REINISCH, LEO. 1893. Die Bedauyesprache in Nordost-Afrika. Wien.
—— 1895. Wörterbuch der Bedawie-Sprache. Wien.
ROPER, E. M. Poetry of the Haḍenḍiwa. Sudan Notes, **10**, 1927, pp. 147–58.
—— 1929. In Bedawie. An elementary handbook for the use of Sudan Government officials. Pp. 288. London: Sudan Government Office.
WATSON, C. M. 1888. Comparative vocabularies of the languages spoken at Suakin: Arabic, Hadendoa, Beni-Amer. Pp. 16. London: S.P.C.K.
    The 'Beni-Amer' given here is Tigre. *See* Leslau, Bibl.

2. AGAU

ABBADIE, ANTOINE D'. Notice sur les langues de Kam. Bull. Soc. Philol. 1872, pp. 67–71.
    Contains numerals of 'Kam*t*iga, Aw*g*a, Y*a*mma, Naa, Xe, Do͏́qua, Gazamba, Dawrowa, Ka*facc*o, Gonga, B*ij*a'. *See also under* JANJERO.
BEKE, CHARLES TILSTONE. On the languages and dialects of Abyssinia and the countries to the South. Proc. Philol. Soc. **2**. 33, 1845.
    Pp. 97–107 consist of tables of the following languages: 'Hhamara' (Agau of Waag), 'Falasha, Agaw' (Agau of Agaumider), 'Gafat, Gonga, Kaffa, Wolamo (Wolaitsa), Yangaro, Shankala of Agaumider' (Gumuz), 'Galla of Guderu, Tigré' (Tigrinya), 'Harargie (Hurrur)'. *See* Leslau, Bibl.: *see also under* JANJERO.
BRUCE, JAMES. 1790. Travels to discover the sources of the Nile in the years 1768–73. 5 vols. Edinburgh.
    Vol. 2 contains (pp. 494–7 of the second edition, 1804) vocabularies of 'Amharic, Falashan, Gafat, Agow and Tcheretch Agow'. *See* Leslau, Bibl.
CAPOMAZZA, ILARIO. Un testo bileno. Riv. Studi Orient. **4**, 1911–12, pp. 1049–56.
CONTI ROSSINI, CARLO. Note sugli Agau. 1. Appunti sulla lingua Khamta dell' Averghele, 2. Appunti sulla lingua Awiyā del Dangheià. G. Soc. Asiatica ital. **17, 18**, 1904–5.
    Also published separately as a reprint: Note sugli Agau, 1 and 2.
—— Racconti e canti bileni. Actes du XIVe Congr. Int. des Orientalistes, 1907, pp. 331–94.
—— 1912. La Langue des Kemant en Abyssinie. Pp. viii+316. Sprachkommission Akad. Wiss. Wien, **4**.
HALÉVY, J. Essai sur la langue Agaou. Actes Soc. Philol. 1873.
    Deals with the 'Falasha' dialect.
MUNZINGER, WERNER. [A vocabulary of Bilin.]
MURRAY, A. 1808. Account of the life and writings of James Bruce . . . Edinburgh.
    Contains vocabularies taken from Bruce, Travels . . . (*q.v.*).
PRAETORIUS. [A grammatical note.] Z. dtsch. morgenländ. Ges.
REINISCH, LEO. 1882. Die Bilin Sprache in Nordost-Afrika. Wien.
—— 1883–7? Die Bilin-Sprache. 1, Texte der Bilin-Sprache; 2, . . . Leipzig and Wien?
—— 1884. Die Chamirsprache in Abessinien. Wien.
—— 1885–7. Die Quara-Sprache in Abessinien. 3 vols. Leipzig.
SALT, HENRY. 1814. A voyage to Abyssinia and travels into the interior of that country. London.
    Appendix contains vocabularies of Tigre, Tigrinya, Amharic, Agau, Saho, Afar, Galla, and other languages. *See* Leslau, Bibl.; *see also under* SAHO, AFAR, GALLA. There is also a German version, 'Heinrich Salt's neue Reise nach Abessinien', published in Weimar in 1815.
SAPETO, ——. 1857. [A vocabulary in a book of travels.] Roma.
SCHWEINFURTH, G. A. Abyssinische Pflanzennamen. Abh. Akad. Wiss. Berlin, 1893. Pp. 84.
    A list of plant names in Tigre, Tigrinya, Amharic, Agau, Bilin and Saho. *See* Leslau, Bibl.; *see also under* SAHO.
WALDMEIER, TH. 1868. Wörter-Sammlung aus der Agau-Sprache. St. Crishona.

3.   SIDAMA LANGUAGE GROUP
GENERAL

CERULLI, ENRICO. I resultati linguistici dei miei viaggi in Etiopia dal 1926 al 1931. Congr. Inst. Int. Langues et Civilisations Afr. Paris, 1931, pp. 158–64.

COHEN, MARCEL. Du verbe Sīdama (dans le groupe couchitique). Bull. Soc. Ling. Paris, **27**, 1927, pp. 169–200.
MORENO, MARTINO MARIO. Le mie indagini linguistiche nel Galla-Sidama. Oriente Moderno, **18**, 1938.
—— I recenti studi italiani sulle lingue 'Sidama orientali' e la loro classificazione. Ann. Afr. Italiana, **1**, 3–4, 1938, pp. 1081–7.

JANJERO

ABBADIE, ANTOINE D'. Notice sur les langues de Kam. *See under* AGAU.
BEKE, CHARLES TILSTONE. On the languages and dialects of Abyssinia. . . . *See* Leslau, Bibl.; *see also under* AGAU.
CECCHI, ANTONIO. 1885–7, another edition 1892. Da Zeila alle frontiere del Caffa. 3 vols. Rome.
　Vol. 3, pp. 459–61, Vocaboli della lingua Giangerò. *See also under* SIDAMO, KAFFA, AFAR, GALLA.
CERULLI, ENRICO. 1938. Studi Etiopici, 3. Il linguaggio dei Giangerò ed alcune lingue Sidama dell' Omo (Basketo, Ciara, Zaissè). Pp. 231. Roma: Ist. per l'Oriente. *See also under* OMETO. Reviewed by Westermann (Africa, 1939), Cohen (Bull. Soc. Ling. Paris, 1939), Moreno (Riv. Studi Orient. 1939), Conti Rossini (Ann. Afr. Italiana, 1939).

SIDAMO

BORELLI, JULES. 1890. Éthiopie méridionale. Paris.
　Pp. 463–82, vocabularies of Tambaro and Hadia. *See also under* OMETO.
CECCHI, ANTONIO. Da Zeila alle frontiere del Caffa.
　Vol. 3, pp. 465–7, Vocaboli della lingua Adijà. *See under* JANJERO.
CERULLI, ENRICO. Note su alcune popolazioni Sidama dell' Abissinia meridionale. 1. I Sidama orientali. Riv. Studi Orient. **10**, 1925, pp. 597–692.
　Deals with Hadiya (Gudiela), Kambatta, Sidama (Sidamo).
—— 1938. Studi Etiopici, 2. La lingua e la storia dei Sidamo. Pp. 263. Roma: Ist. per l'Oriente. See also important reviews by Moreno in Riv. Studi Orient. **17**, 1938, and Oriente Moderno, **18**, 1938.
MORENO, MARTINO MARIO. Appunti sulla lingua Darasa. R. C. Accad. Lincei, **13**, 1937, pp. 211–40.
—— Appunti di Cambatta e di Alaba. R. C. Accad. Lincei, **14**, 1938, pp. 269–79.
—— 1940. Manuale di Sidamo. Grammatica—Esercizi—Testi—Glossario. Pp. 326. Milano: Mondadori.
—— Nuove notizie sull' Alaba e sugli Alaba. Rass. Studi Etiop. **1**. 1, 1941. Pp. 43+53.
　Includes vocabularies of Alaba, Sidamo, Kambatta, Gudella.
SIMONI, ANTONIO. 1940. I Sidamo fedeli sudditi dell' Impero. Pp. viii+270. Bologna: Cacciari.
　Pp. 221–62. Dizionarietto italiano–sidamo e sidamo–italiano. Reviewed by Conti Rossini (Rass. Studi Etiop. 1941).

OMETO

ABBADIE, ANTOINE D'. Notice sur les langues de Kam. *See under* AGAU.
BEKE, CHARLES TILSTONE. On the languages and dialects of Abyssinia. . . . *See* Leslau, Bibl.: *see also under* AGAU.
BORELLI, JULES. Éthiopie méridionale.
　Pp. 449–62, vocabulary of 'Koullo'. *See also under* SIDAMO.
CERULLI, ENRICO. Note su alcune popolazioni Sidama dell' Abissinia meridionale. 2. I Sidama dell' Omo. Riv. Studi Orient. **12**, 1929, pp. 1–69.
　Deals with Walamo, Zala, Gofa, Badditu.
—— Studi Etiopici, 3. Il linguaggio dei Giangerò ed alcune lingue Sidama dell' Omo (Basketo, Ciara, Zaissè). *See under* JANJERO.
CHIOMÌO, GIOVANNI. 1938. Lingua Uollamo (A.O.I.): Grammatica e dizionario. Pp. xlvi+240+46. Torino: Ist. Missioni Consolata.
　Gives equivalent Galla words, also numerals in Burji, 'Meso' (=?), Konso, Gidole, Gowaze. *See also under* GALLA, BURJI–GELEBA group.

CONTI ROSSINI, CARLO. Contributi per la conoscenza della lingua Haruro. R. C. Accad. Lincei, **12,** 1936.
LUCHON, PASQUALE DA. 1938. Grammatica della lingua Uallamo. Roma.
   Favourably reviewed by Moreno (Riv. Studi Orient. 1940).
MORENO, MARTINO MARIO. 1938. Introduzione alla lingua Ometo. Pp. 193. Milano: Mondadori.
   Reviewed by Westermann ('Africa' 1939), Conti Rossini (Oriente Moderno, 1938), Cohen (Bull. Soc. Ling. Paris, 1939).
TRENTO, GABRIELE DA. Vocaboli in lingue dell' Etiopia meridionale. Rass. Studi Etiop. **1.** 2, 1941, pp. 203-7.
   Vocabularies of 'Uollamo, Male, Borana, Conso, Cule, Arbore, Somalo, Gheleba, Bacco, Amarr Cocche, Turcana Bume'. *See also under* SOMALI, GALLA, BURJI–GELEBA.

GIMIRA

ABBADIE, ANTOINE D'. Notice sur les langues de Kam. *See under* AGAU.
CONTI ROSSINI, CARLO. Sui linguaggi dei Naa e dei Ghimirra (Sce) nell' Etiopia meridionale. R. C. Accad. Lincei, **1,** fasc. 7/8, 1925, pp. 612-36.
   Material taken from d'Abbadie and Montandon, with notes.
—— Il popolo dei Magi nell' Etiopia meridionale e il suo linguaggio. Atti del 3° congr. studi coloniali, **6,** 1937, pp. 108-16. Firenze.
MONTANDON, GEORGES. 1913. Au pays Ghimirra. Neuchâtel: Attinger frères.
   Contains an attempt at classifying the languages of Abyssinia, some linguistic material including a vocabulary of 'Dizou–Bennecho (Ghimirra)', and comments by Meinhof. This book has been used as a basis by later writers.
TOSELLI, G. (Senior). 1939. Lingua Magi. Grammatica e dizionario, con alcuni cenni sulla popolazione Magi a cura del P. G. Chiomio. Pp. 43+44. Torino: Ist. Missioni Consolata.

KAFFA

ABBADIE, ANTOINE D'. Notice sur les langues de Kam. *See under* AGAU.
BEKE, CHARLES TILSTONE. On the languages and dialects of Abyssinia. . . . *See* Leslau, Bibl.: *see also under* AGAU.
BIEBER, FRIEDRICH J. Dizionario della lingua Cafficio. Boll. Soc. Geogr. ital. 1908.
—— Beiträge zu einem erotischen Lexicon der Abessinier (Amhara), Galla und Kaffitscho. Leipzig, Antropophyteia **5,** 1908, pp. 18-24. *See* Leslau, Bibl.; *see also under* GALLA.
CECCHI, ANTONIO. Da Zeila alle frontiere del Caffa.
   Vol. 3, pp. 401-51: Appunti grammaticali e vocaboli di lingua Caffecciò: Novelle traddotte dall' abissino, dal galla e dal caffecciò. *See under* JANJERO.
CONTI ROSSINI, CARLO. 1937. Etiopia e genti di Etiopia. Firenze.
   Contains short introductions to Tigrinya, Amharic, Somali, Galla and Kaffa. *See* Leslau, Bibl.: *see also under* SOMALI, GALLA.
MASERA, C. 1936. Primi elementi di grammatica caffina e dizionario. . . . Pp. 285. Torino: Ist. Missioni Consolata (lithogr.).
MORENO, MARTINO MARIO. Appunti di caffino. Riv. Studi Orient. **18,** 1940, pp. 373-85.
REINISCH, LEO. 1888. Die Kafasprache in Nordost-Afrika. 3 vols. Wien.

SHINASHA

ABBADIE, ANTOINE D'. Notice sur les langues de Kam. *See under* AGAU.
BIRD, ——. [A small dictionary or vocabulary of Shinasha.] J. Bombay Geogr. Soc. 1845.
CONTI ROSSINI, CARLO. Studi su popolazioni dell' Etiopia, 5, Appunti di lingua gonga. Riv. Studi Orient. **6,** 1914-15, pp. 404-15.
   Vocabularies taken from d'Abbadie and Beke, with notes.
CROSBY, O. T. Notes on a Journey from Zeila to Khartoum. Geogr. J. **18,** 1901.
   Contains a small vocabulary of Shinasha.
GROTTANELLI, VINIGI L. Gli Scinascia del Nilo Azzurro ed alcuni lessici poco noti della loro lingua. Rass. Studi Etiop. **1.** 3, 1941, pp. 234-70.
   Incorporates the vocabularies of d'Abbadie, Beke, Crosby, Schuver.

KAN, C. M. De reizen van Juan Maria Schuver in het gebied van den Blawen Nijl. Amsterdam, Tijdschr. van het Aardrijkskundig Genootschap **7**, 1883.
    Pp. 98–100 contain 'Kleine wordenlijst der Sienetjo–taal'.
SCHUVER, JUAN MARIA. Reisen im oberen Nilgebiet, Erlebnisse und Beobachtungen auf der Wasserscheide zwischen Blauem und Weissem Nil, und in den ägyptisch–abessinischen Grenzländern 1881 und 1882. Petermanns Mitt., Ergänzungsheft **72**, Gotha 1883.
    Contains a vocabulary of 120 Shinasha words.

Unpublished material:
CERULLI, ENRICO. Linguistic material on:
    SIDAMO, DARASA;
    GIMIRA: NAO, MAJI, BIENESHO, SHAKKO;
    KAFFA, GARO, MOCHA;
    ANFILLO;
    SHINASHA.

4.   SAHO–AFAR LANGUAGE GROUP
SAHO

ABBADIE, ANTOINE D'. Lettres à M. Jules Mohl: 2. Sur la langue Saho. J. Asiatique, **3**, série 4, 1843, pp. 108–18.
CAPOMAZZA, ILARIO. L'Assaorta–Saho. Vocabolario italiano–assaorta–saho ed assaorta–saho–italiano. Boll. Soc. Afr. ital. 1910–11.
    According to Major Duncanson, the spelling is most inconsistent and therefore largely incomprehensible.
CONTI ROSSINI, CARLO. Al Rágali. Boll. Soc. Ital. Esplorazioni Geogr. e Commerciali 1903–4.
    Also published as reprint, 1904, pp. 62. Pp. 31–3, notes on the Saho language.
—— Schizzo del dialetto Saho dell' alta Assaorta in Eritrea. R. C. Accad. Lincei, **22**. 5, 1913, pp. 151–246.
JAHN, ALFRED. Lautlehre der Saho-Sprache in Nordabessinien. 24. Jber. K. K. Staats-Realschule 23. Gemeindebezirk Wien, 1909–10, pp. 1–38.
KIELMAIER, C. Sammlung von Wörtern aus den Sprachen der Küstenbewohner des östlichen Afrika zwischen dem neunten bis sechzehnten Grad nördl. Breite. Ausland, München, **1**, 1840.
    Pp. 303 ff. contain 80 words in German, 'Schiho', Danakil, Somali, Harari, Galla. See Leslau, Bibl.; *see also under* AFAR, SOMALI, GALLA.
LOTTNER, ——. The Saho–Galla is related to the Semitic, yet they are not one family. Trans. Philol. Soc. 1860–1.
MÜLLER, ——. [A grammatical note.] Orient und Occident, **3**.
PERINI, R. Gl'idiomi parlati nella nostra colonia. See Leslau, Bibl.; *see also under* BEJA.
REINISCH, LEO. Die Saho Sprache. Z. dtsch. morgenländ. Ges. **32**, 1878, pp. 415–56.
    Deals especially with the 'Toroa' dialect, i.e. the dialect of the Assaorta.
—— Die Sprache der Irob–Saho in Abessinien. S.B. phil.-hist. Klasse. Akad. Wiss. Wien, 1878.
—— 1889–90. Die Saho-Sprache. 1. Texte der Saho-Sprache. 2. Wörterbuch. Pp. 315. Wien: Hölder.
    Deals especially with the 'Miniferi' and 'Rasamo' (Dasamo) dialects—the Dasamo being a section of the Miniferi tribe.
SALT, HENRY. A voyage to Abyssinia.... *See* Leslau, Bibl.; *see also under* AGAU.
SCHWEINFURTH, G. Abyssinische Pflanzennamen. *See* Leslau, Bibl.; *see also under* AGAU.
YUSHMANOV, NICOLAI V. 1936. Sur les langues de l'Éthiopie. Leningrad: Sovetskaya etnografia.
    In Russian, with French résumé. Vol. 1, pp. 40–4, contains text in Saho and Amharic, in transliteration and with Russian translation. *See* Leslau, Bibl.

AFAR

ARPINO, LUDOVICO D'. 1938. Vocabolario dall' italiano nelle versioni galla (oromo)–amara–dancala–somala. Pp. viii+353. Milano: Hoepli. *See* Leslau, Bibl.; *see also under* SOMALI, GALLA.

CANDEO, G. Vocabolario dancalo. Boll. Soc. Afr. ital. 1893, pp. 135–9, 157–63, 191–9.
CAPOMAZZO, ILARIO. 1907. La lingua degli Afar. Pp. 197.
CECCHI, ANTONIO. Da Zeila alle frontiere del Caffa.
    Vol. 3, pp. 487–90, Vocaboli e modi di dire afar. *See under* JANJERO.
COLIZZA, GIOVANNI. 1886 (1887?). La lingua 'Afar nel nord-est dell' Africa: grammatica, testi e vocabolario. Pp. xii+153. Wien.
DERCHI, FELICE. Dizionario e frasario italiano–dáncalo (afar). Mem. Soc. Geogr. ital. **5**, 1895, pp. 294–324.
ISENBERG, CARL WILHELM. 1840. A small vocabulary of the Dankali language. Part 1. English and Dankali; Part 2, Dankali and English. London.
KOENIG, E. 1839. Vocabulaires appartenant à diverses contrées ou tribus de l'Afrique recueillis dans la Nubie supérieure. Paris: Delaporte.
    Contains a vocabulary of Dankali. *See also under* SOMALI.
LUCAS, MAURICE. Renseignements ethnographiques et linguistiques sur les Danakils de Tadjourah. J. Soc. Afric. **5**. 2, 1935, pp. 181–202.
    According to Cerulli, this is the only work on Afar as spoken in French Somaliland.
OEHLSCHLAGER, —. 1891. Vocabulaire Dankali. Melun: Imprimerie administrative.
PAULITSCHKE, PHILIPP. 1896. Ethnographie Nordost-Afrikas. Berlin: Dietrich Reimer.
    Vol. 2, pp. 78–90 contain remarks on Dankali, Somali, and Galla. *See also under* SOMALI, GALLA.
PERINI, R. Gl'idiomi parlati nella nostra colonia. *See* Leslau, Bibl.; *see also under* BEJA.
REINISCH, LEO. 1883–7. Die Afar-Sprache. 3 vols. Wien and Leipzig.
RIGBY, CHRISTOPHER PALMER. Specimen of the language spoken on the Western shore of the Red Sea and Gulf of Aden. Trans. Bombay Geogr. Soc. **6**, 1844, pp. 93–4.
    Vocabulary in English, Dankali, Somali, Amharic, Galla. *See* Leslau, Bibl.; *see also under* SOMALI, GALLA.
SALT, HENRY. A Voyage to Abyssinia. . . . *See* Leslau, Bibl.; *see also under* AGAU.
SERRA-CARACCIOLO, PIETRO. Saggio di vocabolario della lingua danakil. Napoli, L'Esploratore, **1**. 1, 1883, pp. 84–7.

Unpublished material
KEANY, J. 1943. Simple Sao.
    Grammatical notes and vocabulary of Saho. MS. in the possession of the School of Oriental and African Studies, London.

5. SOMALI

ANON. 1908 (2nd edition). The first Somali standard. Pp. 40, Berbera.
ARMSTRONG, L. E. The phonetic structure of Somali. M.S.O.S. **37**. 3, 1934, pp. 116–61.
ARPINO, LUDOVICO D'. Vocabolario dall' italiano nelle versioni galla (oromo)–amara–dancala–somala. *See* Leslau, Bibl.; *see also under* AFAR.
BERGHOLD, KURT. Somali Studien. Z. Afr. Ozean. Sprachen, **3**, 1897, pp. 1–16.
—— Somali Studien. Wiener Z. Kde Morgenland. **13**, 1899.
BURTON, SIR RICHARD FRANCIS. 1856. First footsteps in East Africa, or an exploration of Harar.
    Contains some linguistic material on Somali.
CARCOFORO, E. 1912. Elementi di somalo e ki-suahili parlati al Benadir. Pp. viii+154. Milano: Hoepli.
    Reviewed by Ferrario (Riv. Studi Orient. 1917), who describes it as unreliable and inaccurate at every point.
CARESSA, FERRUCCIO. 1938. Dizionario africano. Italiano–amarico–tigrino–arabo (A. O., Egitto, Asia)–arabo (Libia, Africa sett.)–galla–migiurtino-benadirese. Pp. 238. Milano: Sonzongo. *See* Leslau, Bibl.; *see also under* GALLA.
CERULLI, ENRICO. Di alcune presunte consonanti nei dialetti somali. Riv. Studi Orient. **7**, 1918, pp. 877–83.
—— Testi Somali. 1. Canti e proverbi nel dialetto degli Habar Auwal. 2. Testi di diritto consuetudinario dei Somali Marrehan. Riv. Studi Orient. **7**, 1918, pp. 797–836.

CERULLI, ENRICO. Somali songs and little Texts. J. Afr. Soc. **19–21**, 1920–1.
—— Nota sui dialetti somali. Riv. Studi Orient. **8**, 1921, pp. 693–9.
CHIARINI, G. Raccolta di vocaboli dei Somali–Isa. Mem. Soc. Geogr. ital. **1**, 1879, pp. 209–15.
CONTI ROSSINI, CARLO. 1937. Etiopia e genti di Etiopia. Firenze.
    Contains a short introduction to Somali and Galla. *See also under* GALLA.
COSTAGUTI, MARCHESA MARIA AFAN DE RIVERA. 1909. Manuale pratico di lingua somàla ad uso dei viaggiatori nella valle di Giuba. Pp. vi+133 (?). Roma; Casa editrice Italiana.
    Reviewed by Ferrario (Riv. Studi Orient. 1914–15).
CZERMAK, W. Zur Phonetik des Somāli. Wiener Z. Kde Morgenland. **31**, 1924, pp. 82–102.
—— Somāli-Texte im Dialekt der Habr Ja'lo. Wiener Z. Kde Morgenland. **31**, 1924, pp. 113–36.
—— Zum Gebrauch des Infinitivs als 'Futurum' in Somali. Nijmegen–Utrecht, Donum Natalicium Schrijnen, 1929, pp. 182–9.
FERRAND, GABRIEL. 1886. Notes de Grammaire Çomalie. Pp. 28. Alger: P. Fontana et Cie.
    See also Boll. Soc. Geogr. ital. 1892, pp. 599–608, a letter to the society from Robecchi-Bricchetti condemning this book ('La grammatica somali del Ferrand').
FERRARIO, BENIGNO. *Ingir* < *$\bar{I}ng\check{i}'\check{i}l$* in Somalo. Riv. Studi Orient. **7**. 1, 1916–18, pp. 717–19.
—— L'accento in Somâlo. Riv. Studi Orient. **6**, 1914–15, pp. 961–7.
—— Note di fonologia somâla. Riv. Studi Orient. **7**. 1, 1916–18, pp. 199–217.
HENRY, L. 1897. Essai de vocabulaire pratique français-issa (Somalis). Melun.
HUNTER, F. M. 1880. A grammar of the Somali language. Bombay.
JAHN, ALFRED. Somali Texte gesammelt und übersetzt. S.B. Akad. Wiss. Wien, **152**. 5, 1906.
JANSEN, PIETRO GERARDO. 1936. Guida alla conoscenza dei dialetti dell' Africa Orientale. Pp. 126. Milano: Le lingue estere.
    Part 4, 'Le lingue e i dialetti della Somalia', deals with the Darod and Hawiyya dialects.
KIELMAIER, C. Sammlung von Wörtern aus den Sprachen der Küstenbewohner.... *See* Leslau, Bibl.; *see also under* AFAR.
KIRK, J. W. C. 1903. Notes on the Somali Language. London: Oxford University Press.
—— 1905. A Grammar of the Somali Language. Pp. 216. Cambridge University Press.
    Includes a section on the dialects of the outcaste tribes Yibir and Midgan.
KOENIG, E. Vocabulaires appartenant à diverses contrées ou tribus....
    Contains a vocabulary of Somali. *See also under* AFAR.
KOENIG, M. 1839. Recueil de voyages et de mémoires. Paris: Soc. Géogr.
    Vol. 4, pp. 35–46, Vocabulaire de l'idiome des Saumals.
LANG, CARL. Repetition, Reduplikation und Lautmalerei in der Somali-Sprache. Biblioteca Africana, **1, 2**, 1925, pp. 98–104.
LARAJASSE, —DE. 1897. Somali-English and English-Somali grammar of the Somali language. Pp. xvi+265. London.
—— 1897. Somali-English and English-Somali dictionary. Pp. xviii+301. London: Kegan Paul.
—— and SAMPONT, [CYPRIEN DE]. 1897. Practical grammar of the Somali language. London: Kegan Paul.
LIGHT, R. H. 1896. English-Somali sentences and idioms, for the use of sportsmen and visitors in Somali-land. Bombay: Thacker.
MEINHOF, CARL. Die Sprachen der Hamiten.
    Chap. 6, Somali: also a comparative vocabulary, pp. 230–40. *See under* BEJA.
ORANO, MARCELLO. 1931. [A manual of Somali.] Milano: Hoepli.
    See B. Ducati, in Atti del 1º congr. di studi coloniali 1931.
—— 1936. La lingua somala parlata nella Somalia settentrionale, nell' Ogaden e nel Benadir. Pp. 182. Roma: Casa ed. Mediterranea.
PALERMO, GIOVANNI MARIA DA. 1914. Grammatica della lingua somala. Pp. vi+357. Asmara.
    Reviewed by Cerulli (Riv. Studi Orient. 1917).
PAULITSCHKE, PHILIPP. Ethnographie Nordost-Afrikas. *See under* AFAR.
PRAETORIUS, F. Über die Somali-Sprache.
    Possibly the 'Grammatical note' referred to by Cust as appearing in Z. dtsch. morgenländ. Ges. 1870.

REINISCH, LEO. 1900, 1902, 1903. Die Somali-Sprache. 3 vols. Pp. 287, 540, 126. Wien: Hölder (Südarabische Expedition 2).
1. Texts, 2. Dictionary, 3. Grammar.
—— 1904. Der Dschäbärtidialekt der Somali Sprache. Wien.
RIGBY, CHRISTOPHER PALMER. Specimen of the language spoken on the Western shore of the Red Sea. . . . *See* Leslau, Bibl.; *see also under* AFAR.
—— On the Somauli Language. Trans. Bombay Geogr. Soc. **9**, 1849.
ROBECCHI-BRICCHETTI, LUIGI. Testi Somali. R. C. Accad. Lincei 1889.
—— Lingue parlate somali, galla e harari. Note e studi raccolti ed ordinati nell' Harar. Boll. Soc. Geogr. ital. 1890. *See* Leslau, Bibl. (*under* Bricchetti-Robecchi); *see also under* GALLA.
—— 1892. La grammatica somala. Roma.
—— Note sulle lingue parlate somali, galla e harrari, raccolte ed ordinate nell' Harrar. Boll. Soc. Afr. ital. **14**. 1895–7. *See* Leslau, Bibl.; *see also under* GALLA.
SACCONI, ——. [Vocabulary and sentences.] Napoli, L'Esploratore 1878, pp. 105–11.
SAMPONT, CYPRIEN DE. 1905. Grammaire Somalée. London and Berbera: Mission Catholique.
—— 1905. Dictionnaire Somalé. London and Berbera: Mission Catholique.
—— 1920. Grammaire de la langue Somalie. Pp. xvi+237. Roma.
SCHLEICHER, A. W. 1892. Die Somali Sprache. Berlin.
—— *ed*. REINISCH, LEO. 1890. Somali-Texte. Wien.
SMEE, TH. Specimens of different languages used on the East Coast of Africa (Suaheli, Somali, Galla). Proc. Bombay Geogr. Soc. **6**, 1844, pp. 50–5. *See also under* GALLA.
STORACI, E. 1935. Il poliglotta africano. Vademecum per l'Africa orientale: italiano, arabo, swahili, somalo, galla, tigrino, tigrè. Raccolta dei vocaboli più usati. Pp. 64. Milano: Bietti. *See* Leslau, Bibl.; *see also under* GALLA.
TILING, MARIA VON. Die Vokale des bestimmten Artikels in Somali. Z. Kol. Sprachen, **9**, 1918–19, pp. 132–66.
—— Adjektiv-Endungen im Somali. Z. Eingeb. Sprachen, **10**, 1919–20, pp. 208–40.
—— Die Sprache der Jabarti, mit besonderer Berücksichtigung der Verwandtschaft von Jabarti und Somali. Z. Eingeb. Sprachen, **12**, 1922, pp. 17–162.
—— Jabarti Texte. Z. Eingeb. Sprachen, **15**, 1925, pp. 50–64, 139–58.
TRENTO, GABRIELE DA. Vocaboli in lingue dell' Etiopia meridionale. *See under* OMETO.

6. GALLA

ANON. 1936. Nomenclatura elementare ed espressioni nelle lingue amarica, galla, arabo (dialetto tripolino). Pp. 48. Roma: Ist. Coloniale Fascista. *See* Leslau, Bibl.
—— Piccoli studi etiopici. Appunti galla in lingua amhara. Z. Assyriologie, **27**, 1912, pp. 373–83. *See* Leslau, Bibl.
—— 1928. Vocabulaire français, oromo, abyssin. Pp. xvi+127. Diredawa: Imprimerie St. Lazare. *See* Leslau, Bibl.
ARENZANO, IRENEO D'. 1940. Grammatica della lingua galla. Con esercizi di traduzione, nomenclatura, conversazione e vocabolario. Pp. 287. Harar: Il Seminatore.
ARPINO, LUDOVICO D'. Vocabolario dall' italiano nelle versioni galla (oromo)–amara–dancala–somala. *See* Leslau, Bibl.; *see also under* AFAR.
BEKE, CHARLES TILSTONE. On the languages and dialects of Abyssinia. . . . *See* Leslau, Bibl.; *see also under* AGAU.
BIEBER, F. J. Beiträge zu einem erotischen Lexicon der Abessinier. . . . *See* Leslau, Bibl.; *see also under* KAFFA.
BOCEGUILLAS, J. M. DE. 1922. Vic. Apost. Notions grammaticales sur la langue Galla ou Oromo. Pp. vi+152. Diredawa.
BORELLO, MARIO. 1939. Grammatica di lingua galla (oromo). 1. Fonetica e morfologia. Pp. 308. Torino: Ist. Missioni Consolata (lithogr.).
Written for a course of instruction for officials in Addis Ababa.
—— 1945. Proverbi Galla (prima serie). Roma: Ist. per l'Oriente. Studi Etiopici raccolti da Conti Rossini, pp. 111–30.
CARESSA, FERRUCCIO. 1935. Manuale linguistico per l'Africa Orientale coi principali vocaboli delle

lingue amarica, galla, tigrina; e versione in italiano e francese, ad uso dei militari, funzionari, uomini d'affari, turisti, ecc. Pp. 96. Torino: Edizioni Spes. *See* Leslau, Bibl.

CECCHI, A. Da Zeila alle frontiere del Caffa.
 Vol. 3, pp. 1–100, Grammatica della lingua oromonica (compiled by Prof. E. Viterbo); pp. 101 ff., vocabulary ('oromonico–italiano'); pp. 269–398, vocabulary ('italiano–oromonico'). *See under* JANJERO.

CERULLI, ENRICO. 1922. The folk-literature of the Galla of Southern Ethiopia. Massachusetts, Harvard African Studies, **3**.
 Reviewed by Werner (Z. Eingeb. Sprachen, 1924), Conti Rossini (Riv. Studi Orient. 1923).

CHIOMÌO, GIOVANNI. Lingua Uollamo. *See under* OMETO.

CONTI ROSSINI, CARLO. Il 'Nagara Galla'. R. C. Accad. Lincei, **13**, 1904, pp. 307–24, 329–44.

—— Etiopia e genti di Etiopia. *See under* SOMALI.

[DUCATI, BRUNO]. 1935. L'amharico, il suahili, il galla. Dizionarietto delle tre principali lingue parlate in Abissinia. Pp. 30. Roma: L'azione coloniale. *See* Leslau, Bibl.

DUCATI, BRUNO. 1936. Corso di lingua galla in dodici lezioni. Milano: Soc. An. Naz. del Gramofono.
 Gramophone course.

—— 1937. Dizionario galla–italiano e italiano–galla. Roma: Ist. Coloniale Fascista.

FOOT, E. C. 1913. A Galla–English, English–Galla Dictionary. Pp. 118. Cambridge University Press.
 Reviewed by Werner (J. Afr. Soc. 1914), Meinhof (Deutsche Literatur-Zeitung 1913).

GUBERNATIS, ANGELO DE. La lingua dei Gallas sui materiali raccolti dal Capitano Cecchi e ordinati dal Prof. Viterbo. Boll. Soc. Afr. ital. (Sezione Fiorentina), **4**, 1888, pp. 27–38.

HODSON, A. W., and WALKER, C. H. 1922. An elementary and practical grammar of the Galla or Oromo language. Pp. 272. London: S.P.C.K.
 Favourably reviewed by Werner (J. Afr. Soc. 1921–2).

JANSEN, PIETRO GERARDO. Guida alla conoscenza dei dialetti dell' Africa orientale. *See* Leslau, Bibl.; *see also under* SOMALI.

JAROSSEAU, ANDREA. 1922. Notions grammaticales sur la langue Galla (ou Oromo). Pp. vi+52. Diredawa: St. Lazare.

KIELMAIER, C. Sammlung von Wörtern aus den Sprachen der Küstenbewohner. . . . *See* Leslau, Bibl.; *see also under* SAHO.

KRAPF, J. L. 1840. Elements of the Galla language.

—— 1842. Vocabulary of the Galla language. London.

—— 1850. Vocabulary of six East-African languages—Kisuaheli, Kinika, Kikamba, Kipokomo, Kihiau, Kigalla. Tübingen.

MASSAIA, G. 1867. Lectiones grammaticales pro Missionariis qui addiscere volunt linguam amaricam seu vulgarem Abyssiniae, et linguam oromonicam seu populorum Galla nuncupatorum. Pp. xix+501. Paris. *See* Leslau, Bibl.

MAYER, J., *ed.* KRAPF, L. 1878. Kurze Wörtersammlung in Englisch, Deutsch, Amharisch, Gallanisch, Guraguesch. Pp. 32. Basel: St. Crishona. *See* Leslau, Bibl.

MIZZI, A. 1935. I proverbi Galla (prima serie). Pp. 59. Malta.

MORENO, MARTINO MARIO. 1935. Favole e rime galla. Pp. vii+204. Roma: Tipografia del Senato.
 Texts, edited, translated, and annotated.

—— Alcuni racconti galla. Riv. Studi Orient. **14**, pp. 98–122.

—— 1939. Grammatica teorico-pratica della lingua galla con esercizi. Pp. 254. Milano: Mondadori.
 Reviewed by Cohen (Bull. Soc. Ling. Paris. 1939).

NESIB, ONES. 1894. The Galla spelling book. Moncullo.

PAULITSCHKE, PHILIPP. Ethnographie Nordost-Afrikas. *See under* AFAR.

PICCIRILLI, TITO. 1938. Dizionario di alcune lingue parlate nell' A.O.I. (Amarica–Tigray–Galla–Tigré) con la relativa traduzione italiana e trascrizione secondo la fonetica italiana. Pp. 813. Napoli: Arti grafiche, Caparrini. *See* Leslau, Bibl.

PIOVANO, GIOVANNI. Nomi galla di vegetali. Rass. Studi Etiop. **2**. 3, 1942, pp. 312–30.

PRAETORIUS, F. 1893. Zur Grammatik der Galla-Sprache. Berlin.
—— Eine Gallafabel. Aus Karl Tutscheks Nachlass mitgeteilt. Z. Afr. Sprachen, 1889–90, pp. 77–9.
RIGBY, C. P. Specimen of the language spoken on the western shore of the Red Sea. . . . *See under* AFAR.
ROBECCHI-BRICCHETTI, LUIGI. Lingue parlate somali, galla e harari. . . . *See* Leslau, Bibl.; *see also under* SOMALI.
—— Vocaboli della lingua oromonica. Boll. Soc. Afr. ital. 1891–2.
—— Testi nelle lingue harar e galla. R. C. Accad. Lincei 1892, pp. 254–63. *See* Leslau, Bibl.
—— Note sulle lingue parlate somali, galla e harrari. . . . *See* Leslau, Bibl.; *see also under* SOMALI.
SALT, HENRY. A voyage to Abyssinia. . . . *See* Leslau, Bibl.; *see also under* AGAU.
SCHMIDT, P. Abriss der Shoagalla-Grammatik. Z. dtsch. morgenländ. Ges. (?)
   Described by Cust as a sketch of the Shoa dialect, based on an analysis of the translation of St. Matthew's Gospel by Krapf.
SCOLART, LUCIO. 1885. Grammatica oromonica ossia della lingua parlata nel paese dei Gallas e nell' Abissinia. Pp. viii+63. Napoli.
—— 1888. Frasario e vocaboli in lingua amarica–oromona–araba–inglese, con le preghiere in etiopico, ad uso dei viaggiatori in Abissinia. Pp. 71. Napoli. *See* Leslau, Bibl.
SMEE, TH. Specimens of different languages. . . . *See under* SOMALI.
STORACI, E. Il poliglotta africano. *See* Leslau, Bibl.; *see also under* SOMALI.
THIENE, GAETANO DA. 1939. Dizionario della lingua galla. Pp. xl+340+153. Harar: Vicariato Apost.
   From MS. material left by Jarosseau. Reviewed by Moreno (Riv. Studi Orient. 1940).
TRENTO, GABRIELE DA. Vocaboli in lingue dell' Etiopia meridionale. *See under* OMETO.
TUTSCHEK, C. 1844–5. Grammar and dictionary of the Galla language. 2 parts. Munich.
   Described by Cust as 'a wonderful performance, considering that the author was never in the country'.
VITERBO, ETTORE. 1892. Grammatica e dizionario della lingua oromonica (galla). Vocabolario della lingua oromonica compilato delle note ed appunti dell' ing. Giovanni Chiarini e del missionario P. Léon des Avanchers. 2 vols. Pp. vi+150, lxiv+105. Milano.
   Vol. 1, Galla–Italian vocabulary; Vol. 2, Grammar and Italian–Galla vocabulary.

7.   BURJI–GELEBA LANGUAGE GROUP

CERULLI, ENRICO. Il linguaggio degli Amar Cocchè e quello degli Arbore nella zona del lago Stefania. Rass. Studi Etiop. **2**. 3, 1942, pp. 260–72.
CHIOMIO, G. Lingua Uollamo. *See under* OMETO.
CONTI ROSSINI, CARLO. Studi su popolazioni dell' Etiopia, 6. I Bambala di Amarr Burgi e il loro linguaggio. Riv. Studi Orient. **6**, 1914–15, pp. 415–25.
   Vocabularies taken from Bottego, with comparisons with other languages.
—— 1927. Sui linguaggi parlati a nord dei laghi Rodolfo e Stefania. Festschrift Meinhof, pp. 247–55.
   Deals briefly with Geleba, Arbore, Konso and other languages.
MORENO, MARTINO MARIO. Note di lingua burgi. Riv. Studi Orient. **17**, 1938, pp. 350–98.
—— Notizie sul ghidole e sul gowazé. Ann. Ist. Univ. Orient. Napoli, Nuova serie, **2**, 1943.
   Scritti dedicati alla memoria di Francesco Gallina, pp. 233–7.
SMITH, A. DONALDSON. 1897. Through unknown African countries. London and New York.
   Pp. 445–6, vocabulary of 'Arbore–Amarr', i.e. Arbore, and Konso.
TRENTO, GABRIELE DA. Vocaboli in lingue dell' Etiopia meridionale. *See under* OMETO.
WELLBY, M. S. 1901. Twixt Sirdar and Menelik: an account of a year's expedition from Zeila to Cairo through unknown Abyssinia. London.
   Pp. 407–8, vocabulary of 'Hammer Koki', i.e. Arbore, and 'Galloppa', i.e. Geleba.

Unpublished material
CERULLI, ENRICO. Linguistic material on:
   KONSO, BURJI, GARDULLA.
SHACKLETON, —. Linguistic notes on 'MARILLE' (GELEBA), in the possession of A. C. A. Wright.

VERNACULAR LITERATURE

SEMITIC LANGUAGES

TIGRE

'The Tigre language is still in the first stages of literary development. . . . The Tigre speaking population is very largely illiterate. . . . There is hardly anything at all printed in Tigre with the exception of the Gospel, Psalms and a few other biblical books.'[1]

TIGRINYA

'Owing to the absolute domination of Ge'ez no noteworthy literature has developed in Tigrinya hitherto. There are, however, some translations, especially of the New Testament, Imitatio Christi and some prayer books. . . . With the help of the British Senior Civil Affairs Officer the traditional law-code of the Serae division was printed some little time ago. An important feature of contemporary Tigrinya literature is a regular weekly newspaper in Tigrinya which was founded in 1942 by the British Ministry of Information in Eritrea. This is, in fact, the first and only regular publication in this important Abyssinian language. The British Military Administration's Education Department, too, deserves mention for the publication of a number of Tigrinya text books. The Swedish Mission and the Missione Francescana have edited a small number of Tigrinya texts.'[2]

AMHARIC

'The oldest literary documents of Amharic date back to the 15th and 16th century. . . . King Menyelik paid much attention to Amharic literature and also the present Emperor does everything in his power to stimulate literary creation in Amharic. The establishment of a printing office in Addis Ababa has had a beneficial effect on literary production. . . . The Ethiopian Press and Information Bureau deserves mention for the publication of newspapers, periodicals and booklets, among them an Amharic grammar written in Amharic.'[3]

Parts of the New Testament have been translated into Amharic, and there are also several religious and educational books in existence.

GURAGE

Roman Catholic missionaries have produced a catechism in the Chaha dialect.

CUSHITIC LANGUAGES

There is very little vernacular literature in these languages. Single Gospels have been translated into the AGAU dialects 'BOGOS' (BILEN) and 'FALASHA KARA' (KAYLA) and the SIDAMA dialects GOFA, WALAMO, 'GUDEILLA' and SIDAMO.

The whole Bible has been translated into 'Northern' GALLA, the New Testament into 'Central' GALLA, and single Gospels into 'SHOA', 'BARARETTA' and 'BORAN'.

There are several Gospels in SOMALI published both by the British and Foreign Bible Society and by Roman Catholic missions, as well as some catechisms and other religious books, including a translation of 'Pilgrim's Progress'.

---

[1] E. Ullendorf, *Exploration and Study of Abyssinia*, p. 69.
[2] Ibid., pp. 68–9.   [3] Ibid., p. 67.

THE DISTRIBUTION OF THE NILOTIC AND NILO-HAMITIC LANGUAGES OF AFRICA

M. A. BRYAN

LINGUISTIC ANALYSES

A. N. TUCKER

LONDON AND NEW YORK

First published in 1948 by Oxford University Press

This edition first published in 2018
by Routledge
2 Park Square, Milton Park, Abingdon, Oxon OX14 4RN

and by Routledge
711 Third Avenue, New York, NY 10017

Routledge is an imprint of the Taylor & Francis Group, an informa business

© 1948 International African Institute 1948

All rights reserved. No part of this book may be reprinted or reproduced or utilised in any form or by any electronic, mechanical, or other means, now known or hereafter invented, including photocopying and recording, or in any information storage or retrieval system, without permission in writing from the publishers.

Trademark notice: Product or corporate names may be trademarks or registered trademarks, and are used only for identification and explanation without intent to infringe.

British Library Cataloguing-in-Publication Data
A catalogue record for this book is available from the British Library

ISBN: 978-1-138-08975-4 (Set)
ISBN: 978-1-315-10381-5 (Set) (ebk)
ISBN: 978-1-138-09586-1 (Volume 12) (hbk)
ISBN: 978-1-138-09621-9 (Volume 12) (pbk)
ISBN: 978-1-315-10552-9 (Volume 12) (ebk)

Publisher's Note
The publisher has gone to great lengths to ensure the quality of this reprint but points out that some imperfections in the original copies may be apparent.

Disclaimer
The publisher has made every effort to trace copyright holders and would welcome correspondence from those they have been unable to trace.

Due to modern production methods, it has not been possible to reproduce the fold-out maps within the book. Please visit www.routledge.com to view them.

DISTRIBUTION OF THE NILOTIC AND NILO-HAMITIC LANGUAGES OF AFRICA

BY

M. A. BRYAN

LINGUISTIC ANALYSES

BY

A. N. TUCKER

Published for the
INTERNATIONAL AFRICAN INSTITUTE
by the
OXFORD UNIVERSITY PRESS
LONDON NEW YORK TORONTO
1948

Oxford University Press, Amen House, London E.C. 4
GLASGOW NEW YORK TORONTO MELBOURNE WELLINGTON
BOMBAY CALCUTTA MADRAS CAPE TOWN
Geoffrey Cumberlege, Publisher to the University

This study is one of a series of publications issued in connexion with the Handbook of African Languages which the International African Institute is preparing with the aid of a grant made by the Secretary of State under the Colonial Development and Welfare Acts, on the recommendation of the Colonial Social Science Research Council.

PRINTED IN GREAT BRITAIN

PREFACE

THE International African Institute's *Handbook of African Languages* is to appear at its first level as a general survey of existing information in four volumes, covering, respectively, Bantu Africa, North Africa, West Africa, and North-east Africa. The present pamphlet is concerned with one section of the North-east volume, and is to be regarded as something in the nature of a 'kite'. Its arrangement has been devised in consultation with the editors of the other volumes and especially with the editor of the West African volume, since the linguistic frontiers between these two volumes have been defined, to some extent, by criteria of practical expediency.

As was explained in the foreword to a previous paper—*Distribution of the Semitic and Cushitic Languages of Africa*—the LANGUAGE or the DIALECT CLUSTER is the basic unit. These basic units, where the information permits, are classified under GROUPS, e.g. the LWO Group of Nilotic languages or the NANDI Group of Nilo-Hamitic languages. If, within the group, there is a further alinement of some of the languages exhibiting similar traits, this is noted, but no attempt is made to label it a 'sub-group'; e.g. there are at least two alinements of languages within the Lwo Group, but it is not proposed here to call the Southern Lwo languages a 'sub-group' of the Lwo languages, nor the ACOLI-LANGO a 'sub-sub-group' of these.

It is possible sometimes to put the groups themselves into larger units such as the Nilotic Languages and the Nilo-Hamitic Languages.[1] These, though convenient units, are not an essential part of the system, which is primarily concerned with Languages and Dialect Clusters and the Groups to which they belong. The relationships between languages and dialects within the group are briefly described, and the authorities for statements on such relationships are quoted. This is considered to be important as indicating the reliability of information as well as the gaps in existing knowledge.

For each language, data are given on locality, number of speakers, use for educational and religious purposes, and the extent of vernacular literature. The linguistic material is set out in phonetic script with tone marks, though reference is made to current standard orthographies where these exist.

This paper has been issued in advance of the volume on North-east African languages, of which it is a part, because the number of experts on Nilotic and Nilo-Hamitic languages is probably greater than in any other part of the non-Bantu linguistic field. It is to be expected, therefore, that much useful criticism and correction of the linguistic material here presented will be forthcoming. Such criticism will be welcomed with much gratitude, and incorporated in the North-east African volume which should be ready for publication in a year's time.

A. N. TUCKER

[1] In this connexion it may be remarked that the all-embracing terms 'Sudanic' and 'Hamitic', because of their vagueness, have little classificatory value beyond a rough division into little-inflected and highly inflected languages. This can be seen from the author's previous attempts at defining them in *Survey of the Language Groups in the Southern Sudan* and *The Eastern Sudanic Languages*, Vol. I. With further definition as 'Eastern Sudanic', 'Nilo-Hamitic', 'Chado-Hamitic' they may still serve a useful purpose, and are so used here.

PREFACE

THE author and the Linguistic Advisory Committee desire to express their thanks to numerous officials and missionaries who have provided information. In particular, acknowledgement is made to:

MR. A. J. ARKELL; FATHER CRAZZOLARA; MR. G. W. B. HUNTINGFORD; MR. G. JANSON SMITH; FATHER KIGGEN; MR. G. R. KING; FATHER VAN DER LOOY; FATHER MCGOUGH; FATHER MURATORI; MR. PARIS J. REIDHEAD; FATHER SANTANDREA; MR. R. A. SNOXALL; MR. J. C. WILD; MR. J. WILLIAMSON; DR. W. A. WILSON; M. L'ADMINISTRATEUR TERRITORIAL, MAHAGI, BELGIAN CONGO; PROVINCIAL COMMISSIONER, N. PROVINCES, UGANDA; EDUCATION OFFICER, KISUMU, KENYA.

INTRODUCTORY NOTES

Nomenclature

The following linguistic and tribal names are given:

1. Name of language or dialect, and of tribe, used by Europeans (Language: Roman Capitals; Tribe: Italic Capitals).
2. Other names used by Europeans (Roman or Italic Capitals in brackets).
3. Name by which known to the speakers of the language, in the accepted orthography (certain languages only) (Roman or Italic Capitals).
    Note: Native names of Nilotic and most Nilo-Hamitic languages consist of the phrase 'mouth (language) of the So-and-so'.
4. Phonetic rendering of (3), with tone marks where known (heavy type, lower case).
5. Other names by which known to neighbouring tribes (Roman or Italic Capitals).
6. Phonetic rendering of (5) (heavy type, lower case).

It has not been possible to give all these names in every case; context and type should, however, make it clear which are used in each instance.

Orthography

1. A standard orthography has been accepted for use in the following languages:

Nilotic: DINKA, NUER, SHILLUK, ACOLI, LANGO, ALUR, LUO (provisional);

Nilo-Hamitic: BARI, LOTUHO, TOPOSA, TESO.

The following are the main symbols in use:

th, dh, nh	dental *t, d, n*.
c	as in English 'church', but often pronounced as pure palatal.
ny	palatal nasal, as in French 'Boulogne'.
ŋ	velar nasal, as in 'singing'.
'	glottal stop.
'b, 'd	implosive *b* and *d*.
ɣ	voiced velar fricative, as Arabic ﻉ
ɛ, ɔ	open *e* and *o*.
ä, ö	centralized vowels.

} in the Southern Sudan only.

2. For the phonetic rendering of names, and in the linguistic sections, the following additional symbols are used here:

ʋ	bilabial fricative.
ţ, ḍ, ṇ	dental *t, d, n*.
θ, ð	dental fricatives, as in 'thick' and 'this'.
ṭ or ṛ	alveolar fricative (like voiceless r).
ç	palatal fricative, as in German 'ich'.
ʃ	post. alveolar fricative, as in 'ship'.

INTRODUCTORY NOTES

x   voiceless velar fricative, as in Scotch 'loch', Arabic ﺥ.
i   as in English 'seat'.
i̯   tense sound as in French 'lit'.
ɪ   lax sound as in English 'sit'.
u   as in English 'fool'.
ʉ   tense sound as in French 'foulé'.
ᴜ   lax sound as in English 'full'.
ə   neutral vowel.
h after a vowel denotes 'breathy voice'.

The tonal diacritics are ´ (high tone), ` (low tone), (falling tone). Mid tone is unmarked.

TRIBAL STATISTICS

Where the figure given is that of taxpayers, this is indicated by the letters TP. To obtain approximate total figures, the taxpayer figure should be multiplied by four.

An asterisk * shows that the figure is taken from recent (1945–7) official sources.

SOURCES OF INFORMATION

Where an authority is quoted without footnote reference, the information cited was given verbally or in correspondence.

LINGUISTIC WORK AND THE PRODUCTION OF LITERATURE

Anglo-Egyptian Sudan. A Language Bureau was set up in 1940 at Southern Education Headquarters, with group language committees for the purpose of research, agreement on matters of orthography and spelling, and the promotion of vernacular literature. The latter is encouraged by Government grants, and some thirty books and pamphlets have been produced each year. A Language and Publications Bureau with a linguist in charge and five Sudanese translators is to be set up in 1949.

East Africa. The East Africa Literature Bureau, with headquarters at Nairobi, is performing similar functions for the languages of Kenya, Uganda, and Tanganyika.

NILOTIC LANGUAGES[1]

LANGUAGE GROUP: DINKA

DINKA, own name THOD (DE) JIED. (ʈoŋ (de) jieŋ). DIALECT CLUSTER.

Spoken by: *DINKA*, call themselves *JIED* (jièŋ, jiaŋ).

Number of speakers: Total estimated by Tucker[2] at about 500,000.

Area where spoken: In the southern part of the Anglo-Egyptian Sudan.

The *DINKA* tribes are divided, geographically, under four headings:

(*a*) Northern: Mostly in Northern District, Upper Nile Province, but also on the left bank of the Nile as far as the Bahr el Zeraf and on the right bank around Lake No and as far as the Bahr el Ghazal;

(*b*) Eastern: On the right bank of the Nile, from south-east of Ayod to around Malek;

(*c*) Central: On the left bank of the Nile, between Shambe in the north and Malek in the south, and westwards nearly as far as Tonj;

(*d*) Western: West of the *NUER*, mostly in Jur River and Aweil Districts.

Dialectal differences correspond approximately to geographical; each sub-tribe or section has dialectal variations, but within each area the dialects are more or less inter-intelligible. All four main dialects of DINKA are used in education in both Government and Mission schools, and for administration. The New Testament has been published in BOR dialect, and parts of the New Testament in other dialects. There is a fair number of readers and other elementary school books. Linguistic research planned for the Anglo-Egyptian Sudan includes comparative work on the DINKA dialects to see if a central dialect can be found, intelligible over the whole DINKA area, or if not, whether a 'standard DINKA' can be evolved.

Dialect: PADANG, own name PADAD.

Spoken by: *PADANG* (padaŋ), a general name, used to cover the following tribes:

ABIALANG, call themselves *ABIALAD*, sometimes known as *DINKA IBRAHIM*. They consist of:

BAWOM (BOWOM), call themselves *BAWOM*, estimated total 2,500*, north of Renk on the right bank of the Nile. The most northerly of all Nilotic tribes, their territory marches with that of the Arabs of the White Nile.

AKON, call themselves *AKƆƆN*, estimated total 2,000*, south of the *BAWOM*.

GIEL, estimated at 2,700*, south of the AKON.

PALOC (PALOIC). The name, originally a geographical term, is used to denote:

AGER (AGEIR), call themselves *AGER*, estimated at 4,400*.

---

[1] The term Nilotic is preferred here to the terms **Jii** and **Jɔɔ** introduced by Crazzolara.

[2] 'Survey of language groups in the Southern Sudan', *B.S.O.S.* 7, 4, 1935, pp. 861–96 (hereafter referred to as 'Survey').

ABUYA, estimated at 1,300*, an offshoot of the AGER.

BER, call themselves BƐR, estimated at 2,900*.

NIEL (NYEL), call themselves NIƐL, estimated at 4,800*. Mainly south of Melut, on the banks of Khor Adar.[1]

DONGJOL (DONJOL), call themselves DƆŊJƆL, estimated at 9,000*, on or near River Wol, on the right bank of the Nile opposite Kodok.

The dialect of the DONGJOL has been chosen as literary PADANG.

The following tribes speak dialects which are nearer to PADANG than to other DINKA dialects, but whether PADANG will serve as the literary dialect for all these tribes is uncertain. A beginning has been made at using NGOK for educational purposes.

Note: PANCIEN is a general name used by the PADANG to cover all non-PADANG DINKA in the area south of the River Sobat.

NGOK (NGORK), call themselves ŊOK, estimated at 16,000*. They live along both banks of the River Sobat from the SHILLUK boundary 35 miles from its junction with the Nile, for about 60 miles upstream to the NUER boundary; also some on Khor Filus (Fellus) as far up as Lat. 8.45. The BALAK (of ANUAK origin) live in the east of this area. Another large section of the NGOK, also known as JOK (5,000 TP*) is in Western Kordofan.

THOI, call themselves THƆI (tɔi), 366 TP*, on Khor Filus in Central Nuer District.

RUT, 515 TP*, on the right bank of the Bahr el Zeraf.

LUAC (LUAIC), call themselves LUAC, 695 TP*, on Khor Filus.

Note: Both the THOI and the RUT speak NUER as well as their own dialects of DINKA.

RUWENG (RUENG), call themselves RUWEŊ. The tribe consists of 4 sections in Western Nuer District:

KWIL, 2,881 TP*, in an area between the Bahr el Ghazal east of Long. 30 and Kordofan Province boundary, i.e. north and west of Lake No to about 45 miles inland along the Lake No–Abiad road.

AWET, 1,557 TP*, in the same area as the KWIL and northwards to Lake Abiad.

ALOR, 1,779 TP*, in an area bounded on the north by the territory of the HUMR ARABS, on the south by the Bahr el Ghazal, on the east by the BUL NUER, and on the west by the NGOK (JOK) DINKA, to whom they are closely allied.

PAWENG (**paweŋ**), 480 TP*, on the left bank of the Nile, between the KWIL and the SHILLUK; also 1,142 TP* in Central Nuer District on Khor Atar.

[1] Not to be confused with Khor Atar in Central Nuer District.

Dialect: BOR.

Spoken by: *BOR* (*BOR GOK*), call themselves *BOR*, or sometimes *GOK*, 5,813 TP*, at and around Bor on the right bank of the Nile.

BORATHOI (*BOR ATHOIC*), call themselves *ATHOC* (aṯoc), 5,230 TP*, in Bor District, north of the *BOR*.

Closely related dialects are spoken by the following tribes:

GHOL, call themselves *ɎOL*, 2,051 TP*, south of the *GAWAAR NUER*, whose dialect they also speak.

NYARWENG (*NYARREWENG, NYARRWENG*), call themselves *NYA-RUEIJ*, 1,980 TP*, south of the *GHOL*. They also speak the dialect of the *LOU NUER*.

TWI, 8,825 TP*, south of the *NYARWENG*.

Dialect: AGAR.

Spoken by: *AGAR*, 16,000,[1] south-east of Tonj, north of Rumbek.

Closely related dialects are spoken by the following tribes:

ALIAB, consisting of:

AKER, 552 TP,[1] south-east of the *AGAR*.

THANY 508 TP*, south of the *BOR*, in small fishing villages on the right bank of the Nile; also a few on the left bank.

GOK, call themselves *GƆK*, also (*MUƆNY*) *JAIJ*, 6,064 TP,[1] between the *AGAR* and the *REK*, in Jur River and Lakes Districts. Their dialect is largely influenced by AGAR, but also slightly by REK, and contains a number of ARABIC loan-words.

CIEC (*CIC, CHICH*), call themselves *CIƐC*. The tribe consists of:

KWAC, 2,641 TP.[1]

AJAK, 1,718 TP.[1]

ADOR, 1,172 TP.[1]

in Lakes District, on the left bank of the Nile.

Note: These are probably the *KESH* (*SHESH*) mentioned by some writers.[2]

Dialect: REK.

Spoken by: *REK* (*RAIK*), call themselves *RƐK*, 39,050 TP*, in Jur River District, from Wau in the south-west and Tonj in the south, to Meshra in the east, and across the Jur River in the north; also in Aweil District. The tribe consists of 24 sections, of which the chief are:

APUK, AWAN, AGWOK, LAU.

Closely related dialects are spoken by the following tribes:

LUAIC, call themselves *LUAC*, 3,510 TP*, east of the *REK*, south-east of Meshra, on the eastern edge of Jur River District.

---

[1] Figures collected by Dr. Tucker from local Government sources (probably now out of date).
[2] e.g. S. L. Cummings, 'Sub-tribes of the Bahr-el-Ghazal Dinkas', *J. R. Anthrop., Inst.*, 1904.

TWIJ (TWIC, TWICH, TUIC), call themselves TUIC, 12,600 TP*, north of the REK. The tribe consists of 13 sections, of which the chief are:

THON, ADHIANG, AMIOL, NYANG.

PALIET (BALIET), call themselves PALIET, a branch of the REK between the Aweil road and the River Lol, on both banks of the River Pongo (Kpango). The tribe consists of:

AJAK, 1,520 TP*.
KONGDER (KONDAIR), call themselves KOŊDEER, 810 TP*.
BUONCUAI (BWON SHWAI), call themselves BUƆNCUAI, 1,200 TP*.
THANY BUR (TAINBOUR), call themselves THANY BUR (ṭany bur), 840 TP*.

MALUAL (MALWAL), call themselves MALUAL, between the Bahr el Arab in the north and River Lol in the south. The tribe consists of:

KOROK, call themselves KƆRƆK, 3,900 TP*.
ATOKTHOU (ATOKTO, ATOKTAU), call themselves ATOKTHƆU (atokṭɔu), 2,250 TP*.
PETH, call themselves PETH (peṭ), } 2,240 TP*.
MAKEM, call themselves (M)AKƐM, }
DULIT (DULUIT), call themselves DULIT, 1,020 TP* (see also under ABIEM below).

PALYOUPINY (PALIOPING), call themselves PALYOUPINY, south and south-west of the MALUAL. The tribe consists of:

GOMJUER (GOMJIER), call themselves GOMJUƐR, 3,200 TP*.
CIMEL (CEMEL, CHEMIEL), call themselves CIMEL, 1,780 TP*.
AJUET (AJWET), call themselves AJUET, 1,270 TP*.
AKUANG AYAT (AKWAK AYAT, AKWAK AYAK), call themselves AKUAŊ AYAT, 2,280 TP*.

ABIEM, a general name used to cover several tribes in the area between the MALUAL and the PALIET, from the Bahr el Arab in the north across the River Lol in the south:

DULIT (southern section of the tribe), 1,120 TP*.
WUNDING (WUNEDING), call themselves WUNDIIŊ, 970 TP*.
AKANY JOK (AKERN JOK), call themselves AKANY JOK, 1,980 TP*.
APUOTH (APWOT), call themselves APUƆTH (apuɔṭ), 2,490 TP*.
AJUONG THI, call themselves AJƆŊ THI (ajɔŋ ṭi), 1,630 TP*.
ANEI (WUN ANEI), call themselves ANƐI, 1,300 TP*.
AJUONG DIT, call themselves AJƆŊ DIT, 3,070 TP*.
LOU (LAU), call themselves LƆU, 1,240 TP*.

REK DINKA is now also used as the medium of education and literacy for the JUR (LWO-speakers), and is spoken as a second language by all speakers of the THURI Dialect Cluster.

NILOTIC LANGUAGES

LANGUAGE GROUP: NUER

Consists of: NUER Dialect Cluster.
ATUOT Dialect Cluster.

NUER, own name THOG NAATH (ṭoġ nàȧð). DIALECT CLUSTER.

Spoken by: NUER, call themselves *NAATH* (náàð).

Number of speakers: Estimated total: 260,000*.

Area where spoken: In the southern Sudan, mostly in Upper Nile Province, the main *NUER* territory being around the triangle formed by the Bahr el Zeraf and Bahr el Jebel (often referred to as Zeraf Island); also extending up the River Sobat across the Ethiopian border.

NUER is used in education and administration. A few vernacular books (Gospels and elementary religious and educational books) have been published.

There are several main dialects, roughly corresponding to the geographical divisions of the *NUER* tribes. Both the JIKANY dialects (Eastern and Western) were formerly used in education and for literature. The dialect of the *THIANG*, who occupy a central position, has now been adopted as standard NUER. The present policy of Government is that THIANG should form the grammatical and vocabulary basis of the standard language, but should be enriched by words from other dialects.

Dialect: THIANG.

Spoken by: THIANG, call themselves *THYÄŊ* (ṭyäŋ), 2,516 TP*, west of the Bahr el Jebel.

Closely related dialects are spoken by the following tribes:

BUL, 5,860 TP*, in 8 sections, north of the Bahr el Ghazal.
LEEK (LEIK), call themselves *LEEY*, 4,825 TP*, in 5 sections, south of the *BUL*.
JAGEI, 2,377 TP*, in 4 sections, south of the *LEEK*.
LAK, call themselves *LAAK*, 6,706 TP*, north of the *THIANG*.
GAWAAR (GAWEIR), call themselves *GAWÄÄR*, 7,244 TP*, east of the Bahr el Jebel on Bahr el Zeraf, mainly on Zeraf Island.
 The dialect of the *GAWAAR NUER* is also spoken by the *DINKA* living amongst them.

Dialect: JIKANY (Western).

Spoken by: *JIKANY (JEKAIN, JEKAING, JIKAIN)*, call themselves *JIKÄNY*, (western section of the tribe), 2,935 TP*, in 4 sub-sections, on the Bahr el Ghazal north of the *LAK*.

Closely related dialects are spoken by the following tribes west of the Bahr el Jebel, who call themselves *DAR CIEŊ* ('in the centre'):

DOK, call themselves *DƆK*, 2,752 TP*.
AAK, 1,193 TP*.

Dialect: LOU.

Spoken by: *LOU* (*LAU*), call themselves *LƆU*, 12,499 TP*, east of the *GAWAAR*, extending towards the River Sobat.

This dialect differs considerably from THIANG.

Dialect: JIKANY (Eastern).

Spoken by: *JIKANY* (eastern section of the tribe), 17,600 TP*, in the region of Nasser (Nasir) and the upper Sobat; also extending across the Ethiopian border (numbers not known).

This dialect is the farthest removed phonetically and in vocabulary from all other known dialects of NUER.

> *Note*: The *NUER* towards and in Ethiopia are called *ABBIGAR* by the Ethiopians (*ABIGARO* by the *MAO*); this name is used by Montandon, Cerulli, and others.

Other dialects are spoken by the

NYUONG call themselves *NYUOŊ*, 1,123 TP*,

DOR (*DOOR*), 1,553 TP*,

west of the Bahr el Jebel. A Gospel in NYUOŊ has been published.

NUER (various dialects) is also spoken as a second language by the *DINKA* living along Khor Filus and near Fangak.

ATUOT (ATWOT). DIALECT CLUSTER.

Spoken by: *ATUOT* (*ATWOT*), call themselves *ATUOT*, in Lakes District near Yirrol, in an enclave among the *DINKA*. There are two dialects:

Dialect: APAK (AFAK).

Spoken by: *APAK* (*AFAK*), 2,265 TP.[1]

Dialect: ARIL.

Spoken by: *ARIL*, 5,636 TP.[1]

LANGUAGE GROUP: LWO

Consists of:	SHILLUK	Language.
	ANUAK	Language.
	BURUN	Two Dialect Clusters?
	LWO	Language.
	THURI, &c.	Dialect Cluster.
	BOR	Language.
	ACOLI	Language.
	LANGO	Language.
	'CHOPI'	Language.
	ALUR	Language.
	DHOLA	Language.
	LUO	Language.

This Language Group has previously been known as the SHILLUK Group, but

[1] Figures collected by Tucker from local Government sources (probably now out of date).

concensus of opinion, fortified by the recent investigations of Dr. Tucker in the field, would seem to indicate that the term LWO is more appropriate. The name is actually used by many tribes; it is also acknowledged by many more as being the original tribal name.[1]

The spelling LWO has been accepted by speakers of the LWO languages, with the exception of the so-called 'Nilotic Kavirondo' who retain the spelling LUO.

Area covered by the group. Much scattered: in the southern Sudan, extending into Ethiopia, in Uganda, the north-eastern corner of the Belgian Congo, and the north-western part of Kenya.

SHILLUK, own name DHƆ CƆLƆ (ɖɔ cɔlɔ). LANGUAGE.

Spoken by: SHILLUK, call themselves CƆLƆ; called tɛat by the NUER.

Number of speakers: About 92,000*.

Area where spoken: In Upper Nile Province, Anglo-Egyptian Sudan, between the Nile and Kordofan Province boundary, from Lat. 11 in the north to about 80 miles west of Tonga; also on the right bank of the Nile, round the junction of the River Sobat with the Nile and for about 20 miles up the Sobat.

SHILLUK is used in education. Some elementary readers and religious books have been published; the New Testament is in preparation.

ANUAK, own name DHƆ ANYWA (ɖɔ anywaa). LANGUAGE.

Spoken by: ANUAK (ANYWAK), call themselves JO ANYWA, ANYUAA; called NURO by the TOPOSA, SHAKKO (ʃakko) or K'ORIO by the MAO. The name YAMBO is used by the Ethiopians, and is officially recognized in correspondence with them.

Number of speakers: Estimated by Lyth at 40,000, by Crazzolara[2] at 45,000. (Of these, about 10,000* are in the Sudan.)

Area where spoken: In the Anglo-Egyptian Sudan on the lower Akobo River, from Akobo Post to Lat. 6.45; in Ethiopia, on the right bank of the Akobo and on the Baro and Gila (Bako) Rivers.

Also spoken by: PARI (FARI, BERRI), call themselves PÄRI; called by other tribes LOKORO (lɔkɔɔrɔ), 1,337 TP*, on Lafon Hill north-east of Torit; also a few among the so-called MADI or ACOLI of Opari District (404 TP[3]).

ANUAK is beginning to be used in education, and there is a very small amount of vernacular literature.

BURUN. DIALECT CLUSTERS?

Little is as yet known about the languages or dialects known as BURUN, spoken in Blue Nile Province, Anglo-Egyptian Sudan. The name BURUN or BARUN is used by the Arabs, and has been adopted by Europeans, to refer to a number of tribes in Blue Nile Province (including some whose languages are not Nilotic, such as the

---

[1] See also Crazzolara, 'The Lwoo People', *Uganda Journal*, 5, 1, 1937, pp. 1–21.
[2] Op. cit.
[3] Figures collected by Tucker from local Government sources (probably now out of date).

UDUK and *KOMA*). It is here used, however, only to refer to the Nilotic languages or dialects spoken in this area and to some of the people speaking them.

It is not known whether there are several languages, at present together designated as BURUN, or whether they are dialects in one, or two, clusters. The latter appears probable, from the material at present available.

Tribes speaking the BURUN languages or dialects are:

BURUN (*BARUN*), also known as 'Hill *BURUN*', '*BURUN* proper', or 'Northern *BURUN*', called **laŋɛ** by the *ACOLI*, **cai** by the *NUER*. They are estimated at 1,800*, and live in Fung District, on Jebels Mayah (Maiak), Kurmuk, Jerok, Mufwa, Mughaja, Abuldugu, &c. It does not appear that they call themselves by any one name; Evans-Pritchard[1] records the following:

The people of Kurmuk call themselves *TARAK* or *BOIT*, and are called *MEKORMUK* by the people of Jebel Ulu;
The people of Mughaja call themselves *MUMUGADJA*;
The people of Mufwa are called *MOPO* by those of Kurmuk;
The people of Abuldugu are called *BOGON* by those of Jebel Ulu, *MUGOMBORKOINA* by those of Mughaja.

RAGREIG, estimated at 3,500*, east of the *BURUN*, an enclave among the *BERTA*.

These peoples constitute the 'Northern *BURUN*' of Evans-Pritchard.

MABAN (*MAABAN*, *MEBAN*), also known as 'Southern *BURUN*'; called *GURA* by the *BERTA*. They are estimated at 20,000*, and live on the border between Blue Nile and Upper Nile Provinces, between the Rivers Yabus and Tombak in the north and Khor Daga in the south. According to Evans-Pritchard they are called *TUNGAN* by the people of Kurmuk, *BARGA* by those of Ulu, *TONKO* by the *JUMJUM*.

JUMJUM, estimated at 4,500*, along Khor Jumjum on Jebels Tunga (Tunya), Terta, and Wadega. According to Reidhead[2] 'some members of the tribe refer to themselves as *WADEGA*, but possibly this is true only of those people who live on the hill of that name'. Evans-Pritchard distinguishes between the *JUMJUM* and the people of Wadega. The *JUMJUM* are called *BERIN* by the people of Kurmuk, *OLGA* by those of Ulu.

Evans-Pritchard includes the *JUMJUM* under the general heading of 'Southern *BURUN*', also the people of Ulu (called *BEGU* or *MUNULU* by the *JUMJUM*) and Jebel Gerawi.

The BURUN languages or dialects have for some time been recognized as being largely Nilotic in vocabulary.[3] The material on MABAN and JUMJUM collected by Reidhead shows that they are also Nilotic in grammatical structure.

There are phonetic differences between 'Northern' and 'Southern' BURUN.

---

[1] 'Ethnological observations in Dar Fung', *Sudan Notes*, **15**, 1, 1932, pp. 1–61.

[2] Report of Linguistic Survey among tribes Berta, Ingassana, Koma, Uduk, Jum Jum, Maban (duplicated 1946).

[3] See Seligman, *Pagan Tribes of the Nilotic Sudan*, pp. 421–3; Evans-Pritchard, op. cit., pp. 53 ff.; Tucker, 'Survey', p. 880.

NILOTIC LANGUAGES 15

Evans-Pritchard reports that the *MABAN*, *JUMJUM*, and the people of Jebel Ulu can all understand each other, but cannot understand the 'Northern *BURUN*'.

LWO (LUO), own name DHE LWO (ɖé lúo). LANGUAGE.

Spoken by: *JUR*, call themselves *JO LWO* (jo lúo).

Number of speakers: 4,120 TP* in Jur River District, 660 TP* in Western District.

Area where spoken: North of Wau towards Aweil, south-east of Wau as far as Tonj.

LWO was formerly used in schools, but owing to the present Government language policy, its place has been taken by DINKA (REK dialect). A few religious books (catechisms, &c.) have been published.

    Note: The name *JUR ABAT*, which Tucker[1] gives as a tribal name, is said by Santandrea[2] to be a nickname for the *JUR* (*LWO*).

THURI, &c. DIALECT CLUSTER.

Dialect: THURI, own name ɖɛ ṭùrí.

Spoken by: THURI (SHATT), call themselves **jo ṭùrí**, 372 TP* (on the increase), on the Raga–Nyamlell road adjacent to the *PALYOUPINY*; also on the Wau–Dem Zubeir road.

Dialect: Own name ɖɛ bɔdɔ.

Spoken by: *BODHO* (*DEMBO*, *DOMBO*, *DEMEN*), call themselves **jo bɔɖɔ** (bɔðɔ or bwɔɖɔ), called **bwɔɖe** by the *JUR*, 197 TP*, between Wau and Aweil.

Dialect: Own name ɖe cɔlɔ.

Spoken by: *JUR SHOL*, call themselves **jo cɔlɔ**, in the same area as the *BODHO*. According to Tucker[3] they number about 405 TP, but his figure includes a few *THURI* and *BODHO*.

Dialect spoken by: *MANANGEER* (*JUR MANANGER*), call themselves **mana-ŋɛɛr**, 350 TP*, among the *REK DINKA* between the Rivers Jur and Lol.

    Note: Tucker[4] gives '*JUR WIR*' as a nickname of the *MANANGEER*; there is, however, a section of the *REK DINKA* north of Tonj, called *JURWEIR*.

All these tribes also speak DINKA and are practically absorbed into the *DINKA*.

BOR, own name ɖé bor. LANGUAGE.

Spoken by: *BOR* (the Nilotic section of the *BELANDA*),[5] call themselves **jo bor**, called *RODI* by the *BVIRI* (the non-Nilotic section of the *BELANDA*).

Number of speakers: Estimated by Santandrea[6] at about 3,000 near Raffili, and as

[1] 'Survey', p. 879.
[2] 'Minor Shilluk sections in the Bahr-el-Ghazal', *Sudan Notes*, 21, 2, 1938.
[3] Information obtained from local Government sources.
[4] 'Survey', p. 880.
[5] *BELANDA* is the name used by Europeans and others to denote a single cultural unit (called *ABARE* by the *ZANDE*), consisting of members of two tribes speaking totally different languages, but living together, intermarrying, and sharing the same customs, &c. The two tribes are:
  (a) *BOR*, called by the *BVIRI* and others *RODI* (*MBERODI*, *MVERODI*, also rendered *MBERIDI*). Language: BOR (Nilotic);
  (b) *BVIRI* (*BIRI*), called by the *BOR* and others *GUMBA*, *GAMBA* (*MBEGUMBA*, also rendered *MVEGUMBA*). Language: BVIRI (Eastern Sudanic: NDOGO-BANGBA group).
[6] 'Shilluk Luo Tribes in the Bahr-el-Ghazal', *Anthropos*, 1942–5.

many or more scattered among the *ZANDE*; by Crazzolara[1] at 5,000. More accurate figures are impossible to obtain, as the *BOR* and *BVIRI* are so much intermingled.

Area where spoken: Mainly along the Wau–Tombora (Tembura) road near Raffili, between Rivers Bo and Bussere; also farther south towards Tombora.

BOR is much influenced by BVIRI in both pronunciation and grammar.

ACOLI (ACHOLI), own name LOG ACOLI; sometimes known as GANG. LANGUAGE.

Spoken by: *ACOLI* (*ACHOLI, ACOOLI, SHULI*), call themselves *ACOLI* (àcólí); also known by the nickname GANG (gaŋ), (logaŋ or jo-gaŋ being the name by which the *LANGO* and others call the *ACOLI*).

Number of speakers: Estimated at about 180,000* (total population of Acholi District 205,506*, but this includes some members of other tribes).

Area where spoken: Acholi District, Uganda. The boundaries of the District are the tribal boundaries, except in the north where the *ACOLI* overlap into the Anglo-Egyptian Sudan in Opari District (the Acholi Hills), where they are much mixed with LOTUHO-speaking peoples.[2] They are also to be found scattered through most parts of Uganda in the police, army, &c.

Note: The *OBBO* mentioned by Baker[3] are, to judge from the vocabulary given, *ACOLI*.

Dialects: There are various mutually intelligible dialects of *ACOLI*, varying not so much in grammar as in vocabulary and pronunciation. The 'standard' is generally taken as being the dialect spoken by the *PAYIRA* clans, whose headquarters lie some 25 miles north-east of Gulu.

ACOLI is used in education (Government and Mission schools) and in administration. Vernacular literature includes the New Testament, *Pilgrim's Progress*, and other religious books, and some readers and school books. A book on *ACOLI* history by an African author is in preparation. The *Acoli Magazine* appears at regular intervals; a fortnightly news sheet in ACOLI was distributed to *ACOLI* troops during the war.

LANGO, own name LEB LADO. LANGUAGE.

Spoken by: *LANGO*, call themselves *LAŊO* (láŋò); called *OMIRU* (òmírû) by the *ACOLI* (a nickname).

Note: The tribal name *LANGO* is of Nilo-Hamitic origin, and these people seem to have been formerly known as *LANGODYANG*.[4] When they moved to their present habitat they adopted a dialect of ACOLI which they call LANGO, and which is now considered as a separate language, but still retain many Nilo-Hamitic words (especially the names of plants, which are almost identical with

---

[1] 'The Lwoo People.'
[2] 'Survey', p. 881.
[3] *Albert Nyanza*, 1866.
[4] Driberg, *The Lango*.

NILOTIC LANGUAGES

TESO). The *LANGO* in the Anglo-Egyptian Sudan speak a Nilo-Hamitic language (*see under* LOTUHO, p. 29).

Number of speakers: 276,119*.

Area where spoken: In Lango District, and in part of Acholi District, Uganda.

The *LABWOR* (*LABUR*) on the western border of Karamoja District (761 TP*) are reported to speak a dialect closely akin to ACOLI or LANGO.

The language of the *KUMAM* in Kaberamaido County is said to be akin to LANGO as well as to TESO (*see under* TESO, p. 31).

LANGO is used in education, but the use of ACOLI is encouraged by Government. LANGO is also used (in C.M.S. schools) in Kaberamaido among the *KUMAM*, but it is possible that TESO may be used in the future. Vernacular literature is very slight.

'CHOPI'. LANGUAGE.

Spoken by: *CHOPI* (*JAFALU, SHIFALU, SHEPALU*), call themselves **jò pàluo** (*CHOPI* being a nickname, according to Crazzolara); called *LOLOKA* (**lɔlɔka**) by the *ACOLI*.

Number of speakers: Estimated at 5,000* in Bunyoro District; total estimated by Crazzolara[1] at 6,000.

Area where spoken: Mostly in the south-eastern part of Acholi District and the northern part of Bunyoro District, Uganda.

ALUR, own name DHO ALUR (**ɖo alûr**). LANGUAGE.

Spoken by: *ALUR* (*ALURU, ALULU, LUR*), call themselves *JO ALUR* (**jo àlûr**).

Number of speakers: In Uganda: 81,164*; in the Belgian Congo: 92,987* in Mahagi Territoire (according to Fr. van der Looy, total about 140,000, on the increase).

Area where spoken: In Uganda, north of Lake Albert, in West Nile District; in the Belgian Congo, west of Lake Albert, extending westwards from Mahagi.

Dialect: A dialect of ALUR is spoken by the *JONAM* (**jò naam**) between the Nile at Pakwach and the Alur escarpment to the west (17,422*).

Note: The *BAMBISA* or *MAMBISA* round Kilo in the Belgian Congo are a branch of the *ALUR*, but now speak LENDU (MORU–MADI group of Eastern Sudanic languages).

ALUR is used in education, both in Uganda and the Belgian Congo. The Bible has been published, also various religious books and elementary readers.

DHOLA (BUDAMA), own name **ɖo pa ɖɔlà**. LANGUAGE.

Spoken by: *DHOLA*, call themselves **jo paɖɔlà** or **jò p'àɖɔlâ**; called *BADAMA* by their Bantu neighbours (*BUDAMA* being the name of the district, but used by Europeans to denote the people and their language).

[1] 'The Lwoo People.'

Number of speakers: 49,683 (Uganda Census 1931); estimated by Crazzolara[1] at 52,000.

Area where spoken: West of Mount Elgon on the Kenya–Uganda border, in Mbale District.

LUO, own name DHOLUO (ɖɔ luò); also known as 'Nilotic Kavirondo'. LANGUAGE.

Spoken by: *LUO* ('Nilotic Kavirondo'), also known as *NYIFWA*, *NIFE* (*NIPE* being the name of one of the tribal divisions); call themselves *JOLUO* (jò luò). The name *GAYA* has in the past been applied to those in the south of the area.

Number of speakers: Estimates vary between 200,000 and 600,000.

Area where spoken: Mainly in Central and South Kavirondo Districts, Kenya; also in North Kavirondo, and extending southwards into the northern part of Tanganyika. The *LUO* are also to be found scattered throughout Kenya in the larger towns (especially Nairobi, Nakuru, and Mombasa), in considerable numbers.

LUO is a collective name applied to a great number of hardly distinguishable tribes speaking one language; dialectal differences are slight, and the language may be regarded as uniform.

LUO is used in education and religious teaching by missions (SWAHILI being the language of Government). There is an increasing volume of vernacular literature; the New Testament has been published and the Old Testament is in preparation, and there are various religious and school books. Two books on tribal customs have been written by Africans. Two periodicals in LUO are published.

[1] 'The Lwoo People.'

LINGUISTIC SURVEY OF THE NILOTIC LANGUAGES

By A. N. TUCKER

A. *Nilotic Characteristics*

1. The Nilotic Languages have a peculiar pronunciation of their own which at once distinguishes them from most other sorts of languages. The outstanding points are:

   (a) Dental consonants, ṯ, ḓ, ṉ (written *th*, *dh*, *nh*, and to be differentiated from the alveolar consonants, t, d, n).

   (b) Pure palatal consonants, c and j (quite different from the Sudanic and Bantu equivalents which resemble more the sounds in 'church' and 'jump').

   (c) Slurring of final consonants under conditions usually controlled by grammar: p>f, ṯ>θ, t>ţ ('fricative t'), c>ç, k>x or h. (Most noticeable in NUER and BOR Dinka.)

   (d) A complicated vowel system: on the whole there seem to be seven vowel phonemes, a, ɛ, e, i, ɔ, o, u, with varieties including centralized forms of most of them (varying according to dialect for the most part); diphthongs are very common; vowel length is an important feature.

   (e) Voice quality as a linguistic feature: there is normal and 'breathy' voice; variations in voice quality may indicate lexical and grammatical distinctions.

2. Intonation is present to a high degree, and plays a grammatical role. Semantically, however, tonal doublets are not very common.

3. The words in their ultimate analysis are monosyllabic. The words consists for the most part in Consonant+Vowel+Consonant.

4. Compound nouns are common, but not compound verbs.

5. Formative elements are relatively few; the main noun formatives are **a-, o-, la-**, and the adjective-relative formatives **ma-** and **me-**. The characteristic prefixes and suffixes of Bantu and Hamitic languages are missing.

6. Except in the Southern LWO languages words are inflected by internal change: nouns show plural[1] and verbs show voice or species in the following ways:

   By change in vowel quality, e.g. a>ɛ, a>ä centralized;

   ,, ,, vowel length, ,, a>aa;

   ,, ,, voice quality, ,, a>a*h* (normal to 'breathy' voice);

   ,, ,, voice pitch, ,, á>à (high tone to low tone);

   ,, ,, final consonant, ,, l>t, w>ţ.

   Another characteristic of this form of inflexion is that analogy seems to play little or no part; most words have specific plural and other derived forms and can use or reverse any of the above processes or any combination of them, so that few rules can be laid down.

7. There is no grammatical gender.

---

[1] Both NUER and ACOLI, however, frequently indicate plurality by means of a suffix **-í**.

8. Inflexion of nouns for case varies from group to group. (See further 22.)

9. Verbs seem to fall into two main classes according to their tonal behaviour.

(REK) DINKA		NUER		SHILLUK	
I. yɛn abá.	I come.	lieŋá jè.	I hear it.	yí cwolá ŋɔ?	You call whom?
II. yɛn ájàl.	I go.	nɛanà je.	I see it.	yí nàkà ŋɔ?	You kill whom?

10. Not only is there a distinct passive voice, but also two active voices, one for use with definite objects, expressed or understood (Applicative), and the other for indefinite objects or when no object is implied (Qualitative).

In DINKA and the Northern LWO languages the passive is used much more than in European languages.

Note that NUER and the Southern LWO languages have no passive. (See further 26.)

11. There are many derivative species of the verb (except in Southern LWO), formed almost entirely by internal change in the stem. (See further 27.)

12. There are three main verb tenses—present, past, and future.

13. Negation varies from group to group, but is distinctive within the groups. (See further 21.)

14. The verb stem is inflected for person in all tenses in NUER, in some tenses in DINKA, and in no tenses in the LWO languages.

15. The word order in a sentence seems to demand that the important noun in the sentence should come first, the verb being active or passive according to the sense. Thus:

Important noun+active verb+object.
Important noun+passive verb+agent.

Examples:

DINKA: raan átêm tìm. The man is cutting a tree. (Active.)
tìm átéém ráán. The tree is being cut by the man. (Passive.)

NUER: wút cam-è rîŋ. The man is eating meat. (Active.)
(Note verb with personal suffix.)

SHILLUK: yá mana yìn. I hate you. (Active.)
yá mána yîn. I am hated by you. (Passive.)

ACOLI: làbòr cámó rìŋu. The lion eats meat. (Active.)

16. In the genitive construction the possessor (nomen rectum) normally follows the possessed (nomen regens),[1] which may be inflected as to its final consonant in the singular. (In NUER the possessor is inflected internally). In all languages except NUER there is an optional linking particle.

---

[1] Note, however, in SHILLUK: witɔm or tɔm wän, owner of the lyre. DINKA: dɛl də yá-cin, skin of my hand.

DINKA: tík, woman: tíŋ Bòl or tíŋ (d)ə Bòl, Bol's wife.
NUER: lɛp, tongue, ciék, woman: lɛb cièɣ, tongue of a woman.
SHILLUK: coogó, bone: coŋ (ə) ḍâno, bone of a person.
ACOLI: wìc, head: wì danɔ, head of a person.[1]
            tìc, work: tìc pà mon, women's work.
Kenya LUO: tiɛlɔ, leg: tiɛnd ḍánò, leg of a person.
            kɔm, chair: kom (mar) rwoṭ, chair of the chief.

17. The adjective follows the noun it qualifies, and is introduced by a prefix **ma-** or **me-** in all languages except DINKA. (In DINKA, and sometimes in SHILLUK, the final consonant of the noun is nasalized.)

DINKA: moc, man: **mony** dìht, big man.
NUER: wúṭ, man: **wúṭ mé-dììd**, big man.
SHILLUK: lyec, elephant: **lyéc má-dwɔŋ**, or **lyeny dwɔŋ**, big elephant.
ACOLI: lyèc, elephant: **lyèc ma-dît**, big elephant.
Kenya LUO: líèc, elephant: **liec ma-dwòŋ**, big elephant.

B. *LWO Characteristics*

18. The LWO Language Group shows certain traits which distinguish it immediately from DINKA–NUER. The most outstanding is the suffix **-o (-ɔ, -u)** attached to many nouns and most verbs:

LWO group		DINKA–NUER
riŋo, riŋu	meat	riŋ
rɛmɔ, remu	blood	riɛm
kwalɔ	steal	kwal

19. The second is the absence of inflexion for person (apart from shortened pronouns used as prefixes) in verb conjugation. The following two verbs **ŋac**, to know, and **kuc**, not to know,[2] are used here: note that the DINKA and SHILLUK conjugation is typically passive:

	NUER (active)		DINKA (passive)[3]	
1.	ŋácà[4] je	kwéyá jè	áŋiɛc	ákuɔc
2.	ŋácì je	kwíyí jè	áŋic	ákuc
3.	ŋácé je	kwíyé jè	áŋiic	ákuuc
1.	ŋáckó jè	kwèçkò je	aníckù	akúckù
	ŋácné jè	kwèçnè je		
	ŋácné jè	kwéçné jè		
2.	ŋácé jè	kwèçè je	aníɛckà (or -kè)	akúɔckà (or -kè)
3.	ŋácke jè	kwèçkè je	aníckì (or -kè)	akúckì (or -kè)

[1] Final consonant change is rare in ACOLI, however.
[2] A distinct verb indicating 'not to know' is also typical of Nilotic languages.
[3] '(It) is known by me . . . by you . . . by him', &c.
[4] a in this paradigm is centralized and je=jɛ, but owing to shortage of type with tone diacritics cannot be so represented here.

	ACOLI (active)		SHILLUK (passive)[1]		
1.	à-ŋéyô	à-kwíyâ	áŋáj (y)ì yan	ákwíc (y)ì yan
2.	ì-ŋéyô	ì-kwíyâ	,, yin	,, yin
3.	ŋéyô	kwíyâ	,, ɛn	,, ɛn
1.	wà-ŋéyô	wà-kwíyâ	,, wan	,, wan
			,, wɔn	,, wɔn
2.	wù-ŋéyô	wù-kwíyâ	,, wun	,, wun
3.	ɡì-ŋéyô	ɡì-kwíyâ	,, ɡɪn	,, ɡɪn

20. Another important clue is the tense formation. In DINKA–NUER the following auxiliary verbs are characteristic:

cə (neg. pres.)+present stem of the verb.
cə (past pos.), ke (past neg.), bə (fut. pos.)+past stem of the verb.

(BOR) DINKA (important noun+auxiliary+second noun+verb stem).
(Active)
ɣán ci Dèŋ cɔl. I am not calling Deng (I have not called Deng).
ɣan cí (kén) (bí) Deŋ cóól.[2] I have called Deng (I will call Deng).
(Passive)
ɣan cíí Deŋ còl.[2] I am not called by Deng.
ɣan cíí (kéén) (bíí) Deŋ cóól.[2] I was (was not) (will be) called by Deng.

NUER (auxiliary+object+verb stem).
(Active only)
cí lòny wäl càm. The lion does not eat grass.
cí (ké) (bí) nàár jè nɛɛn. Mother has (has not) (will) see(n) it.

In the LWO languages such auxiliaries are largely absent[3] and the difference between present and past tense is shown predominantly by *intonation*.

SHILLUK (I light fire) (I blow fire) ACOLI (I eat meat) (The man eats meat)
Present: yá cwinya màc. yá kóóṭá mac.
acámó[2] rìŋu. dánó[2] cámó rìŋu.
Past: yáá cwinyà mac. yáá kòòḍà mac.
àcamò rìŋó. dánó[2] òcàmò rìŋu.

Kenya LUO (I beat the child) (He beats the child)
Present: áɡɔyó[2] nyàṭî. óɡɔyó nyàṭî.
Past: aɡôyò nyàṭî. ɔɡôyò nyàṭî.

21. In the LWO languages, further, the negative particle is not conjugated, and precedes the verb.[4]

SHILLUK (important noun+negative+verb+second noun).
yá ba kóṭ mac. I am not blowing the fire. (Active.)
mac ba kóóḍ yi yán. The fire is not blown by me. (Passive.)

---

[1] '(It) is known by me ... by you ... by him', &c.
[2] The vowel should be ə in these examples, but o is used here owing to shortage of type with tone diacritics.
[3] Note -bí- (fut.) in ACOLI, LANGO, and ALUR, and -sé- (past) in Kenya LUO.
[4] The negative *postposition*, which occurs occasionally in ACOLI, seems to be an Eastern Sudanic borrowing: ɛn cámó lùm kù (it does not eat grass).

ACOLI
lòtɪnò pe gì-máṭó kòŋò.[1] Children don't drink beer.
Kenya LUO
ok á-góyɔ[1] nyàṭî. I did not beat the child.

22. All nouns are inflected for case in NUER (gen. and loc.), a few for case in DINKA (loc.), none in the LWO languages.

23. Finally, there is a much closer vocabulary correspondence between DINKA and NUER than between either and the LWO languages.

C. *Linguistic subdivisions in LWO*

24. Within the LWO Language Group there are important subdivisions, the most important being between:

Northern LWO (SHILLUK, ANUAK, BURUN, LWO ('JUR'), BOR, &c.) and Southern LWO (ACOLI, LANGO, ALUR, Kenya LUO, &c.).

The two subdivisions are separated geographically by a belt of MORU–MADI and BARI languages. Northern LWO has more in common with DINKA–NUER than has Southern LWO, which seems to have come under Eastern Sudanic influence.

25. The outstanding linguistic difference here lies in verb conjugation:
In Northern LWO (see 10 above) most verbs have three voices (I use here the terminology employed by Kohnen and Crazzolara):

SHILLUK

Active: { Applicative: yá gwɔka byɛl. I'm preparing the grain.
{ Qualitative: yá gɔɔga (byɛl). I'm preparing (grain).
Passive: byɛl agwɔɔga yân. Grain is prepared by me.

In Southern LWO only traces of the qualitative voice are to be found in a few verbs:

ACOLI
ànɛnɔ dánɔ. I see the man.
ànénô. I see (i.e. I am not blind.)

26. In Northern LWO the passive is preferred to the active, especially in the past tense.

SHILLUK
gwok acám yi óṭwoŋ. The dog has been eaten by a hyena.
óṭwóŋ gwok ácám yi yɛn. The hyena, the dog has been eaten by him.

In Southern LWO there is no passive construction at all:

ACOLI   Kenya LUO
làlúr òcàmò gwôk.   ondíèk òcàmò gwòk.

[1] The vowel should be ɔ in these examples, but o is used here owing to shortage of type with tone diacritics.

Note the use of 3rd person active when no agent is implied:

ACOLI	Kenya LUO
gú-càm-a	gí-câm-a

They have eaten me (i.e. I've been exploited).

27. In Northern LWO (as in DINKA–NUER) verb stems vary according to direcion to or from the speaker, or whether the action is 'dative' or repetitive, &c.

SHILLUK

tɛl ɣot. Pull it into the house (speaker outside).
lél ɣot. Pull it into the house (speaker inside).
yá gɔká jâgo. I prepare (food) for the chief.
jago ágɔɔk i yân. (Passive of above.)
ɖáno akác yi kwɛc. The man is bitten by a leopard.
ɖáno ákääc yi kwɛc. The man is bitten by a leopard (lots of times).
yá ŋáj i yîn. You know me (I am known by you).
yá ŋác i yîn. You told me (I am made to know by you).
yá ŋíc i yîn. You recognize me (I am come to be known by you).

Only relics of such distinctions are to be found in the Southern LWO languages. But note the following regular construction in ACOLI and LANGO:

acwál-ɛ. I sent him.   acwáll-ɛ cèntè. I sent him money.

28. The following phonetic differences are also well established: c and j are not pure palatals in the South, but correspond to the sounds in 'church' and 'jump'; there are nine distinct vowels in Southern LWO (2 varieties of i, 2 of u, 2 of e, 2 of o, one of a). There is no centralization (except of a, see below, 32)[1].

gɨn	thing	gɪn	they	Orthographically:	gin,	gin
bʉr	pit	bʊr	ulcer		bur,	bur
kec	hunger	kɛc	bitter		kec,	kec
toŋ	cut	tɔŋ	spear		toŋ,	toŋ
		rac	bad			rac

D. *Linguistic Subdivisions of Southern LWO*

29. The Southern LWO languages themselves may be subdivided, this time from the phonetic aspect. This subdivision roughly alines ACOLI, LANGO, 'CHOPI' against ALUR and 'JONAM', 'BUDAMA' and (Kenya) LUO. The former languages have lost the dental consonants, while the latter (with the exception of 'JONAM') retain them:[2]

ACOLI		Kenya LUO	
dano	person	ɖano	Orthog.: dhano
latet	smith	jaʈeʈ	jatheth

[1] In paragraphs 28–31 tone diacritics are omitted owing to shortage of type.

[2] In certain LUO words the dental sound is missing (except in certain dialects of North Kavirondo): it—scorpion.

30. A more outstanding feature, however, is the intrusion of a voiced explosive in the nasal consonant *in certain words* in the latter languages:

ACOLI		Kenya LUO	
rɔmɔ	be sufficient	rɔmɔ	Orthog.: romo
rɔmɔ	sheep	rɔmbɔ	rombo
nɛnɔ	see	nɛnɔ	neno
nınɔ	sleep	nındɔ	nindo
wɛlɔ	visit	wɛndɔ	wendo
wınyɔ	bird	wınyɔ	winyo
wi̧nyo	hear	wi̧njo	winjo
waŋɔ	burn	waŋɔ	waŋo
caŋɔ	heal	caŋgɔ	cango

It is interesting to note that this phenomenon is to be found in the Northern LWO area in BOR ('RODI') only.

Whether this 'intrusive' explosive is to be regarded as *introduced* into LUO, &c., or as an original Nilotic component *preserved* in LUO, &c., is for philologists to decide.

31. In ACOLI and LANGO there is a slurring of consonants **t**, **k** between vowels, but it has no grammatical significance. It does not occur in ALUR, LUO, &c.

ACOLI		LUO	
but̯u or bur̯u	lie	buto	lie in wait
nɛxɔ or nɛɣɔ	kill	buɖo	lie
		nɛgo	kill

32. In ACOLI and LANGO the vowel **a** is centralized by a following **i** or **u**. In ALUR and Kenya LUO a different vowel often results:

wàŋ eye   ACOLI: **wäŋí**   ALUR: **weŋí** your eye.

NILOTIC WORD LIST[1]

	DINKA (BOR dialect)	NUER (Crazzolara)	SHILLUK	ACOLI (Crazzolara)	LUO
axe	yieht/yiep	jop/jopni	dɔro/dori	lɛ	lɛ/leɖi
belly	yac/yaahl	jıc/jiiç	yıc/yiet̯	ı(c)	ı(c)/ıyɛ
bird	dıt/diɛht̯	dıd/dıid	winyo/winy	wınyɔ	wınyɔ/wıny
blood	riem/rım	riɛm	rɛmo/rɛm	remu	rɛmɔ
cow	wɛŋ/ɣɔk	yaŋ/ɣɔk	ɖyaŋ/ɖok	dyaŋ/dyäŋi	ɖyaŋ/ɖok
dog	jo(ŋ)/jɔ(k)	jiok/jyooɣ	gwok/guok	gwok/gwogi	guok/guogi
ear	yic/yiiθ	jiθ/jit̯	yit̯/yıt̯	i̧t	i̧t/i̧te
egg	twɔŋ/toŋ	tuɔŋ/toŋ	tɔŋ	tɔŋ	tɔŋ(g)
elephant	akɔɔhn/akohn	guor/gwor	lyɛc/liɛc	lyec/lyeci	liɛc/liec
eye	nyın/nyihn	waŋ/nyin	waŋ/nyiŋ	waŋ/wäŋi	waŋ/weŋge
fire	mac/mɛhi	mac/mäc	mac	mac	mac/mec
foot	cohk/cok	cioɣ/cyoh	tiɛlɔ/tyɛl	tyen	tiɛlɔ/tiende

[1] Owing to shortage of type, intonation marks have had to be omitted.

	DINKA (BOR dialect)	NUER (Crazzolara)	SHILLUK	ACOLI (Crazzolara)	LUO
goat	tɔh(k)/tọ(k)	dɛl/deht	dyɛlɔ/dyek	dyɛl/dyegi	diɛl/diek
hair	ɲiem/ɲɪm	ɲiam/ɲihɛm	yeyo/yiɛr	yɛr	yier
hand	cin/cɪn	tɛht̪/tɛt̪	cino/ciŋ	cɪŋ	cɪŋ
head	ŋom/ɲɪm	wic/woṭ	wic/wuät̪	wi̧c	wi̧c/wi̧ye
honey, bee	cɛhi/ciɛc	tuar	kih/kɪc	ki̧c	ki̧c
hut	ɣöt/ɣööt	hot/hod	(w)ɔt/wuti	ɔt/odi	ɔt/udi
knife	pal/paal	ŋɔm/ŋɔamni	paalo/paal	pala	pala/pelni
leopard	kwɛc/kwec	kwac/kwacni	kwac/kwanyi	kwac	kwac/kwec
meat	rihŋ/rɪŋ	rihŋo/riŋo	riŋo	ri̧ŋu̧	ri̧ŋo/ri̧ŋ
milk	ca/caak	caak/cähɣ	cak	cak	cak/cege
moon	pɛi/pɛhi	pai/pät	dwäy/dwat	dwe	dwe/dwece
mouth	ṭok/ṭook	ṭok/ṭuuh	ɖɔk/ɖɔk	dog	ɖɔ(k)
nose	wum/wuum	wum/wuum	um	u̧m	u̧m/u̧mbe
spear	tɔŋ/tɔɔŋ	mud/muṭ	tɔŋ/tɔŋ	tɔŋ/toŋi	tɔŋ/tɔŋɛ
sun	akɔl/akol	cäŋ	caŋ	ceŋ	cieŋ/cieŋge
tongue	lyep/liehp	lɛp/lɛɛf	lɛp	lɛb	lɛp
tooth	leih/lec	lei/lɛc	leejo/lek	lak	lak/leke
tree	tim/tiim	jiaṭ/jɛn	yat/yeṇ	yat/yädi	yaṭ/yeɖe
water	piu	pi	pi	pi̧	pi̧/pi̧ge

NILO-HAMITIC LANGUAGES

LANGUAGE GROUP: BARI

Area covered by the group: South of Lat. 6, in the Nile valley and to the west, mostly in the Anglo-Egyptian Sudan, but extending into Uganda and the Belgian Congo.

BARI, own name **kutuk na bari**. LANGUAGE, with subsidiary dialects.

Spoken by: *BARI*.

Number of speakers: 7,049 TP*.

Area where spoken: On both banks of the Nile—south of Terakeka on the left bank, Mongalla on the right bank, as far as the Kajo Kaji escarpment (i.e. from Lat. 5.30 on the left bank, Lat. 5.15 on the right bank, to just south of Lat. 4.15).

Note: The Rejaf Conference Report[1] mentions over 8,000 *BARI* in the Belgian Congo. These are, however, probably the *BARI-LOGO*, who speak LOGO (MORU–MADI Group of Eastern Sudanic languages).

BARI is used in education and administration for all speakers of BARI dialects in the Sudan. It is spreading rapidly and is understood not only by speakers of BARI dialects, but by most of the *LULUBA* and in parts of *LOTUHO* and *MADI* country; it is replacing the mother-tongue of the '*LOKOYA*'. Several books of the New Testament have been published, also other religious books, readers, and elementary school books (*see also under* KAKWA).

Dialect: NYEPU.

Spoken by: *NYEPU (NYEFU, NYEPO, NYPHO)*, call themselves *NYEPU*, 2,806*, north-west of Kajo Kaji, between the *KAKWA* and *KUKU*.

Note: According to Janson Smith, their dialect is the most closely related to BARI; they claim to be of *PÖJULU* origin.

Dialect: MONDARI.

Spoken by: *MONDARI(MANDARI, MUNDARI)*, call themselves *MONDARI*, 5,397 TP*, in 4 areas:

(*a*) on the right bank of the Nile opposite Terakeka;
(*b*) on the left bank, north of Terakeka as far as Tombe;
(*c*) round Tindalu (a few only);
(*d*) round Tali.

Note: The dialect spoken in areas (*a*) and (*b*) is identical; the dialects spoken in areas (*c*) and (*d*) differ slightly.

Note: Several writers refer to the *SHIR (CHIR, KIR)*. They are probably identical with the *MONDARI*, as the '*SHIR*' east of the Nile habitually refer to themselves as *MONDARI*.

[1] *Report of the Rejaf Language Conference*, Sudan Government Office, 1928.

Dialect: PÖJULU.

Spoken by: *PÖJULU* (*PÄJULU, FAJULU, FAJELU, FADJULU*), call themselves *PÖJULU* (**päjulu, fäjulu**), 2,348 TP*, in 4 areas:
- (*a*) between Lat. 4.35 and 4.45, Long. 31 and 31.45 (approx.);
- (*b*) between Lat. 5 and 5.15, Long. 31.15 and 31.30 (approx.);
- (*c*) round Loka, mainly to the north-west;
- (*d*) in the Belgian Congo, a tiny enclave on the border north of Aba, among the *KAKWA*.

> *Note*: On Maes and Boone's map[1] they are shown as occupying a continuous strip of territory round the north-east of the *KAKWA*, from Loka in the east over the border into the Belgian Congo in the west.

PÖJULU is also spoken by about 1,200 so-called *MADI* in two areas near Opari.[2]

Dialect: NYANGWARA.

Spoken by: *NYANGWARA* (*NYANGBARA, NYAMBARA*), call themselves **nyamgbara**, 2,764 TP*, in 3 areas:
- (*a*) between Lat. 4.45 and 5.15, Long. 31.45 and 31.15 (approx.);
- (*b*) between Lat. 5.15 and 5.30, Long. 31 and 31.15 (approx.);
- (*c*) between Lat. 5.15 and 5.30, Long. 31.15 and 31.30 (approx.).

Dialect: KUKU.

Spoken by: *KUKU*, 23,563*, on the Kajo Kaji plateau in the Sudan; 1,123 (Uganda Census, 1931) in Acholi District, Uganda.

KUKU is also spoken by a few so-called *MADI* (about 250) living among the *KUKU*.[2]

Dialect: KAKWA.

Spoken by: *KAKWA* (*KAKUA, KAKWAK*), in Yei District, Anglo-Egyptian Sudan, extending into the Belgian Congo in the west, at Aba, and in the south, in Mahagi Territoire; in West Nile District, Uganda. Distributed as follows: Yei District: 42,186*; Aba, 5,000, Mahagi Territoire, 9,801*; West Nile District: Koboko County, 17,802*, Obongi Wakilate, Madi sub-district, total population about 3,000*, of whom practically all speak KAKWA, Rigbo Wakilate, Madi County, about 2,000*, also some in Ajai (included in Government figures for *LUGBARA*).

> *Note*: On Maes and Boone's map[1] they are wrongly shown occupying a continuous territory in the Belgian Congo; the salient of *KELIKO* separating the Aba and Mahagi *KAKWA* is omitted.

A beginning was made at using KAKWA as a medium of education and literacy, and a few vernacular books exist, including a Gospel in KAKWA of the Sudan and some religious books in KAKWA of the Belgian Congo. This dialect is the farthest removed from BARI, the differences being mainly in vocabulary, but there are also some phonetic and grammatical differences. KAKWA is closely related to KUKU.

---

[1] *Les Peuplades du Congo Belge*, Brussels, 1935.
[2] Tucker, *The Eastern Sudanic Languages*, vol. i, p. 7.

The *KULUBA* (921*) living among the *KAKWA* in Koboko County, West Nile District, Uganda, are described by Spagnolo[1] as remnants of a BARI-speaking tribe.

Note: The *LIGGI* are referred to in the writings of Czekanowski and others. They are, however, not a tribe, but a hunting clan. Other clans or submerged peoples among the BARI-speaking tribes are the *TOMONOK* (smiths) and the *'DUPI*. Though the *'DUPI* at least are distinguished in stature and general physiognomy from the *LUI* (the true *BARI*), they have no language of their own, but speak BARI.

Language Group: LOTUHO

Area covered by the group: A considerable part of Torit District, Anglo-Egyptian Sudan.

LOTUHO. Language, with subsidiary dialects.

Spoken by: *LOTUHO (LOTUKO, LATUKO, LATUKKA)*, call themselves **otuxo'**.

Number of speakers: About 3,500 TP*.

Area where spoken: In the plains round Torit, mainly to the north and east; also spoken by some of the so-called *ACOLI* (the *ILERIJI*) in the neighbourhood of Opari.

LOTUHO is used in education for all speakers of LOTUHO dialects, also the *PARI* (ANUAK-speaking) and the *IRENGE* (DIDINGA-speaking). A few elementary religious books and school readers have been published.[2]

Dialect: (name not known) spoken by the *LOUDO*, 370 TP*, north-west of Torit.

Dialect: (name not known) spoken by the *LOPIT (LOFIT)*, about 1,400 TP*, on Lafit Hills (some are bilingual, speaking the IRENGE dialect of DIDINGA as well as their own dialect).

Dialect: (name not known) spoken by the *LOMYA*, call themselves **lɔmya**, 970 TP*, on the Lafit Hills.

Dialect: (name not known) spoken by the *BIRA (LOKATHAN)*, call themselves **ketebo,** 350 TP*, on the Acholi Hills south-east of the *DONGOTONO*.

Dialect: (name not known) spoken by the *LOGIRI*, 1,200 TP*, south-east of the Dongotono Hills, around Ikoto.

Dialect: DONGOTONO.

Spoken by: *DONGOTONO*, call themselves **dɔŋɔtɔnɔ**, called **dɔŋɔtɔlɔ** by the *LOTUHO*, about 1,800 TP*, on the Dongotono Hills east of Torit, with a small offshoot in the Madial area.

[1] *Bari Grammar*, p. xiii.
[2] A bibliography is given in Muratori, *Grammatica Lotuxo*, pp. xxvii-xxviii.

Dialect: (name not known) spoken by the *LORWAMA (LOWAMA)*, south-east of the *LANGO* round Madial.

According to Muratori[1] this dialect closely resembles DONGOTONO, but is not mutually intelligible with LOTUHO.

Dialect: LANGO.

Spoken by: *LANGO*, call themselves **laŋɔ**,[2] about 2,000 TP*, south-east of Torit on the Imatong and southern Dongotono Hills.

> *Note*: The name LANGO is often loosely used to cover several dialects spoken in this area. Some of the so-called *ACOLI* of Torit District speak a LANGO dialect (the *LOLIBAI* and *LOGIRI*—related to the *LOGIRI* of Ikoto).

Dialect: KORIOK (KORIUK).

Spoken by: *KORIOK (KORIUK)*, also known as 'Hill *LOTUHO*', call themselves **xoryok, oxoriok**, about 2,100 TP*, south of the *LOTUHO*, mainly in the Kineti valley; also a few (400 TP*) on the northern side of the Imatong Hills.

KORIOK is also spoken by some of the so-called *ACOLI* of Torit District (the *OBOLONG*).

Dialect: LOKOYA.

Spoken by: *LOKOYA (LOKOIYA)*, call themselves **oyoriok** (not to be confused with *KORIOK*), called **(jo) kɔyɔ** by the *ACOLI*, *LOKOYA* being the name by which they are called by the *BARI*. They number 500 TP*, and are in two sections, calling themselves and their dialects ERYA and OWE, after the hills (Lyria and Lueh on maps) on which they live, north-west of Torit.

LOKOYA is also spoken (as well as BARI) by the *LULUBA*, whose own language belongs to the MORU–MADI Group of Eastern Sudanic languages; also by some of the so-called *ACOLI* of Torit District (the *OFIRIKA*).

Language Group: TESO

Consists of: TOPOSA   Language.
              TURKANA   Language.
              KARAMOJONG   Dialect Cluster.
              TESO   Language.
              and various dialects.

Area covered by the group: Eastern part of Uganda, the north-western part of Kenya, and the south-eastern corner of the Anglo-Egyptian Sudan.

TOPOSA. Language.

Spoken by: *TOPOSA (TOPOTHA, TAPOSA, DABOSSA*, &c.), call themselves **(nyi)toposa, topoθa**; called *AKKARA(AKARU, KARE)* by the *LOTUHO* and others; called *HUMA (KHUMI)*, by the *DIDINGA*, *KUM (KUMI)* by the *MURLE*.

Number of speakers: 7,612 TP*.

---

[1] Op. cit., p. xvi.
[2] To be distinguished from the *LANGO* in Uganda, who speak a Nilotic language.

Area where spoken: On the Singeitta (Thingaita) and Lokalyan Rivers, west and east of Kapoeta in the Sudan. The *TOPOSA* are semi-nomadic, and may be found as far as the Kenya border.

TOPOSA is used in education. There is very little vernacular literature.

TURKANA. LANGUAGE.

Spoken by: *TURKANA*, call themselves **(ŋgi) turkana**.

Number of speakers: 55,000.[1]

Area where spoken: In Kenya, in an area bounded by Lake Rudolf, the *SUK* country, and the borders of Uganda and the Sudan.

The *NYANGATOM* (*NYAMATOM, NYANGATUM*, &c.), also known as *DONYIRO* (*DONGIRO, IDONGIRO*, &c.) and as *BUME* (*BUMA, BUMI*, &c.), appear to be a section of the *TURKANA* living in Ethiopia, mainly on or near the River Kibish. They were estimated at 700 fighting men in 1940. To judge by the short vocabulary available, they speak a dialect of TURKANA.

KARAMOJONG, own name **akaramojoŋ**. DIALECT CLUSTER.

Spoken by: *KARAMOJONG* (*KARIMOJONG*), call themselves **ikaramojoŋ**.

Number of speakers: 10,957 TP*.

Area where spoken: On the Karamoja escarpment, Uganda, south-west of the *TURKANA*.

Dialects: There are considerable differences between the dialects spoken in the north and south of the area. Tucker reports a *TESO* as saying that he could understand southern KARAMOJONG, but not northern.

KARAMOJONG is at present used in Karamoja District as the medium of education, but it is possible that TESO will be used in the future. Some books of the Bible have been published.

TESO, own name **ateso**. LANGUAGE.

Spoken by: *TESO*, call themselves **iteso**; called *IKUMAMA* by the *LANGO* and *KARAMOJONG* (cf. *KUMAM*), *BAKIDI* (*BAKEDI*) by Bantu-speaking peoples.

Number of speakers: Uganda: 387,643 (Uganda Census, 1931); Kenya; numbers not known.

Area where spoken: In Uganda, mostly in Teso District, but some 40,000 are scattered in the northern part of Bugwere and Budama Districts, and there are some settlements among the *KUMAM*. There is a section of the tribe known as *ITESYO* living at Tororo and extending into the western part of North Kavirondo District, Kenya; they are also known as *WAMIA* (to their Bantu neighbours) and as *ELGUMI*.

Dialects: Dialectal differences are slight, and the language may be considered as uniform. According to Fr. McGough the *ITESYO* have preserved an older form of the language. The 'standard' dialect is taken as being that spoken at Ngora.

[1] Figures from G. W. B. Huntingford.

NILO-HAMITIC LANGUAGES

TESO is used in primary education in Government and Mission schools (English being the language of secondary education). The New Testament has been published, but at present little else in the way of vernacular literature exists.

The KUMAM (KUMAN, KUMUM, IKUMAMA), who call themselves IKO-KOLEMU or AKUM (Uganda Census, 1931: 43,916); in Kaberamaido County, between the *LANGO* and the *TESO*, are of *TESO* origin, and speak a language which is akin both to LANGO and to TESO. According to Crazzolara they are in process of becoming assimilated to the *LANGO*. On the other hand, the present tendency of language policy is that TESO should be used as the medium of education for the *KUMAM* (at present, KUMAM is used in Roman Catholic schools, LANGO in C.M.S. schools).

There is at present insufficient linguistic evidence to show what languages or dialects are spoken by the following smaller tribes or sections of tribes:

DODOS (DODOTH, DODOSI, DODOTHO), 2,866 TP*, in Uganda, north of the *KARAMOJONG*, of whom they may be a section.

NYANGEYA (NYANGIYA, NANGIYA, NANGEYA), in Uganda, on the Nyangeya Hills. There appear to be two sets of people, both known as *NYANGEYA*, living on the Nyangeya Hills. Those in the north may be a section of the *TOPOSA*. They are, however, also said to be identical with the *POREN* or *NIPORI*, who are not *TOPOSA*, but probably akin to the *DIDINGA*.[1]

OROM (ROM), in the mountains south of Madial. Seligman[2] calls them a section of the *DODOS*. According to J. C. Wild they call themselves *ACOLI*, but most of them do not speak ACOLI. A short vocabulary collected by Wild shows that their language is undoubtedly related to TOPOSA. The name *OROM* may, however, be only a geographical term.

JIYE (JIE, AJIE, JIWE, NGIYE, NGIJIE, &c.). There is a *JIYE* section of the *TOPOSA*, in the Sudan at Lopet, about 30 miles north of Kapoeta, a *JIYE* section of the *TURKANA*, among the western *TURKANA* in Kenya, and a *JIYE* section of the *KARAMOJONG* (325 TP*), in Uganda (shown on Wayland's map[3] immediately north of the *KARAMOJONG* proper, between them and the *DODOS*). It is thus probable that the *JIYE* have no separate language, but speak TOPOSA, TURKANA, or KARAMOJONG as the case may be.

LANGUAGE GROUP: MASAI[4]

MASAI, own name eŋkútúk ol-maasài. LANGUAGE.

Spoken by: MASAI (MASAE, MAASAE, MASSAI), call themselves **il-máasài**.

---

[1] The other *NYANGEYA* call themselves *UPALE*; their language, of which Driberg gives a vocabulary in his 'Lotuko Dialects' (*American Anthropologist*, 1932) may be related to that of the *TEUSO* on the Karamoja escarpment, and of other small groups of people in Uganda. These languages appear to be unrelated to any other known language.

[2] *Pagan Tribes of the Nilotic Sudan*, p. 363.

[3] 'Preliminary Studies of the Tribes of Karamoja' (*J. R. Anthrop. Soc.*, 1931).

[4] Much of the information on this section, including population figures, was provided by G. W. B. Huntingford.

NILO-HAMITIC LANGUAGES

The name denotes several tribes speaking the same language, with very slight dialectal differences.

Number of speakers: 144,000, made up as follows:
Kenya: *SAMBURU*, 10,000; other tribes, 50,000;
Tanganyika: Agricultural, 47,000; Pastoral, 37,000.

Area where spoken: Round Lake Baringo and to the north-west, Kenya; south of the *KIKUYU* in Kenya, extending into Tanganyika: Masai District, Northern Province, and scattered in other Districts.[1]

MASAI tribes:

SAMBURU, north-west of Lake Baringo. Pastoral.

> *Note*: The *SAMBURU* are administered separately from the other *MASAI*, and it is not always realized that they are *MASAI*.

NJAMUSI (*NJEMPS*), call themselves **en-jamus**; called **il-tiamus** by other *MASAI* tribes. They are agricultural, and live near Lake Baringo.

KAPITI, call themselves **il-kaputiei** (Huntingford), **il-kápútié** (Tucker), mainly around Ngong, Kajiado and Narok, Kenya; also some in Tanganyika. Pastoral.

KISONGO, call themselves **il-kɪsɔŋgɔ**, mainly in Tanganyika, especially round Mondul and Loliondo; a few in Kenya. Pastoral.

> *Note*: The *SONJO* shown on the tribal map of Tanganyika[2] are a section of the *KISONGO*.

> *Note*: There were formerly three other *MASAI* tribes, **il-uasin ɡiʃu** (*UASIN GISHU, GUAS NGISHU*), **il-aikipyak** (*LAIKIPIA, LYKIPIA*), and **en-aipoʃa** (*NAIVASHA*). Remnants of them are now merged in the *KAPITI* and *KISONGO*; a small remnant of *UASIN GISHU* were in 1928 living in North Kavirondo under their own headman.

LUMBWA (**il-lumbwa**), called *IL-OIKOP, EL-OIGOB* by the Pastoral *MASAI*. Agricultural. In Tanganyika, mainly in the neighbourhood of Lakes Natron and Manyara; around Arusha and Meru; east of Kilimanjaro; and in other parts.

The *MASAI* in and around Arusha call themselves **il-arúsà**, and are called *WAARUSHA* by their Bantu neighbours; those around Meru are known as *MERU*, but should be distinguished from the Bantu tribe of the same name.

KWAVI, KWAFI (with Bantu prefix *WAKWAVI, WAKWAFI*), also rendered *KUAFI*, is the name given by SWAHILI-speaking people to the *MASAI*, and is particularly applied to the *LUMBWA MASAI* of Kilosa District.

MASAI is used in elementary education. The New Testament has been published and is now being revised; a few school books exist.

Notes on nomenclature:

1. The name *LUMBWA*, which means 'farmers', is correctly applied only to the

---

[1] 'Survey', p. 58.
[2] Atlas of the Tanganyika Territory, Survey Division, Department of Lands and Mines, Dar es Salaam, 1942.

agricultural *MASAI*. It was, however, erroneously applied to the *KIPSIGIS* by early administrators, and is still so used.

2. The name *BURKENEJI*, used by von Höhnel and others as a tribal name, is a corruption of **il-loo-ibor-keneji** (people of the white goats), a nickname of the *SAMBURU*.

3. Tucker ('Survey', p. 889) gives a number of names of *MASAI* 'sub-tribes'. Huntingford points out that, whereas some of these are the names of tribal sections, others are the names of localities.

LANGUAGE GROUP: NANDI

Consists of: NANDI   Language, with subsidiary dialects.
SUK   Language, with subsidiary dialects.

Area covered by the group: In the western part of Kenya, extending into Uganda; also (scattered) in Tanganyika.

NANDI, own name **ŋalɛk ap nandɪ**. LANGUAGE.

Spoken by: *NANDI* (originally a SWAHILI nickname, but now adopted by the people themselves), called *CHEMWEL* by the *SUK*, **il-teŋwal** by the *MASAI* (the old name for the *NANDI* being *CHEMWAL*); called *MWA* by the *LUO*, *AWAKA-VARE* by the 'Bantu Kavirondo'.

Number of speakers: 50,440.[1]

Area where spoken: In Kenya, on the Nandi escarpment and around Kapsabet; some of the *NANDI* live as squatters on farms.

NANDI is used in elementary education for the *NANDI* and most speakers of NANDI dialects in Kenya. Vernacular literature is slight, but on the increase.

Dialects of Nandi are spoken by the following tribes:

ELGEYO (*ELGEYU*, *KEYU*), call themselves **keyo**, 20,000, in the Kerio valley, east of the *NANDI*.

KAMASIA or *TUGIN* (*TUKIN*, *TUKEN*), call themselves **kamasya** or **tuken**, 33,255, in the Kerio valley, north-east of the *NANDI*.

KABARNET, a small tribe between the *KAMASIA* and Lake Baringo.

KIPSIGIS (*KIPSIKIS*, *KIP-SIKISI*, &c.) call themselves **kɪpsɪkis**, also known as *LUMBWA*,[2] 71,757, south of the *NANDI* in Kericho District.

KIPSIGIS is used in elementary education, and a very small amount of vernacular literature exists. It differs in vocabulary from NANDI, but the two are mutually intelligible, and an attempt is being made at fusion between them.

Note: *BURET* and *SOTIK*, which occur as tribal names,[3] are the names of two districts in the southern part of *KIPSIGIS* country.

[1] Figures for *NANDI* and *SUK* were obtained from Huntingford, unless otherwise stated.
[2] See note on the name *LUMBWA* under *MASAI*.
[3] e.g. Tucker, 'Survey', p. 890.

NYANGORI (*NYANGNORI*), call themselves **terik**,[1] south-west of the *NANDI* in Central Kavirondo District (for numbers see under *MBAI*, &c.)

ELGONYI (*ELGONI*, also known as 'Elgon *MASAI*'), call themselves **kɔny**, 5,200, on the southern slopes of Mount Elgon.

LAGO (*LAKO*), call themselves **pɔɔk**, on the southern slopes of Elgon, west of the *ELGONYI*.

NGOMAMEK, call themselves **ŋgomamek**, a small tribe of *NANDI* stock, closely connected with the *LAGO*, and adjacent to them on the foot-hills of Elgon. They have become largely Bantuized, and are commonly known as *WANGOMA*.

MBAI
SABAUT } in Uganda, on the western slopes of Elgon.
SORE, call themselves **kipsorai**

These three tribes, together with the *NYANGORI* and *ENDO*, together number about 22,000.

SABEI (*SAPEI, SEBEI, SAVEI, SAVE*), call themselves **kamecak** or **sabiny**, 13,477 (Uganda Census, 1931), on the northern slopes of Elgon, in Uganda.

Dialects of NANDI are also spoken by the *DOROBO* (*NDOROBO, NDEROBO*, often with Bantu prefix *WA-*), primitive forest-dwelling hunters living in small settlements scattered in Kenya and Tanganyika, among the *NANDI, MASAI, KIKUYU*, and various Tanganyika tribes. They are unrelated to any of the tribes among whom they live, but, 'wherever they live they speak dialects of NANDI'.[2] The Kenya *DOROBO* call themselves **ɔkiek**, and are distributed as follows (the names given by Huntingford to these *DOROBO* settlements are not tribal, but are names of localities):

Western (in contact with *MASAI* and *NANDI*):

Kipkurerek (226).
Tindiret.
Lo-'l-diani (Londiani).
Ravine.
West Mau.
East Mau.

Central (in contact with *MASAI* and *KIKUYU*):

Dundule.
Saleta.
Kidong.
Digiri.

Eastern (in contact with *MASAI* and *KIKUYU*):

Kisima.
Mount Kenya.

[1] Not to be confused with the *TIRIKI*, a Bantu tribe who live adjacent to the *TERIK*, to the west.
[2] Huntingford, *The Nandi* (Peoples of Kenya, No. 11).

Very little is known about the following tribes in Tanganyika, who are said to be *DOROBO*:

MOSIRO (ELMOSIRO). *MEDIAK* and *KISANKASA* are probably other names for the same people. According to Maguire[1] they number about 1,000, and live on the Talamai Hills east of Kibaya (Masai District).

ARAMANIK (LARAMANIK), scattered in the northern part of the *MASAI* area in Tanganyika.

A NANDI dialect is also spoken by the *TATOGA (TATURU*[2]*)*, call themselves **tatoga**, 3,560 (Tanganyika Census, 1931). Pastoral. In Struck's time they may have been more numerous than they are now; on his map[3] they are shown south of Lake Eyasi between the *IRANGI* in the west and the *IRAKU (IRAQW)* and *FIOME* in the east, with several small enclaves to the north-west towards Lake Victoria in *SUKUMA* country, and to the south. He names several sections:

MANGATI (but see below).
SIMITYEK, called *WANONEGA* by Bantu tribes, on Lake Victoria.
BRARIGA, called *GAMRIT* by the *MASAI*, *WAGAMRITA* by Bantu tribes, scattered on Ukerewe Island and in *SUKUMA* country.
BAYUTA, round Mount Hanang.

The *BARABAIG* are said[4] to be a section of the *TATOGA*, called *MANGATI* by the *MASAI*, and living at the foot of Mount Hanang. They are, however, regarded as a separate tribe for the purposes of the Census (8,977), and shown on the Tribal Map of Tanganyika (on which the *TATOGA* are not shown) in the south of Mbulu District. Nothing is known of their speech, though Dr. Guthrie reports that it is said to be Nilotic, related to LUO.

The dialects of NANDI spoken by the *DOROBO* of Tanganyika have, according to Huntingford, a definite NANDI base, though not so large a proportion of NANDI words in their vocabulary as the dialects of the Kenya *DOROBO*; they do not seem to be mutually intelligible, and are not understood by the *DOROBO* of Kenya.

Note: The name *DOROBO* appears to be used in a general way to denote small remnants of tribes unrelated to, and sometimes speaking a different language from, the tribes among whom they live. Wayland[5] mentions the '*DOROBO*' who live on the Karamoja escarpment in Uganda, and who speak a language of their own. From the short vocabulary he gives, it seems that this language may be related to that of the *TEUSO*.[6] There is also a reference to the '*NDEROBO*' section of the *DONYIRO* in an army report quoted by A. C. A. Wright, but no further information is given.

SUK, own name ŋal pa pɔɔkwut. LANGUAGE.

Spoken by: *SUK*, call themselves **pɔɔkwut (pokot)** (in Uganda: **upe**); called *KIMUKON* by the *NANDI*.

[1] Il-Torōbo (*J. Afr. Soc.*, 1927–8).
[2] Often confused (e.g. by Baumann, *Durch Massailand zur Nilquelle*) with the *NYATURU*, a Bantu tribe.
[3] *Über die Sprache der Tatoga- und Iraku-Leute* (see Bibliography).
[4] Bagshawe, 'Peoples of the Happy Valley', *J. Afr. Soc.*, 1924–5.
[5] Op. cit.
[6] See note on *NYANGEYA*, p. 32.

Number of speakers: 24,633* in West Suk District.

Area where spoken: in the Kerio valley, south-west of the *TURKANA* (the 'Pastoral *SUK*'); west of the 'Pastoral *SUK*', extending into Karamoja District, Uganda (the 'Hill *SUK*').

SUK is used in elementary education. One gospel and a few readers exist.

Dialects of SUK are spoken by the following tribes:

MARAKWET (*MARAGWET, MERKWET*), 18,087, south of the *SUK*.

ENDO (*TO*), call themselves ɛndɔ, called *CHEP-BLENG* by the *SUK*, on the northern part of the Elgeyo escarpment, between the *ELGEYO* and the *SUK*.

KADAM (also extinct) on Mount Debasien in Uganda (referred to by Wayland[1] as *NGIKADAMA*).

Note: The dialects spoken by the *MARAKWET* and *ENDO* are almost identical.

[1] Op. cit.

LINGUISTIC SURVEY OF THE NILO-HAMITIC LANGUAGES[1]
By A. N. TUCKER

1. Phonetically these languages have nothing outstanding in the way of peculiar sounds:

(a) They seem to have the same sort of vowel system as the Southern LWO and Eastern Sudanic languages—2 varieties of **i**, 2 of **u**, 2 of **e**, 2 of **o**, and **a** (which in some languages has a centralized form **ä**)—with well discernible laws of vowel harmony.

Diphthongs and long vowels are common, except in BARI. Vowel 'breathiness' is absent.

BARI		LOTUHO		KARAMOJONG	
gi̧r-ä	gɪr-a	ri̧x-o	gɪt-a	ri̧k-o	ɪlɪm-a
(wipe plate)	(cicatrice)	(lead)	(shave head)	(guide)	(drizzle)
tu̧r-ä	tʊr-a	du̧k-o	xʊt-a	du̧k-o	kʊt-a
(pursue)	(pour)	(build)	(blow)	(build)	(blow)
ker-o	kɛr-a	xej-o	ɪrɛny-a	lep-o	yɛn-a
(steer)	(notch)	(roast)	(squeeze)	(milk)	(learn)
kor-o	kɔr-a	mor-o	rɔj-a	mor-o	bɔk-a
(bore)	(divide)	(insult)	(pinch)	(insult)	(dig)
kär-ä	kar-a	lwäx-ä	mat-a		mat-a
(spoil)	(ruin)	(help)	(drink)		(drink)

Note that in some of the Western BARI dialects these vowel distinctions are not always heard, although the characteristic affixes remain.

BARI	KAKWA
rem, rem-o, rem-bu	**rem, rem-o, rem-bu** (stab with spear)
rɛm, rɛm-a, rɛm-ba	**rem, rem-a, rem-ba** (thatch)

In the following languages vowel varieties have not yet been established, but note the affixes:

TESO		MASAI		NANDI[2]	
pikipik-o (struggle)	*ilip-a* (pray)	*itiŋ-o* (finish)	*idim-a* (be clever)	*pir-o* (strike)	*til-a* (cut)
duk-o (build)	*sub-a* (create)	*iruk-o* (believe)	*suj-a* (follow)	*sup-o* (follow)	
	ner-a (speak about)	*reʃ-o* (trap)	*igwen-a* (talk)	**ker-ɔ** (see)	

[1] Examples in heavy type are taken from: Spagnolo, *Bari Grammar*; Muratori, *Grammatica Lotuxo*; and from information provided by Dr. W. A. Wilson and G. W. B. Huntingford, and from the author's own researches. These are phonetically approximate. Examples in italics have been adapted from the following works not originally written in phonetic script: Kitching, *Handbook of the Ateso Language*; McGough, *Grammar of Teso* (MS.); Hollis, *The Masai, The Nandi*; Africa Inland Mission, *Nandi–English Dictionary*.

[2] According to Huntingford the suffix in each case may be -ɔ *or* -a, with the exception of **kɔɔn-ɔ** (give).

TESO	MASAI	NANDI
kot-o (want) nom-a (beat)	gor-o (be angry) ton-a (sit)	kon-o (give)
mat-a (drink)	laŋ-a (pass) cam-o (love)	nam-a (hold)

(The functions of the above vowel suffixes are explained in par. 10.)

(b) BARI distinguishes implosive or 'glottal' **b** and **d** (written '**b** and '**d**) from explosive **b** and **d**—an Eastern Sudanic trait. None of the other languages does this. In fact with them normal **b** and **d** tend to be implosive, and the latter is retroflex as well, as in SOMALI.[1]

Another feature of these languages (except BARI) is a tendency to soften or slur consonants, especially **k** and **p**, between vowels. This slurring has no grammatical function, however.

LOTUHO: bak and bax-a or baγa (beat)　　neŋòk (<na-xiŋòk) (dog)
　　　　　afɛ and aʋɛ (yes)　　　　　　　　nófítò and nóvítò (rope)
MASAI:　ollódìkà and ollóɽìxà (chair)　　a-ipak (I enjoy it) a-ipaa (<a-ipak-a) (I enjoyed it)
TESO:　　eiŋòk or ekiŋòk (dog)

In TESO the prefixes **ki-** and **ka-** seem to have lost the consonantal element altogether in N. Teso and among young speakers elsewhere; otherwise **k** is not affected in this language.

Compare: LOTUHO: ɔlɔxɔxɔ' pl. axaxalak (thief)
　　　　　TESO:　 ekòkòlan pl. íkókólàk

(c) There are no 'emphatic' consonants as in the Semitic and other Hamitic languages, nor any series of specifically dental consonants as in the Nilotic languages.[2] **c** and **j** are usually post-alveolar (as in 'church' and 'jump'),[3] though the latter is often implosive in the non-BARI languages.

2. Dynamic accent (stress), accompanied by high or falling tone, seems to play a bigger role in these languages than mere syllable pitch.[4]

BARI:　Yatá　Boy's name.　　　　dó nyanyâr nàn? You like which one?
　　　　Yátà　Girl's name.　　　　dó nyanyâr nân? You like me?
　　　　lópír (fat, adj.)　　　　　tì pɔ. He is not coming.
　　pl. lópîr　　　　　　　　　　　tí pɔ. Let him come.
　　　　nân lɔ tótoggù.　　I am cutting.
　　　　nân lɔ tôtóggù.　　I am cutting about in all directions.

[1] See Armstrong, L. E., *The Phonetic Structure of Somali*. I have heard retroflex **d** in the LOTUHO dialects, TESO, TOPOSA, and MASAI. (I have not heard NANDI or SUK spoken.) Note that the phonological relationship is with the *implosive* BARI sound. BARI *explosive* **d** corresponds to **j** or **y** elsewhere.

BARI	'duŋ	LOTUHO	duŋ	MASAI	duŋ	(cut)
	mede		imiji			(village)
	kädini		nayani		òljàni	(tree)

[2] It is true that in TOPOSA, **s** alternates with θ or ð, but no language makes a semantic difference between dental and alveolar consonants.

[3] Pure palatal consonants are found in dialects like MONDARI, bordering on the Nilotic field.

[4] BARI is a tone language *as well* (see 9). Not enough is known about the other languages for a categorical statement at this stage.

LOTUHO: néyalì (oil) náswanì (buffalo)
néyalí (fire-place) pl. náswánì
TESO: ékume (nose) émúduk(í) (blind man) adúkì. I build.
pl. íkúmès ímúdíkyòk adukî. I built.
àkonyeneke (his eyes) kèmìnà Kânà. He loves Kana.
akónyènèkè (his face) kéminá Kànà. Kana loves him.
MASAI: eŋkúmí (nose) olmɔdóónì (blind man)
pl. iŋkumɪʃɪn ilmódók

3. Nilo-Hamitic words are formed mostly with the aid of prefixes and suffixes. The roots in their simplest form, whether of Nilotic origin or not, consist for the most part in consonant+vowel+consonant, as can be seen from the verb stems above. With nouns the roots are often hidden by affixes.

BARI	MASAI	Nilotic
ki-nyòŋ	ol-kí-nyaŋ-î	nyaŋ (crocodile)

There are, however, many non-Nilotic roots which are disyllabic.

BARI		MASAI		
tɔmɛ	pl. tɔmy-à	òl-tɔmɛ	pl. il-tɔmìa	(elephant)
mäyät-í	máyàt	ɔl-máat-î	il-máàt	(locust)

Reduplication of stems, in whole or in part, is very common.

4. Compound nouns are common, and take the form of a contracted genitive.

BARI: **monye-kak** (lit. father-land—village headman).
MASAI: **kutuk-aji** (lit. mouth-hut—door).
NANDI: **kɛl-tepes** (lit. foot-breadth—sole).

5. There are many noun formatives, and the affixes are characteristic. The following are the most common.

Prefix (k)i-

BARI	LOTUHO	TESO	MASAI	NANDI
kɪ-teŋ	neteŋ (<na-xɪteŋ)	a-(k)i-têŋ	eŋ-kɪ-teŋ	(cow)
pl. ki-súk	nesuŋ	a-i-tûk	iŋ-ki-ʃú	(cattle)
kɪ-pyâ' (lightning<pɛ = to flash)	neŋa-t (key<ŋa = to open)	e-(k)-ibuk (churn<ibuk)	eŋ-gi-as (work< as = to work)	ki-ruɔg (counsel <iruɔc = consult)

Prefix (k)a-

kà-'bɔk-à-nit	a-xa-bwax-a-ni	aa-mej-an or e-ka-mej-a-k	ol-a-yer-a-ni	ka-mʊt-ɪn (leader <ɪmʊt)
pl. kà-'bɔk-à-k (digger< 'bɔk)	a-xa-bwax-a-k (digger<bɔk)	aa-mej-a-k or i-ka-mej-a-k (hunter<mej)	il-a-yer-a-k (cook <yer)	

Suffix -ni(t)

bari-nit (a Bari)			ɔl-máásà-ni (a Masai)	nandɪ-ɪn (a Nandi)
kà-dɛr-à-nit	a-xa-irux-o-ni	e-ka-sub-an	ɔl-o-i-bon-i	pɔn-ɪn
pl. kà-dɛr-à-k (cook<dɛr)	a-xa-irux-o-k (believer<iruk)	i-ka-sub-a-k (creator<isub)	il-o-i-bon-ɔ-k (ritual expert< bɔn)	pɔn (witch<pan)

LINGUISTIC SURVEY OF THE NILO-HAMITIC LANGUAGES   41

BARI	LOTUHO	TESO	MASAI	NANDI
Suffix -ti, -to, -ta				
kwɛn-tɪ (bird)	na-xeny-í (bird)	é-tesò-t (a Teso)		
nyar-a-ti	o-nyim-ɔtɔ		*en-jiŋ-a-ta*	
pl. nyar-a-t	o-nyim-ot		*in-jiŋ-a-t*	
(loved one)	(chosen one)		(entrance)	
Suffix -et, -ot, -it				
'bɔk-ɛt	ɛ-bɔx-ɪt	e-bok-et	ol-k-er-is-iot	ki-risw-a
pl. 'bɔk-esi	ɛ-bɔx-ɪt	i-bok-et-a	il-k-er-is-iot (cooking utensil)	ki-riso-n
(spade)	(spade)	(spade)		(hammer)
				ya-ɪtɪɔ
				(badness < ya)

Note that Muratori further gives in KARAMOJONG: **e-ka-bɔk-a-n**, pl. **ŋi-ka-bɔk-a-k** (digger), **a-bɔk-ɛt**, pl. **a-bɔk-ɛt-a** (spade).

6. There are many suffixes indicating number, which seem to be reminiscent of some class system since broken down. The following are the most widely spread:

(*a*) Plural suffixes.

BARI	LOTUHO	TESO	MASAI	NANDI
Suffix -k. See examples under (5) above.				
Suffix -ki, -ka, -ko				
yaya	lä-woru	ek-irio-non		
pl. yaya-kɪ (porcupine)	a-worú-xo-xen (leopard)	luk-irio-ko (black man)		
Suffix -t, -s				
kämiru				kepen
pl. kämiru-ät				kepen-os
(lion)				(cave)
Suffix -ti, -ta, -to				
'buruti	a-ccai	á-pará-n	ol-púkúr-í	
pl. 'buruti-tä	a-cca-ta	a-pará-syà	il-púkúr-tò	
(large pot)	(large pot)	(sun, day)	(milk gourd)	
Suffix -n				
daŋ	(n)ɛbak	á-kuŋ	iŋ-kóítú-í	ɪmbar
pl. däŋ-in	ɛbax-ɪn	á-kuŋ-ɪn	eŋ-kóítò-ɪn	ɪmbar-en
(bow)	(rock)	(knee)	(road)	(field)
Suffix -i, -a, -o				
ŋɛ'dɛp	ä-ŋädyef	e-bukit	ɔl-bítír	ŋecer
pl. ŋɛ'dɛp-à	ä-ŋädyef-ä	í-búkit-ɔ	il-bitir-o	ŋecer-ɔi
(tongue)	(tongue)	(large basket)	(wart-hog)	(stool)
Suffix -jin, -jik, -tin, -tik				
yapa	(n)a-yafà	akwapu	ɔl-ápà	ɔr
pl. yapa-jìn	a-yafa-jin	akwapi-sinei	il-àpà-itin	ɔr-tɪn-wa
(moon, month)	(moon)	(earth)	(moon)	(road)

Note also in MASAI: **ol-kíné** pl. **il-kine-jí** (goat)
ol-kíú pl. **il-kiu-ʃîn** (hill)

(b) Singular suffixes

	BARI	LOTUHO	TESO	MASAI	NANDI
Suffix -i(t)					
pl.	kɔmɔn	xämon	i-samâ	ìl-tɔlàl	
sg.	kɔmɔn-ɪt	xämon-i	é-sàma-i'	òl-tɔlàl-ì	
	(relation)	(relation)	(river)	(monkey)	
Suffix -a, -o, -u					
pl.		(n)ámɔnyɪt	i-mòr	in-tútúny	ŋal
sg.		(n)ámɔnyɪt-a	e-mor-ù	en-tútúny-o	ŋɔl-ɪɔ
		(bowels)	(hill)	(heel)	(word)
Suffix -ni(t), -(n)ut					
pl.	wɪ-jìn	a-tarʊxa	í-jàkâ	in-déró	sakut
sg.	wɪy-ʊt	a-tarʊxa-nɪ	á-jaka-nʊt	en-déró-ni	sakut-ɪn
	(buttocks)	(vulture)	(kingdom)	(rat)	(owner of evil eye)
Suffix -ti					
pl.	mara	(n)á-jaŋá	a-kíro		
sg.	mere-te	(n)á-jaŋá-tì	a-kíro-t		
	(rib)	(fly)	(word)		
Suffix -tat, -tot					
pl.	pioŋ	nófí			ce
sg.	pioŋ-tot	nófí-tò			ceiyɔ
	(drop of water)	(rope)			(drop of milk)

Note that LOTUHO, TESO, and MASAI have *prefixes* for number as well.

NANDI and its dialects KIPSIGIS, TERIK, KEYO, TUKEN, POK, SAPEI, and KONY differ from the rest in that every noun has a primary 'indefinite' form (shown above) and a secondary 'definite' form, both in the singular and in the plural. This form usually has a singular suffix -t, tɔ (or -d, &c.) and a plural suffix -k (sometimes -ka, kɔ), e.g. tiony, pl. tioŋ-in (animal), tion-do, pl. tioŋ-ik (the animal); sɛgɛm, sg. sɛgɛmya (bees), sɛgɛmɪk, sg. sɛgɛmyat (the bees). 'Definite' forms are not, however, found in SUK, ENDO, or MARAKWET.

7. Grammatical gender is present in all languages except SUK. There are three genders (masculine, feminine, and something that appears to be either locative or diminutive), but only TESO seems to have all three fully developed. The sign of the masculine is **lo**, of the feminine **na**, and of the diminutive **i**, and these particles are most commonly to be found in the demonstrative, possessive, and relative pronouns. Examples of 'near' demonstratives.[1]

[1] BARI and TESO have three degrees of proximity, corresponding to 'this', 'that', and 'yonder', e.g. (masc. sg.):

    BARI: (i) (nyɪ)lɔ   (ii) ŋɪlɔ   (iii) **lu**
    TESO: (i)   lo   (ii) ŋol   (iii) **je**

LOTUHO, MASAI, and NANDI have two degrees of 'near' demonstrative and two of 'far' demonstrative. Thus:

    LOTUHO: (i*a*) ɔlɔ   (i*b*) älyä   (ii*a*) lyä   (ii*b*) *a*(la)
    MASAI: (i*a*) *elle*   (i*b*) *elde*   (ii*a*) *illo*   (ii*b*) *lido*
    NANDI: (i*a*) **ni**   (i*b*) **nin**   (ii*a*) **nɔ**   (ii*b*) **nɔn**

LINGUISTIC SURVEY OF THE NILO-HAMITIC LANGUAGES

	BARI	LOTUHO	TESO	MASAI	NANDI
m.	(nyɪ)lɔ	pl. kʊlɔ ɔlɔ pl. **xulo**	*lo* pl. *lu* *elle*	pl. *kullo*	**ni** pl. **cu**
f.	(nyɪ)na	kʊnɛ ana	xʊna *na*	*nu* *enna*	*kunna*
dim.			*yen(i)*	*lu enne*	*kunne(n)* *yu* *uli*

In LOTUHO, TESO, and MASAI, gender is further shown in nouns in their prefix. Only a few BARI nouns have such prefixes (e.g. **la-lɛt** = man, **na-rakwan** = woman).

	LOTUHO	TESO	MASAI
m.	(l)ɔ- pl. (l)a-	e- pl. i-	ol- pl. (i)l-
f.	(n)a- pl. (n)a-	a- pl. a-	en- pl. (i)n-
dim.	i- (in fem. names)	i- pl. i-	e-

Note that NANDI and SUK do not distinguish between masculine and feminine;[1] that whereas TESO uses the third agreement in connexion with a few diminutive words, NANDI and MASAI use it only in agreement with the word for 'place' (*olto* in NANDI, *eweji* in MASAI).

In most languages words are feminine unless referring to specific masculine (or big or strong) objects. In BARI, however, gender allocation is more complex, and seems to follow rough physiological analogies, e.g.

Masculine: big, strong, long, or used as an active agent or instrument.
Feminine: small, weak, soft, round, hollow, flat, or used in a passive sense.

Cases of *polarity* are also to be found, whereby the singular and plural forms of some nouns have different genders, e.g.

BARI: **ber** (age-grade contemporaries)   **luŋsak** (young men) (pl. fem.)
     bertyo (age-grade contemporary)   **luŋsaktyo** (young man) (sg. masc.)
TESO: **ayeyait, eja** (aunt)   **papa** (father)
     pl. **nukeiya** (fem.), **lukeja** (masc.)   **lukapap** (masc.), **atapapa** (fem.)[2]

8. There seems to be no inflexion for case,[3] which is shown by position in the sentence.

9. Verbs in these languages fall mostly into two groups, according to whether the root begins with the vowel **i-** or not.

	LOTUHO	TESO	MASAI	NANDI
I.	**lyof-o** (milk)	(*ko-*)*duk* (build)	*suj* (follow)	*pir* (strike)
II.	**iruk-o** (believe)	(*k-*)*ilip* (pray)	*isuj* (wash)	*isup* (follow)

---

[1] Lexical distinction, however, may be found in NANDI in the noun formative prefixes **kip-** (big, strong, masc.) and **cep-** (small, weak, fem.), and the suffixes **-in** (masc.) and **-ia(t)** (fem.), e.g.:

    (m.) **kɪp-sɪkis-ɪn**   (f.) **cep-sɪkiʊ-ɪa(t)** (Kipsigis)
                    cep-keswet (small knife)

Note that LOTUHO, by omitting the initial consonant of a noun, can deprive it of its sex designation:
    á-tɔmɛ (elephant), **lá-tɔmɛ** (bull elephant), **ná-tɔmɛ** (cow elephant).

[2] No polarity in the pronouns, &c., however.

[3] If one excepts coalescence and sound change in the gender prefix in MASAI, TESO, and LOTUHO (see 16). Note that MASAI has a specific vocative prefix *li-* or *le-*; in BARI, LOTUHO, NANDI, and SUK, on the other hand, the noun itself is usually followed by a demonstrative in such instances. TESO elides the prefix altogether in some adverbial contexts: **aparan** (day), **paran** (by day).

This grouping is not necessarily consistent between languages. Compare MASAI *suj* with NANDI *isup* above, also NANDI ɪlac (dress), ɪŋwal (be lame), ɪnan (think) with SUK lac, ŋwal, nɔn.

In BARI there as no **i-** verbs, but there are two main *tonal* classes.[1]

I. **nân lɔ totók.** I am cutting it.   **nân lɔ tótoġġù.** I am cutting.
   toké! toké-tok! Cut it!   **kɔtók!** Don't cut it!

II. **nân lɔ yíyíŋ.** I hear it.   **nân lɔ yíyiŋgâ.** I am listening.
    yiŋê! yiŋé-yíŋ! Listen!   **kɔ yîŋ!** Don't listen!

10. BARI is the only language group in which the Nilotic three-voice system is fully employed—here by means of suffixes.

Active (Applicative) (short stem): **dɛr** (to cook it)   **pet** (to tether it)
   ,,   (Qualitative)   **dɛr-ja** (to cook)   **ped-du** (to tether)
Passive   (long stem): **dɛr-a** (to be cooked)   **pet-o** (to be tethered)

The other languages have two stems ('short' and 'long'—the latter having the suffix **-a** or **-o** according to the quality of the root vowel, see 1a above). In LOTUHO the long stem indicates composite action,[2] in TESO it indicates continuous action, in MASAI it is a sign of the past tense, and in NANDI of the 1st person object.

LOTUHO	TESO	MASAI	NANDI
a-xɔny nɪ (I bite)	*a-duk-i* (I build it)	*a-suj* (I follow him)	*k-esup* (he followed him)
a-xɔny-a nɪ (I eat)	*a-duk-o* (I am about to build it)	*a-juj-a* (I followed him)	*k-esup-o* (he followed me)

Note that BARI is the only language group to have a passive voice, though MASAI and NANDI have an impersonal form of the verb conjugation ('It follows me' = 'I am followed'), and the 3rd person plural active may be used in an impersonal sense in all languages.

11. Each language has many derived verbal species, formed mostly by suffixes. Here the overall correspondence is most striking. (Note that occasionally a species-suffix in one language will correspond to a tense-suffix in another.)

Suffix **-un**. Directional (towards speaker or principal person concerned)[3]

BARI	LOTUHO	TESO	MASAI	NANDI
'bɔk-ʊn (dig up)	**bɔx-ʊ** (dig up)	*a-boŋ-un(i)* (return here)	**rum-u** (push here)	*isup-u* (follow hither)
'bɔk-ʊn-dya				
'bɔk-wɛ' (pass.)				
(<**'bɔk**)	(<**bɔk**)	(<*boŋ*)	(<*rum*)	(<*isup*)

[1] Tonal research into the verbs of the other languages is still to be done.
[2] This is the nearest summary of Muratori's description, pp. 151–61.
[3] Spagnolo: 'linear movement'; Muratori: 'avvicinamento'.

BARI	LOTUHO	TESO	MASI	NANDI

Suffix **-ar-, -or-.** Directional (away from speaker or principal person)[1]

BARI	LOTUHO	TESO	MASI	NANDI
rem-oro (throw spear at) **rem-od-du** **rem-o-ji'** (pass.) (<**rem**)	**bwax-ara** (dig away)	*a-boŋ-or(i)* (return thither)	**a-rum-o** (push away) *suj-aa* (follow thither) *suj-ari*	**ɪsup-te** (follow thither)

Suffix **-kin.** Dative

BARI	LOTUHO	TESO	MASI	NANDI
ŋa-kɪn (open for or at) **ŋa-kɪn-dya** **ŋa-kɪ'** (pass.) (<**ŋa**)	**bwax-a-k** (dig for) **ŋa-xɪ** (open for)	*a-boŋ-o-kin(i)* (answer)	**duŋ-o-ki** (cut for) (<**duŋ**)	**ɪsup-ci** (*isup-cin, isup-jin* (follow for))

Suffix **-(r)i.** Instrumental[2]

BARI	LOTUHO	TESO	MASI	NANDI
dɛr-a-rɪ (be used for cooking) **dɛr-a-rɪ-kɪn** (<**dɛr**)	**bwax-a-rɪ** (dig with)		*yeŋ-ye* (use for skinning) (<*yeŋ*)	*eŋ-e* (use for skinning) *mwa-i* (talk about)

Further 'instrumental' suffixes in MASAI: *duŋ-iʃore* (cut with), *isuj-ye, isuj-are*, (wash with), *duŋ-iʃore-ki* (be used for cutting).

Suffix **-ta, -itu.** Continuative. (Tense suffix in MASAI)

BARI	LOTUHO	TESO	MASI	NANDI
kɪkɪta-tʊ (keep on working) (<**kɪta**)	**bɔx-ɪta** (dig continuously)	*ilip-itoi* (beg continuously)	**a-duŋ-ito** (I am digging) **a-iʃɪr-ɪta** (I am crying)	**am-ɪsɪe** (be in habit of eating) **mwɔg-se-i** (be in habit of shooting)

Suffix **-yo, -ju.** Continuative, frequentative

BARI	LOTUHO	TESO	MASI	NANDI
kɪkɪta-jʊ (keep on working)	**box-yo** (keep on digging) **bwax-a-tyo** (dig again and again)			

Suffix **-an, -on, -ar, -or.** Incohative

BARI	LOTUHO	TESO	MASI	NANDI
rɔny-an (become bad)	**dar-an** (become red)	**kwaŋ-un** (become white) **kwaŋ-ar** (become whiter)		*lalaŋ-it(u)* (become hot)

Suffix **-i-, -o-.** Impersonal quasi-passive

BARI	LOTUHO	TESO	MASI	NANDI
		duk-io (be built) (<*duk*)	*suj-i* (be followed)	*sup-ot, sup-ok* (be followed)

[1] Spagnolo: 'centrifugal-linear'; Muratori: 'allontanamento'.
[2] Hollis: 'applied'; McGough: 'prepositional'.

Suffix **-(k)e**. Reflexive, reciprocal

*isuj-e*¹ (bathe)   **tɪl-ke** (cut oneself)
   tɪl-ye (cut each other)

There is one important common derivative *prefix*:

Prefix **ɪ-ta-, i-to-**. Causative

to-rem (cause to stab) (stab each other)   **ɪta-duxyo** (get something built) (<duk)   *to-loma* (take out) (<*loma* = go out)   *ita-suj* (cause to follow)²   *i-lapat* (make run) (<*lapat*)

Note that Muratori gives the following for KARAMOJONG: (<**bɔk** = dig): **bɔk-ʊn, bɔk-ar, bɔk-a-kin**; **itu-duk** (<duk = build).

12. Verb tenses are few in number, the most outstanding being present (including future) and past. The following affixes are fairly general:

Suffix **-i** in NANDI and TESO—Present tense.
Prefix **a-** in BARI and TESO—Past or perfect tense.
Prefix **ka-** or **ko-** in BARI, NANDI, and TESO, to indicate that action took place at a specific time in the past. (In both NANDI and TESO this particle is more like a 'mood' than a 'tense' particle, as it may be used to expand both Present and past tense forms.)

The formidable number of 'tenses' given by Hollis for both MASAI and NANDI can be resolved to a great extent by regarding their initial elements as adverbial adjuncts attached to the main tense forms.

13. The negative particle, which precedes the verb, is **mam** in TESO, **ma** in MASAI and NANDI.³

14. Inflexion for person is affected by prefixes, which vary according to verb class, in all languages outside the BARI group; in most of them the subject pronoun may follow the verb optionally. Note the extended stem in the 2nd pers. pl.

	LOTUHO (beat)	TESO (build)	MASAI (follow)	NANDI (take)
I.	a-bak nɪ	a-dúk-í (ɛɔŋ)	a-suj (nanu)	a-nɔm-e
	ɪ-bak ie	i-dúk- (ijɔ)	i-suj (iye)	i-nɔme
	a-bak inyi	e-dúk-í (nes)	e-suj (ninye)	nɔm-e(-i)
	ɛ-bak xɔxɔi	(k)i-dúk-i (isɔ)	ki-suj (iyook)	ki-nɔm-e
	ɪ-bwax-áta itai	(i-)duk-éte (yes)	i-suj-usuju (ndae)	o-nɔm-e
	a-bax-ɪ isi	e-duk-éte (kes)	e-suj (ninje)	nɔm-e(-i)

¹ Note also **duŋ-a** (cut oneself); **duŋ-ara** (cut each other).
² But: *isuj-ye* (cause to wash).
³ LOTUHO **beŋ**, and the BARI infixes **-ti-** and **-ko-** have no apparent affinities elsewhere. BARI shows traces of the **m-** negative in **mɪŋɛ** (deaf), **mɔ'dɔkɛ** (dumb); cp. **yiŋ** (hear), **dak** (palate). Note also BARI **mó'dóké**, TESO **émúduk** (blind).

	LOTUHO (believe)	TESO (pray)	MASAI (buy)	NANDI (follow)
II.	eruk nɪ	elip-i (eoŋ)	á-ínyàŋ	a-sup-i
	iruk ie	ilip-i (ijo)	i-ínyàŋ	i-isup-i
	iruk inyi	ilip-i (nes)	e-ínyàŋ	isup-i
	eruk xɔxɔi	k-ilip-i (iso)	kí-ínyàŋ	ki-isup-i
	irux-ɔtɔ itai	ilip-ete (yes)	inyaŋ-úŋù	o-sup-i
	irux-i isi	ilip-ete (kes)	e-ínyàŋ	isup-i

BARI stands out from the rest in that the verb stem is uninflected for person, and the pronoun precedes it.

nân ... dó ... (nyé) ... yî ... tá ... sé rerém.
(I ... you ... he ... we ... you ... they stab it.)

15. The sentence order (except again in BARI) is typical:
Verb+ subject+object

LOTUHO: itadɔ naŋɔtɛ leitɔ. Bore the woman a child.
MASAI: *eok iŋgera kulle.* ⎫ Drink the children milk.
NANDI: **lue lakok cekɔ.** ⎭

In TESO this order occurs when the subject is pronominal, but not when it is a noun.

akúrikín ɛɔŋ papa-kà. Hoe I for my father.
abérú-ka erukokín toto-ká. My wife grinds for my mother.

In BARI the sentence order is as in Sudanic languages:
Subject+Verb+Object

nân dɛrjá súmutî. I cook fish.
narakwán nío dɛrjá súmutî. My wife cooks fish.

It should be noted that in TESO the subject prefix may vary (between *ka-* and *ki-*) according to the pronominal *object* (see Kitching, pp. 38–9). In MASAI the pronominal object merges with the pronominal subject to form a composite *prefix* (Hollis, pp. 48–9): *e-suj* (he follows him), *aa-suj* (he follows me), *ki-suj* (he follows thee). In NANDI the pronominal object is a suffix. Elsewhere the absolute pronoun is used as object.[1]

16. The possessor (nomen rectum) follows the possessed (nomen regens) in the genitive construction, and is joined to it by the relative particle, which shows gender and number in varying degrees.

	BARI (child of chief)	LOTUHO (child of chief)	TESO (child of chief)
m.	ŋurɔ lɔ matat	leito ɔlɔ xobu	esapat (lo)ka ejakait
f.	ŋurɔ na matat	neito ɔnɔ xobu	asapat (na)ka ejakait
pl.	ŋwajɪk ti matat	läduri xulɔ xobu	isapa (lu)ka ejakait
	(no fem. pl. in BARI)	näduri xunɔ xobu	asapa (nu)ka ejakait
			(thing of chief)
dim.			ibɔre (yeni)ka ejakait
pl.			ibɔro (lu)ka ejakait

[1] Note in TESO, however: **ki-ŋarakin-ai!** (Help me!)

	MASAI		NANDI
	(bone of boy)	(bone of child)	(child of the old man)
sg. m.+m.	*ol-oito lo l-ayoni*	m.+f. *ol-oito le ŋ-gerai*	sg. **lakwet** $_{nepɔ}^{ap}$ **poiyɔt**
pl. m.+m.	(*i*)*l-oik lo l-ayoni*	m.+f. (*i*)*l-oik le ŋ-gerai*	pl. **lakok** $_{cepɔ}^{ap}$ **poiyɔt**
	(thing of boy)	(thing of child)	
sg. f.+m.	*en-doki o l-ayoni*	f.+f. *en-doki e ŋ-gerai*	
pl. f.+m.	(*i*)*n-doki o l-ayoni*	f.+f. (*i*)*n-doki e ŋ-gerai*	

17. The adjective follows the noun it governs; many adjectives show gender by means of the relative particle, and number by means of suffixes.[1]

	BARI	LOTUHO	TESO
	(bad child)	(bad child)	(bad child)
sg. m.	ŋurɔ lɔ-rɔn	leito ɔl-ɔrɔxɔ	esapat le-rono
f.	ŋurɔ na-rɔn	neito ɔn-ɔrɔxɔ	asapat ne-rono
pl. m.	ŋwajık lɔ-rɔk	läduri xul-ɔrɔxɔji	isapa lue-rɔko
f.	ŋwajık na-rɔk	näduri xun-ɔrɔxɔji	asapa nue-rɔko
			(bad thing)
dim.			ibɔre yeni-rono
pl.			ibɔro lue-rɔko

	MASAI	NANDI
sg. m.	*oloiŋoni o-nyukye* (red bull)	sg. *lakwet ne ya* (bad child)
f.	*eŋgiteŋ na-nyukye* (red cow)	
pl. m.	*iloiŋok oo-nyokyo* (red bulls)	pl. *lakok ce yaac*
f.	*eŋgiʃu nee-nyokyo* (red cows)	

The most important points to be borne in mind in defining the Nilo-Hamitic languages are:

(1) a large common vocabulary of Nilotic stems;
(2) a large common vocabulary of non-Nilotic stems;[2]
(3) a large common vocabulary of Hamitic-like prefixes and suffixes.

In all these vocabularies laws of sound change are operative between groups.

It is not sufficient for the classification to rely on purely *grammatical* phenomena, for these are to be found throughout non-Bantu Africa, and in languages with no vocabulary correspondence whatever. For instance, a cursory glance at Meinhof's *Sprachen der Hamiten* (in which MASAI has been included) reveals:

(*a*) Grammatical gender is present in FUL, HAUSA, SHILH, BEDAUYE, SOMALI, and HOTTENTOT.

---

[1] In LOTUHO, TESO, and NANDI, verbs of quality ('verbi qualitativi') are used in a relative sense. These verbs, although they have characteristic plural forms, are nevertheless capable of full conjugation.

[2] See Muratori, *Grammatica Lotuxo*, p. 474, for detailed information on vocabulary correspondence between LOTUHO and KARAMOJONG, MASAI, BARI, SUK, and NANDI, and between BARI and KARAMOJONG, MASAI, SUK, and NANDI.

(b) The sentence order: verb+subj.+obj. is also found in SHILH.
(c) The Nilotic and Nilo-Hamitic word order in the genitive is found in FUL, HAUSA, SHILH, SOMALI, and is common to Bantu languages as well.
(d) All Meinhof's languages employ a host of plural and singular suffixes, which seem to hark back to some sort of class system, and the suffixes *-an*, *-in*, *-un* are even to be found in SOMALI, HAUSA, KHAMIR, and SHILH.

These common 'Hamitic' grammatical phenomena are useful, at a very elementary level, in assigning these languages to some larger and vaguer 'family', but, for the purpose of *classifying* the languages, must be regarded as secondary to the phenomenon of the amalgamation of two basic vocabularies, one Nilotic and the other not, but both revealing phonological laws of sound change, and both employing word-building particles of a characteristic sort.

NILO-HAMITIC WORD LIST

	BARI	LOTUHO	TESO	MASAI	(indef.)	NANDI (def.)
axe	tulu/tulwā	(n)atolu/ătuluo'	ayep/ayepe'	endolu	aiyua/aunoi	aiyuet/aunok
belly	pele'/pelya	nɔxe/nɔxyai	akoik	eŋgɔʃoye/ɪŋgɔʃua	mo/mootɪnwa	moiet/mootɪnwek
bird	kwen	(ŋ)axeŋ	wiɲy	ɔlmɔtɔɲy/ɪlmɔtɔɲyi	tarit¹/tarit	tarityet/taritɪk
blood	sg. kwenti	sg. (n)ăxenyi	sg. ekwenyɪt			
	rima	nɔtɔ/naxɔt	awokot	ɔsarge/ɪsargeta	kɔrɔtɔ/kɔrɔti	kɔrɔtiot/kɔrɔtik
	sg. rɪmatat					
cow	kɪteŋ/kɪsʊk	neteŋ/nesuŋ	a(k)iteŋ/aituk	eŋgɪteŋ/ɪŋgɪʃu	taɲy/tic	teta/tuka
dog	'dioŋ'/dioɲin	ŋepok/(ŋ)apɔxe'	e(k)iŋok/iŋokwo'	oldia/ildiain	ŋɔk/ŋɔɔk	ŋɔɔkɪt/ŋɔɔkɪk
ear	swāt/swatan	(n)eyok/(n)ayăxā	akit/aki'	eŋgiyok/ɪŋgiyaa	iit/iitɪn	iitɪt/iitɪk
egg	katolok	(n)atel	ɑbeet (Ar.)	imɔsor		
	sg. katulukuti			sg. emosori		
elephant	tɔme/tɔmya	sg. (n)ătelyo'	etom/itomi	ɔltome/ɪltomia	pelio/pel	pelot/pelek
eye	koɲe/koɲyen	atome/ătomye	akoɲu/akoɲyɪs	eŋgɔɲʊ/ɪŋgɔɲyek	koŋ/koɲyan	konda/koɲyek
fire	kɪmaŋ/kɪmaŋjɪn	ŋoɲyek/ŋɔpide'	akim/akimia	eŋgima/ɪŋgimaite	maa/mɔɔstɪnwa	maat/mɔɔstɪnwek
foot	mokot/mokosi'	neema'/amatɪ	akeju/akejen	eŋgeju/ɪŋgejek	kel/kelten	keldo/keltek
goat	kɪne'/yidin	neiɲu/ɲejek	a(k)ine/a(k)inei	eŋgine/ɪŋgineji	ara/no	artet/neko
hair	kāpir	nofir	ɪtɪm	ɪlpapit	sume	sumeyet
hand	sg. kāpirāt	sg. nofɪtti	sg. etimat	sg. ɔlpapita		
	kānin/kānisi'	naani/naxas	akan/akanin	eŋgaina/ɪŋgaɪk	sg. sumeyɔ	sumeyot
head	kwe/kusɪk	naxou/nosi'	akou/akwes	elluyunya/illuyuny	e/eun	eut/eunek
honey, bee	sɪwa	neesyo/-jin	esɪke	enaiʃɔ/inaiʃi	met/metoa	metɪt/metoek
		awɔtɔrɔ (bees)	awu'/awak²		kumɪa/kumɪn	kumɪat/kumɪk
hut	sg. sɪwatat	naaji/nasik	akai/akais	eŋgaji/ɪŋgajɪjɪk	kɔ/kɔrɪn	kɔt/kɔrɪk
knife	kadi/kadijɪk	nademi	ekileŋ/ikileŋa	eŋgalem/ɪŋgalema	rɔtwa/rɔtɔi	rɔtwet/rɔtok
leopard	wale/walya	(l)ăworu/ăworuxo	eris/erisai'	ɔlowaru keri/ɪlɔwa- rak kerin	melɪlɔ/melɪlwa	melɪldɔ/melɪlwek
	kɔka/kɔkajin					
meat	lokore/lokoryo	neriŋo/năxɪrɪ	akɪrɪŋ	eŋgɪrɪn/ɪŋgɪri	peɲy/paɲy	pendɔ/paɲyek
milk	le	(n)ale'	akile	kulle	ce	ceko
	sg. letat				sg. ceɪyɔ	sg. ceɪyot
moon	yapa/yapajɪn	(n)ayafa/ayafajɪn	elap/ɪlapyo'	ɔlapa/ɪlapatɪɪn	arawa/araa	arawet/arawek
mouth	kutʊk/kutusen	neetʊk/netuxe	a(k)ɪtuk/a(k)ɪtukwa	eŋgutʊk/ɪŋgutʊkye	kʊt/kʊtʊswa	kʊtɪt/kʊtʊswek
nose	kume/kumejɪn	nemo/amɔse	ekume/ikumes	eŋgumi/ɪŋgumɪʃi(n)	ser/serun	serut/serunek
spear	gor/goro	nafere/nafɛrɪk	akwara/akwaras	eremet³/ɪremeta	ŋɔt/ŋɔtwa	ŋɔtɪt/ŋɔtwek
sun	kɔloŋ/kɔloŋan	ŋɔoloŋ/ɔpitek	akoloŋ	eŋgɔloŋ/ɪŋgɔloŋi	asɪs/asɪswa	asɪsta/asɪswek
tongue	ŋedep/ŋedepa	(n)aŋădyef/ăŋădyefɑ̄	aŋejep/aŋejepa	ɔlŋejep/ɪlŋejepa	ŋelyep/ŋelyepwa	ŋelyepta/ŋelyepwek
tooth	kele/kaɪa	nalai/naala	ekelai/ikela	ɔlalai/ɪlala	kelda/kelat	keldet/kelek
tree	kādini/kaden	(n)ăyăni/ăyănio'	ekitoi/ikito	ɔljani/ɪlkak	ket/ket	ketɪt/ketɪk
water	pioŋ	naari/narya	akipi	eŋgare/ɪŋgarɪak	pei	pek
	sg. pioŋtot				sg. peɪyɔ	peɪyot
	cf. kare/karya (river)					

¹ Cf. MASAI: endarrtikɪ/indarrtik (small bird).
² Cf. MASAI: il-otorok, NANDI: segem (bees). The BARI word sɪ-wa would seem to have a compound stem.
³ Cf. BARI: rem (to stab with a spear).

BIBLIOGRAPHY

Abbreviations of titles of Periodicals used in this Bibliography.

In general, abbreviations used are in accordance with the International Code, with the exception of the following:
M.S.O.S. Mitteilungen des Seminars für orientalische Sprachen (Berlin).
B.S.O.S. Bulletin of the School of Oriental Studies.

GENERAL

CONTI ROSSINI, CARLO. Lingue nilotiche. Riv. Studi Orient. **11**, 1926, pp. 69–168.
   Using the term 'Nilotic' in a wider sense than that used in this Outline, the author deals with the 'Ciòl family' (Shilluk, Anuak, Acoli, Alur, Lango, 'Cavirondo (Gia-luo)'); Dinka; Nuer; also Bari, Masai, Turkana, Nandi, and Suk; also Kunama and Mekan.
CZEKANOWSKI, JAN. 1924. Forschungen im Nil–Kongo Zwischengebiet. 2 vols. Wissenschaftliche Ergebnisse der Deutschen Zentral-Afrika Expedition 1907–8, vol. 6, parts 1 and 2. Leipzig.
   Vol. 2 contains the following vocabularies: pp. 686–700 Kakwa; pp. 707–11 'Lur', 'Nyifwa' and a few words of Dinka; pp. 712–14 'Fadjulu', 'Latuka', Bari.
DREXEL, A. Gliederung der afrikanischen Sprachen. Anthropos, **16/17**, 1921–2; **18/19**, 1923–4; **20**, 1925.
   Vol. 20, pp. 232–43, Die nilotischen Sprachen, includes comparative vocabularies of Shilluk, Dinka; Bari, Masai, Nandi, Suk.
JOHNSTON, SIR H. H. 1904. The Uganda Protectorate. 2 vols. London: Hutchinson & Co.
   Vol. 2, pp. 903 ff., comparative vocabularies, including Acoli, Ja-luo, Lango, Alur; Turkana, Suk, 'Karamojo', 'S. Karamojo', 'Elgumi', Masai, 'Ngishu', Bari, Nandi, Kamasia, Dorobo.
KERKEN, G. VAN DER. Notes sur les Mangbetu. Antwerp: Univ. Colon. Belge.
   Comparative vocabularies include Shilluk, Alur, 'Bahari' (Bari), Kakwa, Lotuho.
MURRAY, G. W. The Nilotic languages. A comparative survey. J. R. Anthrop. Inst. **50**, 1920, pp. 329–68.
   An attempt to prove the common ancestry of Nubian, Bari, Masai, and Shilluk.
SHAW, A. A note on some Nilotic languages. Man, **24**, 16, 1924.
THOMAS, N. W. A note on the Nilotic languages by G. W. Murray. Man, **21**, 69, 1921.
   A criticism of the article by Murray.
TUCKER, A. N. De unificatie der zuidnilotische talen. Kongo-overzee, **12/13**, 5, 1946–7.

NILOTIC LANGUAGES

DINKA

BELTRAME, G. 1870. Grammatica della lingua denka.
—— Grammatica e vocabolario della lingua denka. Mem. Soc. geogr. ital. **3**, 1880. Pp. 283. Rome: Civelli.
—— 1881. Il fiume bianco e i Denka. Verona.
   Pp. 66–71, Raffronti della lingua dei Denka con quella dei Sciluk.
—— Cenni sui Denka e la loro lingua. Riv. Orient. 8, pp. 17 ff.
BRUN-ROLLET, ——. Vokabularien der Dinka-, Nuehr- und Schilluk-Sprachen. Petermanns Mitt. Ergänzungsheft, **7**, pp. 25–30. Gotha, 1862.
CASATI, G. 1891. Dieci anni in Equatoria. Milano.
   Vol. 1, pp. 316–21, Tavola comparativa delle lingue degli Dinca . . . Bari e Lur.
CONTI ROSSINI, CARLO. Lingue nilotiche. See under GENERAL.
CUMMINS, S. L., and TÜRSTIG, R. [vocabularies of Dinka] In: GLEICHEN, COUNT A. E. W. 1905. The Anglo-Egyptian Sudan, vol. 1.
CZEKANOWSKI, JAN. Forschungen im Nil–Kongo Zwischengebiet. See under GENERAL.

DREXEL, A. Gliederung der afrikanischen Sprachen. *See under* GENERAL.
KAUFMAN, A. 1862. Schilderungen aus Central-Afrika. Brixen: Weger.
Pp. 95–100, Notizen über die Sprache der Dinka.
MITTERUTZNER, J. C. 1866. Die Dinka Sprache in Zentral Afrika.
Pp. 307. Brixen: Weger.
MÜLLER, F. 1877–8. Grundriss der Sprachwissenschaft. 4 vols. Wien: Hölder.
Vol. 1, section 2, pp. 48–58, Die Sprache der Dinka; pp. 81–4, Die Verwandtschaftsverhältnisse des Dinka und Bari.
MURATORI, C. Grammatica Lotuxo. *See under* LOTUHO.
Comparative vocabularies include Dinka.
NEBEL, A. [about 1931] [Dinka–English conversation] Wau, A. E. Sudan (duplicated).
—— 1936. Dinka dictionary with abridged grammar. Pp. 171. Verona: Missioni Africane.
—— 1948. [Dinka Grammar.]
NEBEL, A., and TUCKER, A. N. [1932]. Dinka Grammar (cyclostyled).
RÜPPELL, E. 1829. Reisen in Nubien, Kordofan und dem peträischen Arabien. Frankfurt-a-M.: Wilmans.
Pp. 370–3, Vokabularien von sieben Nuba-Sprachen . . ., including 'Dynke' and 'Schilluk'.
SCHUCHARDT, H. Bari und Dinka. Wiener Z. Kde. Morgenland. **26**, 1912, pp. 11–41.
SCHWEINFURTH, G. 1873. Linguistische Ergebnisse einer Reise nach Centralafrika. Pp. 82. Berlin (Z. Eing.-Spr. Supplement).
Pp. 79–82, vocabulary of Dinka.
SHAW, A. Dinka animal stories (Bor dialect). Sudan Notes, **2**, 2, 1919, pp. 255–75.
With translation.
STANLEY, SIR H. M. 1890. In darkest Africa. London.
Vol. 2, pp. 436–9, vocabulary of Dinka.
TRUDINGER, R. 1942, 1944. English–Dinka dictionary. 2 parts. Sudan United Mission (duplicated).
A dictionary of the Dongjol dialect, following the rules for orthography and word-division advocated by Dr. Tucker.
TUCKER, A. N. [1939.] Rules for Dinka spelling and word-division. Pp. 50 (cyclostyled).
WESTERMANN, D. Short vocabularies of the Dinka, Gọ̄lọ (Golo) and Zande languages, M.S.O.S. **15**, 3, 1912, pp. 151–4.
WESTERMANN, D., and WARD, I. C. 1933. Practical phonetics for students of African languages. Pp. xvi+227. Oxford University Press for International Institute of African Languages and Cultures.
Pp. 207–13, phonetic summary of Dinka (Rek dialect).
WILSON, H. H. 1906. English–Dinka vocabulary. . . . Khartoum.

Unpublished

TRUDINGER, R. Dictionary of Padang Dinka. A few copies duplicated.
Comprehensive and full of examples, with tones marked.

NUER

ANON. 1946. Simple English–Nuer phrases for beginners. Pp. 42. Bussere Press, Mill Hill Fathers.
In Thiang dialect.
BRUN-ROLLET, —. Vokabularien der Dinka-, Nuehr- und Schilluk-Sprachen. *See under* DINKA.
CONTI ROSSINI, CARLO. Lingue nilotiche. *See under* GENERAL.
CRAZZOLARA, J. P. 1933. Outlines of a Nuer grammar. Pp. 218+xii. Wien: Anthropos Bibliotek **13**.
'A very careful and thorough exposition of Nuer, illustrated by copious examples' (Tucker). Reviewed by Tucker (Africa, 1934), Doke (Bantu Studies, 1934), Meinhof (Z. Eing.-Spr., 1933–4). In Jikany (Western dialect); now being used with modifications made by Fr. Kiggen.

HUFFMAN, RAY. 1929. Nuer–English dictionary. Pp. 63. Berlin: Dietrich Reimer.
  A useful little book, in spite of some defects and omissions. Reviewed by Driberg (Africa, 1931), Evans-Pritchard (Sudan Notes, 1929), Klingenheben (Z. Eing.-Spr., 1929–30).
—— 1931. English–Nuer dictionary. Pp. viii+80. Oxford University Press.
  Marred by several errors and inexactitudes, and the introduction of foreign words. Reviewed by Driberg (Africa, 1931), Doke (Bantu Studies, 1931), Klingenheben (Z. Eing.-Spr.,1931–2).
—— 1931. The human body. Book 1, parts 1/2, Some Nuer terms in relation to the human body. Pp. 79. Nasser: American Mission.
  A dictionary of Nuer anatomical, physiological, psychological, and pathological terms. Contains also interesting accounts of native customs. Reviewed by Evans-Pritchard (Sudan Notes, 1925).
KIGGEN, J. 1948. Nuer-English dictionary.
  In Thiang dialect.
MARNO, E. 1874. Reisen im Gebiete des blauen und weissen Nil. . . . Wien: Gerold.
  Pp. 481–95, Kleine Vokabularien der Fungi-, Tabi-, Bertat- und Nuehr-Sprache.
STIGAND, C. H. 1923. A Nuer–English vocabulary. Pp. 39. Cambridge University Press.
  Reviewed by E. W. Smith (J. Afr. Soc., 1925).
WESTERMANN, D. The Nuer language. An outline grammar. M.S.O.S. **15**, 3, 1912, pp. 84–141.
WESTERMANN, D., and WARD, I. C. Practical phonetics. . . . *See under* DINKA.
  Pp. 202–7, phonetic summary of Nuer ('Eastern Dialect').

LWO LANGUAGE GROUP

SHILLUK

ADELUNG, J. C., and VATER, J. S. 1812. Mithridates. Berlin: Voss.
  Vol. 3, section 1, pp. 237–8, Sprachproben der Schilluk-Sprache nach handschriftlichen Nachrichten von Dr. Seetzen.
BELTRAME, G. Il fiume bianco e i Denka. *See under* DINKA.
BRUN-ROLLET, ——. Vokabularien der Dinka-, Nuehr- und Schilluk-Sprachen. *See under* DINKA.
CONTI ROSSINI, C. Lingue nilotiche. *See under* GENERAL.
DREXEL, A. Gliederung der afrikanischen Sprachen. *See under* GENERAL.
EVANS-PRITCHARD, E. E. The Mberidi (Shilluk group) and the Mbegumba (Basiri group) of the Bahr-el-Ghazal. Sudan Notes, **14**, 1, 1931, pp. 15–48.
  Contains vocabularies of Shilluk, Lwo, 'Mberidi' (Bor), and other languages.
HEASTY, J. A. Shilluk dictionary (multigraphed).
KERKEN, G. VAN DER. Notes sur les Mangbetu. *See under* GENERAL.
KOHNEN, B. 1923. [Shilluk–German dictionary.] Khartoum.
—— 1931. Grammatica della lingua Scilluk con l'aggiunta di un piccolo dizionario italiano-scilluk. Pp. 201. Cairo: Missioni dell' Africa Centrale.
  Reviewed by Tucker (Africa, 1934).
—— 1933. Shilluk grammar with a little English–Shilluk dictionary. Pp. xvi+317. Verona: Missioni Africane.
  A translation of the preceding.
LATHAM, R. G. 1862. Elements of comparative philology. London: Walter & Maberly.
  Pp. 550 ff. deal with Shilluk.
LEHR , J. Die sprachliche Stellung des Schilluk. Bibliotheka Africana, **1**, 1, 1924, pp. 18–26; **2**, 1, 1926, pp. 235–8.
MÜLLER, F. Grundriss der Sprachwissenschaft. *See under* DINKA.
  Vol. 4, pp. 54–9, Die Sprache der Schilluk.
MURATORI, C. Grammatica Lotuxo. *See under* LOTUHO.
  Comparative vocabularies include Shilluk.
RÜPPELL, E. Reisen in Nubien, Kordofan und dem petraïschen Arabien. *See under* DINKA.

VATER, J. S. 1816. Proben deutscher Volksmundarten. Leipzig.
  Pp. 306–7, Dr. Seetzens linguistischer Nachlass. Wörtersammlungen aus Nordostafrikanischen Sprachen . . ., includes 'Schülluk'.
WAKEFIELD, T. Native routes through the Masai country. Proc. R. Geogr. Soc. **4**, 1882, pp. 742–4.
  Contains examples of the 'Kavirondo', 'Yambo' (Anuak), and Shilluk languages.
WESTERMANN, D. 1911. Short grammar of the Shilluk language. Pp. v+76. Philadelphia: Board of Foreign Missions of the United Presbyterian Church of N. A.; Berlin: Reimer.
—— 1912. The Shilluk people, their language and folk-lore. Pp. lxiii+312. Philadelphia: Board of Foreign Missions of the United Presbyterian Church of N. A.; Berlin: Reimer.

ANUAK

CONTI ROSSINI, C. Lingue nilotiche. See under GENERAL.
MEINHOF, CARL. Sprachstudien im egyptischen Sudan. 26. Anywak. Z. Kolon. Spr. **8**, 1917–18, pp. 50–63.
WAKEFIELD, T. Native routes through the Masai country. See under SHILLUK.
WESTERMANN, D. Some notes and a short vocabulary of the Anywak language. M.S.O.S. **15**, 3, 1912, pp. 142–50.

Unpublished

HUFFMAN, RAY. English-Anuak vocabulary (pp. 50, cyclostyled).
TUNNICLIFFE, E. C. Anuak Dictionary (pp. 100, typed MS.).

ACOLI

ANON. The Acholi–English handbook. Pp. 64. Gulu: Verona Fathers' Mission.
BAKER, SIR SAMUEL. 1866. The Albert Nyanza. 2 vols.
  Vol. 1, p. 297, vocabulary of a few words of 'Obbo' (Acoli), Bari, and 'Latooka'.
CONTI ROSSINI, C. Lingue nilotiche. See under GENERAL.
CRÁZZOLARA, J. P. 1938. A study of the Acoli language. Pp. xv+426. Oxford University Press for International Institute of African Languages and Cultures.
  By far the most accurate and comprehensive study that has yet been published on Acoli. The very narrow system of phonetic notation employed ensures accuracy, but is overcomplicated for practical use. Reviewed by Tucker (Africa, 1939).
EMIN PASHA. Wörterverzeichnisse afrikanischer Sprachen. Z. Ethnol. **14**, 1882.
  Pp. 163–9, 'Shuli'.
HOMBURGER, L. Le genre sexuel dans le sous-groupe choli-shillouk des langues nilotiques. XVIe Congr. Int. Anthrop. Bruxelles, 1935.
  A comparison of gender in 'Choli', Masai, and Teso, with references to Shilluk.
JOHNSTON, SIR H. H. The Uganda Protectorate. See under GENERAL.
KITCHING, A. L. 1907. Outline grammar of the Gang language. Pp. 96. London: S.P.C.K.
—— 1932. Outline grammar of the Acholi language. Pp. 95. London: Sheldon Press.
  A revised edition of the preceding.
MURATORI, C. Grammatica Lotuxo. See under LOTUHO.
  Comparative vocabularies include Acoli.

Unpublished

LAW-RYAN, FR. Grammar of Acoli.
MALANDRA, Fr. Grammar of Acoli.
MURATORI, C. Comparative dictionary: English–Bari–Lotuho–Acoli (nearly completed).

LANGO

CONTI ROSSINI, C. Lingue nilotiche. See under GENERAL.
COX, T. R. F. Lango proverbs. Bull. Uganda Soc. **51**, 1945, pp. 21–9.
  With translation.
—— Lango proverbs. Uganda J. **10**, 2, 1946, pp. 113–23.

DRIBERG, J. H. 1923. The Lango, a Nilotic tribe of Uganda. Pp. 468. London: T. Fisher Unwin.
    The second part of the book deals with language: grammar, vocabulary, fables with translation.
JOHNSTON, SIR H. H. The Uganda Protectorate. *See under* GENERAL.

ALUR

CASATI, G. Dieci anni in Equatoria. *See under* DINKA.
CONTI ROSSINI, C. Lingue nilotiche. *See under* GENERAL.
CZEKANOWSKI, J. Forschungen im Nil–Kongo Zwischengebiet. *See under* GENERAL.
EMIN PASHA. Wörterverzeichnisse afrikanischer Sprachen. Z. Ethnol. **14**, 1882.
    Includes a vocabulary of 'Madi'.
JOHNSTON, SIR H. H. The Uganda Protectorate. *See under* GENERAL.
KERKEN, G. VAN DER. Notes sur les Mangbetu. *See under* GENERAL.
LIESENBORGHS, O. Enkele Nota's over de Bale en Banioro van Belgisch Kongo. Kongo-Overzee, **1**, 4, 1935, pp. 205–18.
    Contains a short vocabulary of Alur for comparison with Lendu, &c.
VANNESTE, M. Regels der welluidendheid in de Alur-taal (Mahagi). Congo, **2**, 1, 1925, pp. 49 ff.
—— De getallen in de Alur-taal. Congo, **2**, 5, 1934, pp. 692–700.
—— 1940. Woordenboek van de Alur-Taal. Mahagi (Belgisch Congo). Pp. [438]. Boechout: Seminarie der Witte Paters (duplic.).
    An extensive Alur–Dutch dictionary. Unfortunately the author does not employ the orthography already recognized in other Nilotic languages. Reviewed by Tucker (Africa, 1946).
—— Vergelijking van een paar Alur-woorden met de taal der Farao's. Kongo-Overzee, **9**, 1943, pp. 160–5.

Unpublished
RINGE, P. C. Grammar of Alur.

LUO (Nilotic Kavirondo)

ANON. 1910. Elementary grammar of the Nilotic Kavirondo language (Dhö Lwo). London: Fathers of St. Joseph's Missionary Society, Mill Hill.
BAUMANN, O. 1894. Durch Massailand zur Nilquelle. Pp. 386. Berlin: Reimer.
    Pp. 364 ff., vocabularies of Masai, Tatoga (Kitaturu [*sic*]), Kavirondo, 'Ndorobbo', and other languages.
CONTI ROSSINI, C. Lingue nilotiche. *See under* GENERAL.
HOBLEY, C. W. 1902. Eastern Uganda. An ethnological survey. Pp. 95. London: Anthrop. Inst. Occasional papers No. 1.
    Contains vocabularies of 'Nilotic Kavirondo (Nife)', Nandi, Elgumi, 'Eldorobo', and some Bantu languages.
JOHNSTON, SIR H. H. The Uganda Protectorate. *See under* GENERAL.
MACDONALD, J. R. L. Notes on the ethnology of tribes met with during progress of the Juba expedition of 1897–98. J. R. Anthrop. Inst. **29**, 1899.
    Contains vocabularies of 'Wanyifa', Masai, 'Latuka', 'Karamojo', Suk, Nandi, 'Wanderobo', 'Save'.
RAVENSTEIN, —. Vocabularies from Kavirondo, British East Africa. Collected by Mr. C. W. Hobley, F.R.G.S. J. R. Anthrop. Inst. **28**, 1899, pp. 338–42.
    Vocabularies of 'Nife', Elgume, Nandi, Lako, and Bantu languages.
WAKEFIELD, T. Native routes through the Masai country. *See under* SHILLUK.

OTHER LANGUAGES

EVANS-PRITCHARD, E. E. The Mberidi (Shilluk group) and the Mbegumba (Basiri group) of the Bahr-el-Ghazal. *See under* SHILLUK.

EVANS-PRITCHARD, E. E. Ethnological observations in Dar Fung. Sudan Notes, **15**, 1, 1932, pp. 1–61.
  Contains vocabularies of Burun languages or dialects: 'Ulu, Southern Burun, Jumjum, Mughaja, Maiak, Kurmuk, Ragreig', as well as other languages.
GHAWI, J. B. 1925. First steps in Jur. Pp. 42. Khartoum (cyclostyled).
PETHERICK, J. and MRS. 1869. Travels in Central Africa. London.
  Contains a few words of 'Baer', i.e. Jur (Lwo).
SANTANDREA, S. The Belanda, Ndogo, Bai and Sere in the Bahr-el-Ghazal. Sudan Notes, **16**, 2, 1933, pp. 161–79.
  Pp. 171 ff. consist of linguistic notes, mainly on languages of the Ndogo Group, but with references to Bor.
—— Shilluk tribes in the Bahr-el-Ghazal. Anthropos, **37/40**, fasc. 1–3, 1942–5, pp. 225–40.
  Appendix on 'The Luo dialects in the Bahr-el-Ghazal': Jur-Lwo, Bor.
—— 1946. Grammatichetta Giur. Pp. xiv+142. Roma: Italica Gens; Verona: Missioni Africane.
SCHWEINFURTH, G. Linguistische Ergebnisse. . . . See under DINKA.
  Pp. 61–72, vocabulary of 'Djur'.
STRUCK, B. An unlocated tribe on the White Nile. J. Afr. Soc., **8**, 1908, pp. 75–8.
  The author quotes the 'Baer' vocabulary given by Petherick (*see above*) and points out that it is Jur (Lwo).

Unpublished

NALDER, L. F. Short vocabularies of 'Barun', Gura (i.e. Maban), Ragreig.
REIDHEAD, PARIS W. 1946. Report of linguistic survey among tribes Berta, Ingassana, Koma, Uduk, Jum Jum, Maban. (Vocabularies, in phonetic script.)
STEVENSON, R. C. Vocabulary of Maban in phonetic script.

NILO-HAMITIC LANGUAGES

BARI LANGUAGE GROUP

BAKER, SIR SAMUEL. The Albert Nyanza. See under ACOLI.
BEATON, A. C. Bari studies. Sudan Notes, **15**, 1, 1932, pp. 63–95.
  Songs, with translation.
—— Some Bari songs. Sudan Notes, **18**, 2, 1935, pp. 277–87; **19**, 2, 1936, pp. 327–44.
CASATI, G. Dieci anni in Equatoria. See under DINKA.
CONTI ROSSINI, C. Lingue nilotiche. See under GENERAL.
COOKE, R. C. 1940. Bari–English conversation. Pp. 43. Lalyo: Southern Education Office (duplicated).
CZEKANOWSKI, J. Forschungen im Nil–Kongo Zwischengebiet. See under GENERAL.
DREXEL, A. Gliederung der afrikanischen Sprachen. See under GENERAL.
HILLELSON, S. The Nyangbara language. Sudan Notes, **5**, 1922.
JOHNSTON, SIR H. H. The Uganda Protectorate. See under GENERAL.
KAUFMANN, A. Schilderungen aus Central-Afrika. See under DINKA.
  Pp. 156–63, Beiträge zur Erforschung der Bari-Sprache.
KERKEN, G. VAN DER. Notes sur les Mangbetu. See under GENERAL.
MELDON, J. A. The Latuka and Bari languages. J. Afr. Soc. **9**, 1910, pp. 193–5.
  A short vocabulary of Bari, and numerals in Lotuho.
MITTERUTZNER, J. C. 1867. Die Sprache der Bari. Grammatik, Text und Wörterbuch. Pp. 262. Brixen.
  Appendix also contains 'Kleines Vokabular der Sprache der Nyang-Bara' by Morlang.
—— Likikiri-lo-kija kua i jur lo Bari. Thiermärchen im Lande der Bari (Central-Afrika). Original-Text mit Übersetzung und sprachlicher Analyse. Z. dtsch. morgenländ. Ges. 1867.

MÜLLER, F. Bari-Text mit Anmerkungen. Z. Völkerpsychol. u. Sprachwiss. **2**, 2, 1861.
—— 1864. Die Sprache der Bari. Grammatik, Lesestücke und Glossar. Pp. 84. Wien: Gerold.
—— Grundriss der Sprachwissenschaft. *See under* DINKA.
 Vol. 1, section 2, pp. 59–80, Die Sprache der Bari; pp. 81–4, Die Verwandtschaftsverhältnisse des Dinka und Bari; vol. 3, section 1, pp. 95–8, Über die Beziehungen der Sprache der Il-Oigob zur Sprache der Bari.
MURATORI, C. Grammatica Lotuxo. *See under* LOTUHO.
 Contains a fable in Bari (from Spagnolo) and a grammatical and phonetic comparison of Bari and Lotuho.
MURRAY, G. W. The Nilotic languages. *See under* GENERAL.
—— The Nubian and Bari languages compared. Sudan Notes, **3**, 1920, pp. 260–70.
OWEN, R. C. R. 1908. Bari grammar and vocabulary. Pp. 164. London: Bumpus.
 A verbatim translation of Mitterutzner's book.
PHILIP, SGT. 1938. Kakwa–English conversation. Lalyo: Southern Education Office (duplicated).
PLAS, V. H. VAN DEN. 1910. Les Kuku. Pp. xliii+407. Collections de monographies ethnographiques, ed. by Van Overbergh, **4**. Bruxelles: Bureau de Document. Ethnogr. du Congo Belge.
 Pp. 301–8, vocabulary of Kuku. Reviewed by J. W. Crowfoot (Sudan Notes, 1919).
RAGLAN, LORD. Some roots common to the Turkana, Lotuko and Bari languages. B.S.O.S. **4**, 2, 1926, pp. 427–8.
SCHUCHARDT, H. Bari und Dinka. *See under* DINKA.
SPAGNOLO, L. M. 1933. Bari grammar. Pp. xxvii+452. Verona: Missioni Africane.
 Reviewed by Whitehead (Africa, 1933), Beaton (Sudan Notes, 1934).
—— 1942. Bari-English-Italian dictionary. Pp. 258. Lalyo: Southern Education Office (duplicated).

Unpublished

MURATORI, C. Comparative dictionary of Bari–Lotuho–Acoli (nearly completed).

LOTUHO LANGUAGE GROUP

ARBER, H. A. 1936. A simple Lotuko grammar and Lotuko vocabulary (duplicated).
BAKER, SIR SAMUEL. The Albert Nyanza. *See under* ACOLI.
CZEKANOWSKI, J. Forschungen im Nil–Kongo Zwischengebiet. *See under* GENERAL.
DRIBERG, J. H. Lotuko dialects. Amer. Anthrop. **34**, 4, 1932, pp. 601–9.
 Deals with Lotuho, Lopit, Lerya, Owe, Dongotono, Lokathan, and Turkana; also Nyangiya[1]).
EMIN PASHA. Wörterverzeichnisse afrikanischer Sprachen. Z. Ethnol. **14**, 1882. Pp. 174–8, 'Lattuka'.
KERKEN, G. VAN DER. Notes sur les Mangbetu. *See under* GENERAL.
MACDONALD, J. R. L. Notes on the ethnology of tribes.... *See under* LUO.
MELDON, J. A. The Latuka and Bari languages. *See under* BARI.
MURATORI, C. 1938. Grammatica Lotuxo. Pp. xxx+498. Verona: Missioni Africane.
 A sound and reliable work. Includes (pp. 471–96) fables in 'Loppit, Lɔkɔya Telegu (Loyirya)', Bari (from Spagnolo), 'Lotuxo, Topossa, Laŋo, Lɔkɔya (Lowoi), Dɔŋɔtɔnɔ, Lɔrwama', and comparative vocabularies of the above and of 'Karimojoŋ', Masai, Turkana, Nandi, Suk, 'Denka, Scilluk', Acoli; also grammatical and phonetic comparisons of Lotuho with Bari, Karamojong, and Masai.
RAGLAN, LORD. The Lotuko language. B.S.O.S. **2**, 2, 1921, pp. 267–96.
—— Some roots common to the Turkana, Lotuko and Bari languages. *See under* BARI.

[1] This 'Nyangiya' is not Nilo-Hamitic. See p. 32.

WAYLAND, E. J. Preliminary studies of the tribes of Karamoja. J. R. Anthrop. Inst. **41**, 1931, pp. 187–230.
    Contains short vocabularies of Labwor, Lango, Karamojong, 'Dorobo'[1]).
WESTERMANN, D. Das Oxoriok. Eine sprachliche Skizze. Nach Aufnahmen von A. C. Beaton bearbeitet von D. Westermann. Afrika, **33**, 1, 1944, pp. 19–46.

Unpublished

MURATORI, C. Comparative dictionary of Bari–Lotuho–Acoli (nearly completed).

TESO LANGUAGE GROUP

ANON. Akarimojong–Swahili–English vocabulary. Pp. 31. Uganda Bookshop Press.
BARTON, J. Turkana grammatical notes and vocabulary. B.S.O.S. **2**, 1921, pp. 43–73.
CONTI ROSSINI, C. Lingue nilotiche. *See under* GENERAL.
DRIBERG, J. H. Lotuko dialects. *See under* LOTUHO.
HALL, C. R. English–Teso vocabulary. Pp. 41. Portsmouth: Charpentier.
HOMBURGER, L. Le genre sexuel dans le sous-groupe choli-shillouk. . . . *See under* ACOLI.
—— Le peul et les langues nilotiques. Bull. Soc. Ling. Paris, **37**, fasc. 1, 1936, pp. 58–72.
    A comparison of 'Massaï' and Teso with 'Peul'.
HULLEY, D. M. 1923. Vocabulary and grammar for use in Turkana, Karamoja and Toposa. Pp. 50. Kampala.
JOHNSTON, SIR H. H. The Uganda Protectorate. *See under* GENERAL.
KIGGEN, J. Grammar of Teso. Pp. 120. Ngora: Mill Hill Mission.
KITCHING, A. L. [1915?] Handbook of the Ateso language. Pp. 144. London: S.P.C.K.
MACDONALD, J. R. L. Notes on the ethnology of tribes. . . . *See under* SHILLUK.
MURATORI, C. Grammatica Lotuxo. *See under* LOTUHO.
RAGLAN, LORD. Some roots common to the Turkana, Lotuko and Bari languages. *See under* BARI.
TRENTO, GABRIELE DA. Vocaboli in lingue dell' Etiopia meridionale. Rass. Studi Etiopici, **1**, 2, 1941, pp. 203–7.
    Includes a vocabulary of 'Turcana (Bume)'.
WAYLAND, E. J. Preliminary studies of the tribes of Karamoja. *See under* LOTUHO.

Unpublished

ANON. Vocabulary of a few words of Jiye and Nyangatom.
HENRIKSEN, FR. Grammar of Teso.
McGOUGH, FR. Grammar of Teso.
WILD, J. C. Vocabulary of a few words and sentences of Orom (Rom).
WILSON, DR. Dictionary of Teso (in preparation).

MASAI LANGUAGE GROUP

BAUMANN, O. Durch Massailand zur Nilquelle. *See under* LUO.
CONTI ROSSINI, C. Lingue nilotiche. *See under* GENERAL.
DREXEL, A. Gliederung afrikanischer Sprachen. *See under* GENERAL.
ERHARDT, J. 1857. Vocabulary of the Enguduk Iloigob as spoken by the Masai tribes. Ludwigsburg.
FOKKEN, H. Einige Bemerkungen über das Verbum im Masai. M.S.O.S. **10**, 3, 1907, pp. 124–54.
—— 1914. Die Sprüchweisheit der Massai. Pp. 37. Leipzig: Verlag d. Evang. Mission. 100 proverbs.
HINDE, H. 1901. The Masai language. Grammatical notes, together with a vocabulary. Pp. ix+359. Cambridge University Press.

---

[1] This 'Dorobo' does not appear to be a Nandi dialect. See p. 36.

BIBLIOGRAPHY

HOLLIS, A. C. 1905. The Masai, their language and folklore. Pp. xxviii+359. Oxford: Clarendon Press.
    Still the standard work on the subject.
HOMBURGER, L. Le genre sexuel dans le sous-groupe choli-shillouk. . . . *See under* ACOLI.
—— Le peul et les langues nilotiques. *See under* TESO.
JOHNSTON, SIR H. H. 1886. The Kilima-Njaro expedition. Pp. xv+572. London: Kegan Paul, Trench & Co.
    Pp. 453–77, notes on Masai grammar; Appendix 1, pp. 501–20, Vocabulary of Masai, with some words of Dinka, Shilluk, Alur, Luo, Bari, and Lotuho.
—— The Uganda Protectorate. *See under* GENERAL.
KRAPF, J. L. 1854. Vocabulary of the Engutuk Eloikop or of the language of the Wakuafination in the interior of equatorial Africa. Pp. 144. Tübingen.
LAST, J. T. A visit to the Masai living beyond the borders of the Nguru country. Proc. R. Geogr. Soc., 1883.
    Includes vocabulary and phrases in Masai.
—— 1885. Polyglotta Africana orientalis. London: S.P.C.K.
    Pp. 190–3 and 234–9, Masai words and sentences; pp. 219–20, 'Kwafi' words; pp. 188–9 and 231, Taturu words.
MACDONALD, J. R. L. Notes on the ethnology of tribes. . . . *See under* LUO.
MAGUIRE, R. A. J. Il-Toróbo. *See under* NANDI.
    Gives a vocabulary of Masai for comparison.
MEINHOF, CARL. 1912. Die Sprachen der Hamiten. Pp. xvi+256. Abh. Hamb. Kolon. Inst. **9**.
    Chap. 7, Masai; pp. 230–40, comparative vocabulary. The vocabulary is taken from Hollis, with alterations in spelling.
MÜLLER, F. Grundriss der Sprachwissenschaft. *See under* DINKA.
    Vol. 3, section 1, pp. 95–8, Über die Beziehungen der Sprache der Il-Oigob zur Sprache der Bari.
MURATORI, C. Grammatica Lotuxo. *See under* LOTUHO.
SCHUCHARDT, H. Zu den Verben mit i- im Masai. Wiener Z. Kde. Morgenland. **24**.

Unpublished
RICHMOND, CHARLES. Grammar of Masai.

NANDI LANGUAGE GROUP

ANON. Nandi–English dictionary. Pp. 94. Africa Inland Mission (duplicated).
BAUMANN, O. Durch Massailand zur Nilquelle. *See under* LUO.
BEECH, M. W. H. 1911. The Suk, their language and folklore. Pp. xxiv+151. Oxford: Clarendon Press.
—— Endo vocabulary. Man, **13**, 42, 1913.
    Suk words given for comparison.
BRYSON, S. M. 1940. Nandi grammar with sentences showing the various parts of speech. Pp. 78. Africa Inland Mission (duplicated).
CONTI ROSSINI, C. Lingue nilotiche. *See under* GENERAL.
DREXEL, A. Gliederung afrikanischer Sprachen. *See under* GENERAL.
HOBLEY, C. W. Eastern Uganda. An ethnological survey. *See under* LUO.
HOLLIS, A. C. 1909. The Nandi, their language and folklore. Pp. 238. Oxford: Clarendon Press.
HUNTINGFORD, G. W. B. Miscellaneous records relating to the Nandi and Kony tribes. J. R. Anthrop. Inst. **57**, 1927, pp. 417–61.
    Gives a list of plant and tree names, and folk tales with translation.
—— Studies in Nandi etymology. Bibliotheca Africana, **3**, 1, 1929, pp. 35–50; **3**, 4, 1930, pp. 317–26.
—— A note on the 'Taturu' language. Man, **28**, 139, 1928.
    A brief note pointing out that the 'Taturu' vocabulary given by Last is a dialect of Okiek (Dorobo). Gives short vocabularies of Taturu, 'Tindiret', Dorobo ('Ravine' and 'Digiri'), Nandi, and Kony.

HUNTINGFORD, G. W. B. Modern hunters: Some account of the Kâmelīlo-Kâpchepkendi Dorōbo (Okiek) of Kenya Colony. J. R. Anthrop. Inst. 59, 1929, pp. 333–78.

 Pp. 354 ff. deal with language: grammatical notes; vocabulary, with Kony, Sapei, and Suk for comparison; names of trees and plants.

—— The Taturu, Mosiro and Aramanik dialects of Dorobo. Man, 31, 217, 1931.

 A criticism of the article by Maguire (*see below*).

JOHNSTON, SIR H. H. The Uganda Protectorate. *See under* GENERAL.

LAST, J. T. Polyglotta Africana orientalis. *See under* MASAI.

LINDBLOM, G. Some words of the language spoken by the Elgoni people on the East side of Mount Elgon, Kenya Colony, East Africa. Le Monde Oriental, 18, 1924, pp. 46–55.

MACDONALD, J. R. L. Notes on the ethnology of tribes. . . . *See under* LUO.

MAGUIRE, R. A. J. Il-Torōbo. J. Afr. Soc. 27, 1927–8, pp. 127–41, 249–68.

 Pp. 256–60 deal with the 'Mósiro' and 'Aramanik' dialects; there is also a vocabulary of Nandi and Masai for comparison, as well as numerals in other languages.

MEINHOF, C. Linguistische Studien in Ostafrika. 13. Ndorobo. M.S.O.S. 10, 3, 1907.

MURATORI, C. Grammatica Lotuxo. *See under* LOTUHO.

PERISTIANY, J. G. 1939. The social organisation of the Kipsigis. Pp. 288. London: Routledge.

 Chap. 12, pp. 230–82, Myths, stories, and songs, with interlinear translation.

RAVENSTEIN, ——. Vocabularies from Kavirondo. . . . *See under* LUO.

STRUCK, B. Über'die Sprache der Tatoga- und Iraku-Leute.

 Pp. 107–32 of JAEGER, F. 1911. Das Hochland der Riesenkrater und die umliegenden Hochländer Deutsch-Ostafrikas. Mitt. aus d. dtsch. Schutzgebieten, Ergänzungsheft 4.

STUHLMANN, F., ed. SCHLEICHER, A. W. and MEINHOF, C. Sammlung von Wörtern der Taturu-Sprache. Z. Kolon. Spr. 6, 1915–16, pp. 154–60.

WERTHER, C. W. 1898. Die mittleren Hochländer des nördlichen Deutsch-Ostafrika. Berlin.

 Pp. 490–3, vocabulary of Taturu.

For Product Safety Concerns and Information please contact our EU
representative GPSR@taylorandfrancis.com
Taylor & Francis Verlag GmbH, Kaufingerstraße 24, 80331 München, Germany

www.ingramcontent.com/pod-product-compliance
Lightning Source LLC
Chambersburg PA
CBHW070725020526
44116CB00031B/1831